Professional Imperialism:
Social Work in the Third World

Studies in Social Policy and Welfare XVI

Professional Imperialism:
Social Work in the Third World

James Midgley

 Heinemann · London

Published by Heinemann Educational Books Ltd
22 Bedford Square, London WC1B 3HH
LONDON EDINBURGH MELBOURNE AUCKLAND
HONG KONG SINGAPORE KUALA LUMPUR NEW DELHI
IBADAN NAIROBI EXETER (NH)
KINGSTON PORT OF SPAIN

Midgley, James
    Professional imperialism. – (International
studies in comparative welfare).
    1. Underdeveloped areas – Social service
    2. Social service
    I. Title   II. Pinker, Robert   III. Series
    361'.9172'4   HV40

ISBN 0-435-82588-7

Typeset by Northumberland Press Ltd,
Gateshead, Tyne and Wear
Printed in Great Britain by Richard Clay (The Chaucer Press) Ltd,
Bungay, Suffolk

Contents

To Dija

Acknowledgements

My interest in social work in the Third World was aroused originally when I practised as a social worker in Southern Africa and found that the problems experienced by the majority of my clients could not be solved through conventional social work methods. Since then I have shared my misgivings about social work's relevance to developing countries with many social workers; my own teachers and many others whom I have met in Third World countries have been receptive to my views and I have benefited from their ideas.

I wish to record my gratitude to the staff of those schools of social work which participated in the study of current trends in social work education in the Third World which is described in this book; they responded openly to requests for information and many were helpful in other ways.

Yvonne Asamoah and Jean Peasah of the University of Ghana were extremely helpful in facilitating the study of social work graduates in Ghana, and I wish especially to express my gratitude to Margaret Hardiman who visited Ghana to interview these social workers; she has given me much encouragement and assistance.

Zsuzsanna Adler, my research assistant, deserves special thanks for her dedication to the study. Thanks also to my secretary, Gay Grant, for her willing help with the typing of the manuscript. The Noel Buxton Trust financed two visits to schools of social work in Africa and I am grateful to the trustees and especially to Mr Gilbert Ponsonby and Sir Bernard de Bunsen for their assistance.

I also wish to express my thanks to the Research Committee of the London School of Economics which met the other research costs and Bob Pinker for his valuable editorial comments. Finally I owe much to Brian Abel-Smith who has given me a great deal of encouragement and advice.

James Midgley
London School of Economics

Introduction

Social work is an approach to the amelioration of social problems which originated in western, industrial countries at the end of the nineteenth century. Since then, social work has experienced considerable academic and professional growth and it now has several characteristics which distinguish it from other ways of meeting human need. It employs professionally qualified workers to help people, who have personal problems, by dealing with them in face to face relationships. These relationships are governed by a distinctive methodology which combines the worker's practical skills with the client's own efforts to find a solution. Social work is a formalised approach which is based on the belief that social problems can best be remedied through the intervention of professional personnel who have the appropriate training, knowledge and skills.

These characteristics contradict the popular image of social workers as kindly individuals who dispense charity to the needy with philanthropic dedication. Social workers argue that this is totally inaccurate; theirs is a professional involvement in which expertise is more important than altruism. Social workers do not only make a distinction between themselves and those engaged in voluntary welfare; they believe that residential care workers, social administrators, youth leaders, community development personnel and others, who are engaged in what is referred to often as social work, are paraprofessionals who lack the skills and training of the professionally qualified social worker.

Social workers point out that, like other professionals, they are required to pursue a specialised course of study at institutions of higher learning, many of which are located at prestigious universities; they take courses in a variety of academic subjects and study the principles and methods of social work. So that they may be prepared adequately for professional practice, theoretical study and practical training is combined. Like the other professions, social work has developed its own body of knowledge. Social work educators are engaged not only in teaching but also in research and writing, and the numerous research publications, textbooks and social work journals which have been produced over the years now comprise a substantial professional literature.

Like other professionals, social workers find remunerative employment; in countries such as the United States and Britain they have good career prospects and some command high salaries. They are employed by private welfare agencies and by local and central government social service authorities and they work in settings as diverse as schools, courts, hospitals, prisons, housing estates and psychiatric clinics. Although the great majority are involved in remedial social welfare work, dealing with the problems of individuals and their families, some social workers are employed in preventive and other fields. Some provide creative leisure activities for both young and old, others undertake research into social problems and other matters related to social work practice; some are concerned with community action and the promotion of welfare rights and others are responsible for planning local welfare services. Some social workers have managerial and executive positions in government social service organisations and some work for large, international development agencies. But these activities are open to relatively few social workers and are regarded as secondary to the profession's primary concern with remedial social welfare.

Social workers belonged to professional associations which, like other professional bodies, seek to promote and protect the interests of their members. They negotiate salaries and conditions of service, accredit training institutions and maintain the status of the profession by setting educational standards appropriate to the requirements of professional practice. These associations exert considerable influence in some countries; they have succeeded in persuading governments to enact legislation providing for the registration of social workers and the standardisation of social work training and, in some cases, have participated in the formulation of national social welfare policies.

Although social work does not enjoy the status and recognition accorded to the older and better established professions, the expansion of social work education, greater employment opportunities for social workers and the growing influence of the professional associations has resulted in the wider recognition of social work in western, industrial societies. Social work is established also in many developing countries; it has been exported to these countries over the last thirty years and while social workers in the Third World do not command the same salaries or enjoy the same degree of recognition, they share a common professional identity with their western counterparts. This has been fostered largely through social work education. Schools of social work have been created in many developing countries and, as in the West, many have been incorporated into universities. Here students are trained to apply the principles of social work in the same way as are students in western countries; they study the same textbooks, read the same journals and are taught the same theories and methods. They find employment subsequently in public and voluntary welfare organisations which attempt to deal with social problems in the same way as do social welfare agencies in the West. As in western countries, the great majority of social workers in the Third World are engaged in remedial social welfare work with individuals and their families.

As a consequence of these developments, the international social work profession has expanded greatly since the Second World War. It can boast of a universal methodology which social workers are taught to apply with equal conviction in countries of disparate economic, political, cultural, social and other characteristics. Through the efforts of the international professional associations and through conferences, journals, academic exchanges and other personal contacts, the diffusion of common professional ideas and ideals is maintained.

Many social workers have approved strongly of these developments, believing that the international acceptance of social work will benefit the profession as well as the countries of the Third World; many have claimed that social work is a modern and scientific way of dealing with social problems which can be used effectively in all societies, and others have argued that social work is a truly international profession since it is compatible with the cultures of all peoples. But the methods which social work formulated in the nineteenth century reflected prevailing European and North American cultural values and political ideo- logies. Individualism, humanitarianism, liberalism, the work ethic and capitalism unrestricted by government intervention were re- garded as virtues by the founders of social work. Social work's dependence on these values and its effectiveness as a method of dealing with social problems has been questioned by some social workers in the West. The effectiveness of social work in the Third World and the relevance of its values to other cultures is even more questionable. In most developing countries, social workers have far fewer public or private resources to draw on than do western social workers; psychiat- ric services, income maintenance provisions and residential care facilities are inadequate and often unavailable in the developing world. Usually, social workers in developing countries have very large caseloads and insufficient time to establish effective interpersonal relationships with their clients. Also, the circumstances and needs of their clients differ greatly from those of the beneficiaries of social work in the West. The majority of those who seek social work assistance in developing countries are in dire need of material aid; many are destitute, unemployed, homeless, in poor health and hungry. The scale of absolute poverty in the Third World defies remedies which rely on professional counselling. Social work is powerless to deal with these problems in its present form and yet the governments of many developing countries have formulated social welfare policies which depend on conventional social work intervention.

These are just some examples of the consequences of professional imperialism in social work. If attempts had been made during the profession's formative years in the Third World to modify its methods and principles so that they would be appropriate to the needs and circumstances of developing countries, many of these problems could have been averted. Instead, western social workers exerted a powerful influence over their Third World colleagues and, claiming that social work had a universally relevant methodology and an international professional identity, they imposed alien theories and techniques on developing countries, which were unsuited to their cultures and development needs.

Professional imperialism in social work, as in medicine, law, economics, education and the other professions, is a reflection of other, far more dramatic forms of dependency. During the last decade, development studies have exposed many of these dependent re-lationships through which inappropriate ideas, institutions and technologies have been replicated in the Third World and through which exploitative links have been established. For example, much has been written about the techniques of economic and political manipu-lation which have been employed to serve the interests of the industrial countries in a more subtle and effective way than old-fashioned colonialism. But there are indications that developing countries are attempting to resist these influences and to assert their independence with more determination; although little has been achieved, the rich nations no longer rule the world with the same confidence which characterised their diplomacy twenty years ago.

This book does not aspire to deal with these complex issues but seeks instead to examine, in a modest way, the nature and consequences of professional imperialism in contemporary social work. Also, it hopes to support those social workers in developing countries who have questioned the uncritical adoption of western social work ideas in their societies. In recent years, some have expressed doubts about the ability of social work to contribute to the amelioration of the pressing problems of poverty and deprivation in the Thirld World and there has been some discussion about the relevance of social work's values to other cultures; also, some alternative and more appropriate forms of involvement for social work in developing countries have been proposed. By reviewing these issues, it is hoped that this book will contribute to the new debate on social work's proper role in development.

In the following chapters, the more important literature about social work is reviewed. An attempt is made to describe the ways in which western and especially North American social work theories and methods were exported to developing countries and their impact on social work education and practice in these societies is examined. Two issues concerning social work practice in developing countries are dealt with in some detail; these are the relevance of social work, firstly to the cultures of Third World peoples and secondly, to the social problems of developing countries. A critical review of some proposals for alternative professional social work roles in the Third World is attempted and, in the final chapter, it is argued that pragmatic forms of social work intervention, which are uniquely appropriate to the requirements of different countries, must be identified if social work is to be of any use in the Third World.

A discussion of the problems of professional imperialism in social work requires an understanding of the nature of the profession as it evolved in the West; the methods and techniques which social workers employ and the principles which govern social work intervention, require further elaboration. These are described in the next chapter.

1 The Theory and Practice of Social Work

Gisella Konopka, an American social work professor, once described social work as: 'An approach to social problems, systematized and based on as much scientific understanding as we have.'[1] Professor Gore, of the Tata Institute of Social Sciences in India, called social work 'the liberal-professional approach' to social problems and argued that its most distinctive feature was its reliance on 'professionally trained personnel who possess the skills and knowledge to solve society's problems'.[2] Many social workers would agree with these definitions and concur also with the view that social work is a modern and scientific approach, characterised by professionalism and skill. But it is necessary to recognise that other approaches, which are very different from social work, have been employed to deal with social problems at different times and in different cultural and historical contexts. An understanding of the ways in which different societies have responded to social problems in the past, and in the present, will clarify the contribution of contemporary social work and offer a better opportunity of understanding its role.

The term 'social problems' is used widely in sociological literature but it is not defined precisely. Sociologists disagree about whether social problems should be regarded as phenomena which are objectively harmful to a society or whether they are events which are perceived subjectively by an influential majority or number of the population as detrimental to their well-being. Both aspects have validity for while social problems may be harmful to a society, they must be perceived as such before steps can be taken to remedy them. The way social problems are dealt with depends also on the way they are defined. If social problems are believed to be the results of the immoral actions of individuals, the reaction is likely to be punitive. On the other hand, if social problems are thought to be the consequences of causes over which individuals have very little or no control, the reaction is likely to be much more sympathetic. This may be illustrated with reference to the changing remedies which have been pre-

scribed over the centuries for the treatment of insanity in western
societies. Punitive remedies were compatible with the view, in the past,
that the mentally ill had dabbled in witchcraft or were in league with
the devil and were therefore responsible for their situation, while contemporary medical treatment is based on the belief that the mentally
disordered are sick people. Existential psychiatry may re-define the
problem eventually and propose new solutions.

Reactions to what different societies regard as social problems vary
considerably; some, like social work are formalised and of recent
origin, while others are non-formal and traditional. Also, these
responses vary in the extent to which they invest responsibility for
dealing with social problems on certain people or groups. They differ
also in their effectiveness and in the degree to which they stigmatise
recipients of help. A number of ideal-typical social reactions to social
problems may be identified: they include the punitive and the
humanitarian; the religious and the familial; the voluntary and the
professional and the collective and the individual.

Contemporary social welfare literature has stressed the humanitarian nature of social responses to social problems but many
problems, which could be regarded as worthy of sympathetic treatment today, have been subjected to penal measures in the past. The
punitive sanctions which were imposed on those with contagious
diseases or on sexual deviants by the Mosaic law and the harsh
penalties which were inflicted on vagrants in early Anglo-Saxon law
are just two examples of this. The punitive approach is still widely used
but in many societies, punitive sanctions have been replaced by more
enlightened alternatives; behaviour which was regarded previously as
socially improper has been decriminalised and overtly punitive
measures are reserved now for a smaller number of criminal offences.
But the punitive obsession has popular appeal and the criminal law is
still used by some ostensibly enlightened legislatures to deal with
problems such as alcoholism, homosexuality, abortion and vagrancy.

Religious charity is an approach to the amelioration of social
problems which is institutionalised in many societies; the established
religions of the world proclaim that it is obligatory for their followers to
have a compassionate concern for the needy and those in trouble. In
Islam, the principles of religious charity are given practical expression
in the poor tax, or *zakaat* and in Christianity, similar principles were
formulated by the early apostolic church; later the medieval monastic
orders assumed much responsibility for the care of those in need. In
India, as Gore pointed out, the religious approach to social problems is

'typified largely by individual charity directly benefiting the needy as when the giver doles out food, grain or clothing'.[3] In Hinduism, as in other religions, the act of charity is thought to have favourable consequences for the after-life and the gift is not given always without an expectation of immediate earthly reward: public acts of altruism bestow merit and increase the donor's standing in the community. While punitive responses seek to suppress social problems, religious charity attempts to alleviate need but usually those dispensing religious charity have little interest in the causes of suffering and it may be regarded as a fatalistic approach which confirms the low status of the beneficiary and fails to deal with the causes of social problems.

Another traditional approach to social problems is the familial. In the past, social needs were met by the family and primary responsibility for dealing with the problems of individuals lay with family members and relatives. In western, industrial countries today, reciprocal obligations of this kind between relations are not strong but in many African and Asian communities, they still operate effectively. These are well defined and understood clearly; relatives and kin have an unavoidable duty to help family members in times of crisis and to care for orphans, widows and the elderly. Similarly, those who find themselves in difficulty expect to be helped. Familial responses to social problems deal also with behaviour which is regarded as deviant by the community; here the involvement of the wider kin is common and restitutive penalties are often imposed on the offender.

Voluntary service is a modern rather than traditional approach to social problems, although many of the philanthropic organisations which were established in nineteenth-century Europe and North America were inspired by religious charity. Often their founders were deeply religious and some were members of the clergy. Although originally motivated by religious ideals, many voluntary agencies became secular and rephrased their objectives to reflect a broader humanitarian, rather than religious, commitment. Voluntary organisations motivated by Christian values in the West have counterparts in other religions: in Hinduism, Buddhism, Islam and Judaism, numerous voluntary organisations have been established, which have aims similar to those of the Christian charities.

Whatever doubts may be cast on the humanitarianism of the pioneering charities of the nineteenth century, there was, as Roof put it: 'A new spirit abroad in the late eighteenth century which gathered strength in the nineteenth and prepared the way for the extension of social services in the twentieth.'[4] Although the voluntary service movement was poorly co-ordinated, ignorant of the need for urgent social reform and blind to the magnitude of social need at the time, it led to a proliferation of voluntary organisations in modern, industrial societies. These are concerned with a great variety of social problems; they vary in size and financial resources and many are well established and respected. However, the character of conventional voluntary service has changed considerably over the years; many voluntary societies are run now as self-help organisations and others operate as radical pressure groups which publicise neglected issues and campaign actively for reform. Voluntary organisations were established also in many developing countries where they were based often on developments in the West. This is true especially of the former colonial territories where colonial administrators and their wives, together with the local, educated élite, established voluntary societies which built children's or old people's homes and engaged in other forms of philanthropic work.

Although the social policy or governmental-administrative approach has been formulated only recently, it is not an exclusively modern response to social problems. Governments and rulers have intervened in social affairs and formulated administrative procedures to deal with social problems since the earliest laws were promulgated. Chambliss pointed out that, despite its punitive character, Hammurabi's Code contained various provisions which were concerned with social need and social justice and prescribed how social problems should be dealt with. 'Numerous articles restrained the rich from exploiting the poor and weak. Taking advantage of an individual in distress was forbidden ... the rights of women and children could not be arbitrarily disregarded.'[5] In England, the Elizabethan Poor Laws are one of the earliest examples of the state's efforts to deal comprehensively with a social problem through legislative and administrative measures. But historically, government policies for dealing with social problems have been formulated poorly, implemented sporadically and dependent often on punitive sanctions.

Growing pressures for reform in the industrial countries led to greater state intervention and more comprehensive public welfare provisions. In countries such as Britain, this was resisted by the rich and influential as well as many of the founders of social work who believed that state involvement in social affairs diminished self-reliance and encouraged indolence and abuse. This view is still widely held; moreover, it is argued frequently that people should be responsible for their own welfare and that human needs for health, education and shelter should be satisfied in the market through individual effort and private means.[6] In the nineteenth century these beliefs were countered by a vocal minority who campaigned for the extension of government action and gradually, as working-class movements increased in influence and strength, the legislature was compelled, as Bruce suggested, 'however reluctantly, to intervene to secure to all at least minimum standards'.[7] Government intervention in matters such as health, education, employment and housing was not motivated primarily by humanitarian concerns but was a consequence of the realisation that poverty and social neglect were socially harmful and politically disruptive. Certainly, Chadwick's sanitary reforms in England and Bismarck's social security legislation in Prussia were based on this reasoning. In spite of this reluctance, these beginnings paved the way for more comprehensive government involvement and led eventually to the creation of the so-called welfare state. With the coming of the welfare state, the social policy approach became the subject of academic study; the creation of this new discipline has permitted the systematic analysis of government social policies and has provided opportunities for research as well as training.[8] University educated social administrators are employed now by some governments to administer social services and to formulate new policies and plans.

These different approaches to social problems are inter-related; punitive methods of dealing with social problems constituted the social policies of the past and, in some cases, the present. Traditional religious beliefs about the virtues of charity inspired the voluntary service approach. While all may be contrasted with modern, professional social work, the merits of social policy and social work are debated most frequently; both are established now as academic disciplines and both claim to be effective. The proponents of social policy believe that the causes of social problems are rooted in the structure of society and not in individual pathology; they believe that social problems should be remedied through government action and they are often critical of social work. Social policy and social work employ different methods to deal with social problems: social policy's instruments are legislation and administration while social work relies instead on professional skills and direct intervention. Although they no longer oppose state intervention vigorously, social workers claim that the sympathetic understanding of a trained worker is a more effective way of helping people than the impersonal, bureaucratic provision of material aid to needy people by government agencies.

Social workers have not defined the concepts of social need or social problems adequately even though these are basic to social work practice. Social workers are concerned primarily with specific social problems such as child abuse or neglect, mental illness, marital disharmony, alcohol or narcotic addiction, illegitimacy, juvenile delinquency and adult crime, family disintegration, homelessness, prostitution, physical handicap and a number of similar personal pathologies or needs. The literature of social work conceptualises these as manifestations of maladjustment and people who experience them are, as Maas put it, 'under stress and in need of help'.[9] Perlman's widely respected textbook on social casework offered an eloquent but characteristically imprecise definition of the social problems social workers deal with: 'Problems of hunger for food and hunger for love, of seeking shelter and of wanting to run away, of getting married and staying married, of feeling afraid, of feeling useless – all these and many other problems of physical and emotional survival as a human being come to the door of the social agency.'[10] While social work deals chiefly with the personal problems of individuals, the concept of need is used also in the profession's literature to denote positive aspects of human welfare. Self-fulfilment, human development, adjustment and social integration are needs which social workers are said to be also concerned with, and social workers point out that they employ different methods of practice to achieve these objectives. While they are concerned primarily with individual and family problems which require treatment, professional social workers are trained also in methods which aim to strengthen group ties, improve social re- lationships and integrate communities.

The Methods of Social Work

There are three methods of social work. These are casework, group work and community work or community organisation as it is called in the United States. The three methods of professional practice are complemented by other social work activities, such as social work research and social work administration, which are a part of the social worker's professional training. Although these are referred to some- times as social work methods, most social workers regard casework, group work and community work as the primary forms of social work intervention through which the profession's ideals are given practical expression.

A fundamentally important characteristic of social casework is what social workers call 'individuation'. By this they mean simply that people who experience social problems should be treated individually and as individuals. Since social workers believe that social problems are manifested as the problems of individuals, their efforts are directed chiefly at helping them and their immediate family members who are affected. Social work's primary concern for individuals is reflected in most authoritative definitions of casework. In one of the profession's first standard textbooks, Mary Richmond defined social casework as a method which has 'for its immediate aim the betterment of individuals and their families, one by one, as distinguished from their betterment in the mass'.[11] Or, as Biestek explained, with great conviction: 'Individuation is based on the right of human beings to be treated not just as *a* human but as *this* human being with his personal differences.'[12]

Another, equally important feature of social casework is the casework relationship. Social workers not only deal with their clients on a face to face basis but must establish close, sympathetic and meaningful relationships with them. While good inter-personal relationships between professionals and clients in law, dentistry or medicine are desirable, they are not essential if the lawyer, dentist or doctor is to provide a useful service. But in casework, 'a good relationship is necessary not only for the perfection but also for the essence of the casework service'.[13] Consequently, social workers are required to establish effective relationships with their clients and to pay careful attention to the emotional and other obstacles which hinder its full development.

Treatment is another essential ingredient of social casework; to remedy personal problems, social workers use the casework relationship therapeutically. For treatment to be effective, 'caseworkers must be able to use skilfully, knowledge of human behaviour in stressful situations'.[14] This knowledge is derived from theories of behaviour and psychopathology, and different schools of casework give emphasis to different psychological approaches. The most popular of these are based on Freudian and other psychoanalytic ideas but recently, behaviourist and other theories have been applied to casework practice. In the therapeutic casework relationship, personal skills are as important as a scientific knowledge of human behaviour and through practical training, caseworkers are taught techniques of interviewing, diagnosis and treatment. As the casework relationship matures, clients are helped to gain insights into their actions and emotions, confidence is instilled and they are encouraged to deal with their problems through their own efforts. It is for this reason that social work has been described both as an art and a science which has the ultimate goal of helping people to help themselves.[15] Caseworkers believe that treatment must involve clients actively and although their skills and knowledge are an important resource, success in casework depends largely on the client's response. Social workers claim that, by involving people in the treatment of their own problems, casework not only deals with immediate personal and family crises but helps to develop the client's personality.

Another method of professional social work is group work which seeks, as one eminent exponent of this method put it: 'to strengthen human capabilities'.[16] Social group work is based on the premise that human beings have a common need to participate in group life which is not satisfied by contemporary, industrial society. Social workers argue that modern societies provide few opportunities for people to establish and enjoy meaningful relationships with each other. Secularism has weakened traditional religious institutions which previously integrated the community. Urbanism and industrialism have brought about greater personal autonomy and anonymity and lessened opportunities for companionship. The family has become smaller and increasingly detached from the wider kin. Today people are more isolated from each other and many are excluded from the benefits of participating in group activities. Whether this is an accurate analysis of the condition of industrial society or not, social workers believe that the loneliness of the aged, delinquency among slum children and the isolation of the unmarried and the widowed are only a few symptoms of the disintegration of traditional social institutions.

Social workers argue that problems such as these could be averted if individuals belonged to groups and took part in group activities more frequently. Also, they believe that group participation develops individuals as human beings, strengthens their personalities and improves social relationships generally. It is the group worker's task to encourage people not only to participate in group life but to do so meaningfully; opportunities for organised group participation are provided by specialised group work organisations and also, to some extent, by family welfare agencies as an extension of their casework services. Different group work agencies use different activities to attract clients and to foster social integration. Youth organisations, clubs for the aged, children's play groups and a variety of leisure and educational activities are just some of the ways in which group interaction is facilitated and the needs of different age groups and different types of clients are catered for.

As in social casework, group workers are required to combine knowledge and skills. The professional group worker must know how individuals behave in groups, understand the causes of group conflict and have a thorough knowledge of the scientific principles which govern group dynamics. The worker's skills are used to help individuals with different personalities to participate effectively; the diffident are encouraged to be more assertive while the self-confident are taught to be more democratic. To foster group integration, group workers play different roles at different times. While their involvement is usually non-directive, they sometimes take an active leadership role in order to stimulate greater interaction. But, as in casework, the emphasis is on self-help; the worker seeks ultimately to let the group operate independently and take its own decisions. As Konopka put it: 'The function of the group worker is a helping or enabling function.'[17]

Much group work is concerned with preventive social welfare; group work activities are directed often at adolescents in poorer areas especially aiming to counteract the attractions of delinquency. Young people are encouraged to join youth clubs and to participate in organised recreation and sport: by creating a healthy atmosphere for group participation, group workers seek to channel young peoples' needs for group experience into socially acceptable activities and to prevent the formation of juvenile gangs. Similarly, by encouraging adults to participate more actively in groups, problems caused by isolation and loneliness are avoided. Group work techniques are employed also in remedial work; therapeutic group work evolved from developments in psychiatry and the involvement of social workers in clinical settings and its purpose, as Stroup suggested 'is to use specialised group placements and group activities to help individuals who reveal abnormal social relations'.[18] Today, therapeutic group work is used widely in general psychiatry, drug rehabilitation and the treatment of alcoholism, child guidance and correctional work.

The third method of professional social work is community work. Because communities have social needs, which can be met only partially by casework and group work agencies functioning independently, social workers believe that community problems must be viewed in their totality and dealt with through the provision of a comprehensive range of social welfare services. These must be planned and co-ordinated properly and involve local people; community workers believe that local citizens must participate fully in the promotion of community welfare. They must be made aware of social need in their areas and be encouraged to take the initiative for dealing with it. Local people should serve on the governing boards of social welfare agencies and should be responsible for their financial management. Also, they should be involved in the co-ordination and planning of existing welfare services so that community resources can be used effectively to deal with local needs. The co-ordination of community welfare endeavour is one of the most important aspects of community work. In what is now accepted as a classic definition, Dunham wrote: 'Community organization is the process of bringing about and maintaining adjustment between social welfare resources and social welfare needs within a geographic area or specific field of service.'[19]

Like caseworkers and group workers, community workers have specialised knowledge; from their sociological understanding of community life, they know how community institutions function, how local political processes operate and how community needs arise. Because they are also concerned with the management and planning of local welfare services, they study the principles which govern formal organisations and learn to undertake administrative tasks. Community workers use their theoretical knowledge of the sociology of communities to obtain specific information about the localities in which they work; they should have a detailed knowledge of the demographic, political and economic characteristics of the community, understand its social structure and be able to undertake research into community needs. Community workers use their professional skills to establish and maintain good relationships with community leaders and citizens. They motivate people to participate in welfare activities and foster an attitude of concern and responsibility in the community. They assist community leaders to take decisions effectively but democratically and are able to deal with problems and conflicts which arise in ways that do not cause resentment.

The community worker is concerned initially, as Carter suggested: 'with establishing a formal structure'.[20] This requires the creation of effective channels of communication and the adoption of procedures by which the community can define and realise its objectives. To achieve this, community workers favour the establishment of local community organisation and planning agencies, many of which exist now in the United States. Staffed by professional workers but governed by lay committees, these provide a base for community organisation; here local needs are identified and plans for action formulated. In communities where welfare services are well established, community work agencies serve as a meeting place where problems of co-ordination and finance are discussed and where unmet needs are identified. Often, community organisation agencies take an overall responsibility for fund raising and are engaged in the financial planning and budgeting of local welfare resources. These agencies are also concerned with publicity; community workers see themselves as educators who seek to change attitudes to social welfare and social problems. Also, they publicise the activities of existing welfare organisations and draw attention to needs which have been neglected or unrecognised.

There is an alternative interpretation of community work which is critical of social work's conventional approach to the provision of organised community welfare services. Some social workers believe that, in poor areas especially, community needs cannot be met adequately through the creation of formal community organisation procedures; in these areas adequate financial resources cannot be raised locally and it is meaningless to suggest that local people should be responsible for their own welfare. Instead, they believe that community welfare is the responsibility of public authorities and that needy people should be encouraged to take action and make demands for improved amenities and welfare benefits. They are sceptical of procedures which are dependent on consensus politics and argue that more radical methods, which confront recalcitrant governmental organisations with demands, are more likely to benefit local citizens than are attempts to establish co-ordinating and fund raising agencies which are staffed by professional social workers.

It is claimed that these three methods of social work practice are of equal importance and that professionally qualified social workers should be able to practise with equal ease in different agencies which specialise in one or more of these methods. While each relies on a specialised body of scientific knowledge, the different methods are said to be no more than different manifestations of a methodology which is common to all forms of social work. Although social workers have promoted a generic approach to professional practice, this methodology is based not on abstract principles but on concepts derived from social work's original dependence on casework method.

Casework was the first method of social work to be formulated and principles and techniques have been taken from it and used to provide a theoretical basis for the subsequent development of the two other methods. Social casework is the most prestigious and best established of the three. It is given far greater emphasis in social work education than the other methods which are sometimes omitted from the curricula of schools of social work entirely. There is a more extensive literature on social casework than group or community work, and while casework has experienced considerable academic refinement through its adoption of psychological and psychiatric theories, the other methods have not enjoyed the same degree of intellectual development. Most social workers are employed as social caseworkers and in many countries, group work and community work are hardly practised. Social casework is so central to the profession that it is used often as a synonym for all forms of social work; this is clearly shown in the literature dealing with principles which govern social work practice.

The Principles of Social Work

The theoretical basis for all social work practice is formulated in what social workers call the 'generic principles'. These reflect also the profession's philosophical beliefs and although they are intended to govern the way social workers deal with their clients, some are more concerned with values and ideals than with practical procedures. The generic principles have been the subject of controversy among social workers; it has been claimed that they are inconsistent and con-tradictory and that many social workers are faced with practical problems which hinder their proper implementation. But these difficulties are usually ignored in standard social work textbooks, which present an idealised account of how the generic principles guide the practitioner and provide the profession with a unitary methodology.[21]

The concept of individuation, which is a basic characteristic of social casework, is enshrined also as a generic principle and expresses social work's belief in what Friedlander described as 'the inherent worth, the integrity and dignity of the individual'.[22] Individuation is said to govern all three methods of social work and each translates it into practice in different ways. Group work may be concerned with group activities but its ultimate purpose is, as social workers themselves admit, 'the development and adjustment of the individual through voluntary group associations'.[23] Similarly in community work, social workers seek to mobilise and co-ordinate community resources so that 'individuals and groups are helped to meet their own needs'.[24] While the literature claims that groups and communities benefit directly from group and community work and that this gives a distinctive character to each method, social work uses these methods primarily to serve the needs of individuals. Groups and communities are not conceptualised as phenomena which have their own reality or which are more than the summation of individual experience. In practical terms, group workers are concerned primarily with strengthening the personalities and improving the social functioning of group members, and in community work, relationships with community leaders and citizens are used in the same way. The profession's literature makes it clear that the individual is at the centre of social work and that individuation is the first of its principles.

Direct intervention is another generic principle which has been abstracted from social casework. In formulating this principle, social workers translated the profession's experience of the casework relationship, through which they dealt with needy people on a face to face basis, into a methodological concept which now governs all forms of social work intervention. All three methods of social work practice are characterised by direct service; social workers deal with their clients directly and seek to establish meaningful relationships with them. This is as important in group work and community work as it is in casework. The knowledge and skills which group workers possess are applied through the interpersonal relationships they have with group members; similarly, community workers must establish good relationships with local leaders and others when attempting to promote a concern for community welfare.

Self-determination and self-help are two generic principles which are accorded canonical status in social work. One reason for the poorly defined use of the concept of need in the profession's literature is because social workers believe that individuals, groups and communities have the right to determine what their needs are 'and how they should be met'.[25] The principle of self-determination prescribes that need should never be imputed; although social workers believe that social problems must be diagnosed properly, they do not tell individuals, groups and communities what their needs are but seek instead to help them to identify and recognise their needs. Similarly, social workers never instruct, cajole or even persuade their clients to take decisions. This is believed to be un-democratic and inimical to personality development for, in social casework, despair, confusion and demoralisation cannot be remedied through solutions prescribed by social workers. Instead, social workers assist their clients to regain confidence and to believe in their ability to solve their own problems. In group and community work, social workers may clarify problems and suggest alternative courses of action but they do not prescribe solutions to their clients. Instead, social workers regard themselves as enablers who help individuals, groups and communities to solve their own problems.

The principle of self-determination has guided social work practice for many years but it has presented the profession with several practical problems. For example, what should social workers do when their clients make the 'wrong' decisions? Because of their knowledge and experience, social workers must be able to judge the consequences of their clients' actions and are bound, as are other professionals, to advise and guide them towards viable solutions. Another problem, the question of individual versus collective rights, has complicated the application of the principle of self-determination. Do individuals have a right to freedom of choice if the consequences of their actions directly or indirectly disadvantage others? For example, this issue has been especially difficult for child care workers who must protect the welfare of children but simultaneously respect the rights of parents to rear their children as they see fit. In response to this problem, social workers are taught that while individuals have a fundamental right to determine their actions, they have equally important responsibilities towards their families and the community. Although social workers are required to demonstrate that individual and social needs are reciprocal, many have found that it is difficult to reconcile individual wants and community needs. This is especially difficult when anti-social conduct is the subject of social work intervention.

The generic principle of acceptance denotes a non-judgemental stance in social work which finds expression in the social worker's attitude of value neutrality. Social workers are taught that they should not have preconceived ideas about moral standards. Because they believe in the inherent worth of human beings, clients are accepted for what they are, irrespective of what they have done or failed to do; social work does not distinguish between 'good' or 'bad' clients. Ultimately, the principle of acceptance is based on the belief that human beings are intrinsically good and naturally virtuous and that they should be treated as such. But social workers also believe that individuals should be accountable for their actions and behave responsibly towards others. In the nineteenth century, social workers dealing with the poor made no pretence at ethical impartiality; poverty was believed to be a consequence of immorality and social workers disapproved especially of the able-bodied unemployed whom they regarded as indolent. Similarly, whenever individual negligence caused dependents to suffer, social workers readily reprimanded the offender. Contemporary social workers are required to use more subtle techniques but most admit that it is difficult to regard the unco-operative and obstreperous client as a person worthy of acceptance. To resolve this difficulty, social work teaches that the practitioner must separate individuals from their deeds; while unacceptable behaviour may require censorship, individuals must be viewed independently of their actions and remain free from moral evaluation.

Confidentiality is another generic principle which governs social work practice. In the same way that medical practitioners, lawyers and the clergy treat intimate information confidentially, social workers believe that their clients have a right to keep their past behaviour and present troubles private. However, social workers are often required to communicate private information to their colleagues, other professionals, public authorities and even to their clients' families. Social workers in fields such as correctional work and psychiatric social work face this problem frequently. Those who learn that their clients have transgressed the conditions of a probation or parole order have a dual loyalty; they have a responsibility to report the offender to the authorities. But if the client made the admission voluntarily, they may feel that they should not divulge it, not only to respect the principle of confidentiality but to maintain the relationship which has been established. Similarly, it is necessary sometimes to reveal information provided by psychiatric patients to family members even though the client may wish this to be kept confidential.

Two further generic principles deal with emotional expression and professional non-involvement. Social workers are taught that they should encourage their clients to express their feelings; in this way, social workers are able to gain deeper insights into their problems and become more sensitive to their needs. Also, emotional expression permits the release of pent up feelings. However, emotional expression must be controlled and used purposefully in social work relationships and should not influence the social worker's professional detachment. Although social workers must be sympathetic and understanding, they must guard against becoming involved emotionally with their clients, as the problems they experience from this detracts from their ability to function rationally and effectively.

The generic principles reveal social work's ultimate objectives which are often phrased in lofty terms in the profession's literature. Guided by the generic principles, social workers are said to develop the individual's personality and to strengthen social relationships between people. Social work claims to bring about a healthy adjustment between individuals and society and to help people to participate in group life more meaningfully. It encourages human beings to be more aware of the needs of others and teaches them to join with their fellow citizens to decide democratically how community needs can be met. Summarising these ideals, one social work educator wrote: 'In this way, social work assists in realising democratic principles and human rights, seeking to secure for all citizens a decent standard of living, social security and the fulfilment of the universal need for love, acceptance, recognition and status.'[26]

These improbable and romantic sentiments belie the profession's involvement with harsh and dismal problems of poverty, neglect and deprivation, which social workers encounter daily. Indeed, many social workers today are critical of the idealism which is enshrined in the generic principles; many recognise that they are not concerned with the promotion of human happiness on a grand scale but with the personal and family crises which are occasioned frequently by material and other forms of deprivation. Others have pointed out that the practical demands which social workers face often require responses which violate these principles. Many social workers are employed in governmental agencies where they are bound by statutory obligations; in fields such as probation, child welfare and after-care, the non-directive prescriptions of social work theory cannot always be implemented. While many descriptions of social work theory and practice, such as the one given in this chapter, equate genericism with social work, it should also be recognised that the theoretical unification of different forms of social work practice through the generic principles is a comparatively recent development which is neither accepted universally nor always implemented. But, in spite of this, the generic approach has been adopted widely. Also, the generic principles reflect the profession's humanitarian and Christian heritage and demonstrate the extent to which social work embodies specific cultural values. Although it has been claimed that these values are applicable universally, social work's pholosophical and ethical ideals are rooted firmly in the profession's experience of nineteenth century, European and North American philanthropy.

2 Social Work's Western Origins

Historically, the emergence of social work in Europe and North America is associated with poor relief. As the rural poor were drawn into and concentrated in the industrialising cities during the nineteenth century, the problem of urban destitution became more acute and conventional public poor relief provisions were strained; social work attempted to provide an alternative which would lessen the burden of public assistance borne by taxpayers, be more humane and seek to rehabilitate the destitute.

The founders of social work were critical of the large numbers of people who were dependent on state relief, but they were also concerned about the punitive provisions of the Poor Law and especially of the way these affected those who had become destitute through no fault of their own. Statutory poor relief had been made unattractive purposefully and public assistance was given reluctantly. Two centuries earlier, the English Elizabethan Poor Laws prescribed that the poor were to be 'set to work' and that those who had left their homes in search of a livelihood were to be apprehended, whipped and returned to their parishes.[1] With the Reformation and the growing influence of puritanism, attitudes towards the poor hardened for puritans believed that work was not only a virtue but a moral duty and that poverty was the just consequence of idleness. John Locke expressed popular views when he claimed that the causes of poverty lay in 'the relaxation of discipline and the corruption of manners'.[2] Eighteenth and nineteenth century liberalism confirmed these attitudes; because it was believed that the poor had chosen to live dissolutely and had shunned the rewards of hard work, temperance and ambition, they should suffer condemnation and be denied public assistance. Public policies which were formulated in the nineteenth century to deal with the poor took account of these views; Bentham, among others, argued that if poor relief was made more unattractive, abuse would be discouraged and the poor would be compelled to seek employment. Chadwick relied greatly on Bentham's ideas when formulating the principle of less elegibility; this featured prominently in the drastic ammendments which were made to the English Poor

Laws in 1834. In order to prevent fraud, deter the idle and coerce the poor to work, applicants for poor relief were required to attend degrading public inquiries and many were committed to workhouses.

Similar practices were adopted in other European countries and in North America. Before independence, many American colonies enacted legislation which was similar to the Elizabethan Poor Laws; one of the earliest, the Virginia Poor Law of 1646, conformed closely to the English statutes. The colonies took special care to prevent the poor from immigrating and settling in their territories; in 1661, the Netherlands passed laws which permitted the deportation of paupers from New York. In most colonies, the Poor Laws provided for outdoor relief to be administered by the church but by the nineteenth century, institutions were being built on a large scale to house the poor. In 1821, the General Court of Massachusetts accepted the recommendation of a commission appointed to revise its Poor Laws; it proposed that outdoor relief be abolished and that those who were dependent on public aid be kept in almshouses. With the enactment of the County Poor House Act in 1824, New York took similar steps. The practice of committing the poor to institutions characterised public poor relief provisions in Britain and other European countries as well and subsequently, these institutions became specialised; different workhouses catered for the aged, women, the infirm, children and other indigent people and this resulted in the separation of families. Also, many were owned privately and abuses were widespread. The appalling conditions in the poor houses and the cruelties inflicted on the inmates by their custodians became common knowledge and attracted much criticism from middle-class philanthropists.

Numerous charities were established in the nineteenth century to provide outdoor relief to the poor and to prevent their committal to these institutions. Also, many were inspired by missionary zeal to rescue the poor of the industrial cities from the purgatory of the urban slums. The middle and upper classes had drawn a distinction between themselves and those who lived in overcrowded and insanitary conditions in these deteriorated areas; the slums were believed to contain the 'dangerous classes' who shared a predilection for vice, indolence, crime and gin. While the temperance movement, the Sunday Schools and the Salvation Army crusaded in an attempt to convert large numbers of slum dwellers, many charities focused their attentions on specific groups whom they thought to be worthy of salvation. The charities distinguished between the 'undeserving' poor, whom they believed to be impoverished because of insobriety, indolence or irresponsibility and the 'deserving' poor to whom no moral blame could be attached. Orphans, young women in moral danger, widows and the indigent aged were deemed to be worthy of salvation while the able-bodied poor were not. Later, the able-bodied were aided, provided that they were of reputable character and had fallen into financial difficulty because of sickness or other circumstances beyond their control. The unemployed and chronically poor were condemned as idle and irredeemable and the charities guarded against being exploited by them.

Most charities were small and had limited resources; they were able to help only a small proportion of those in need and their efforts were unco-ordinated. They were criticised frequently for giving aid indiscriminately and of neglecting to take adequate steps to prevent abuse; many were accused specifically of failing to determine whether a beneficiary of charitable aid was receiving help from another source as well and many were thought to be sentimental about poverty. Among those who called for the reform of these alleged abuses was the Rev Thomas Chalmers, who attacked the charities for being negligent and shortsighted. Although he had great faith in the potential of private philanthropy, Chalmers believed that the charities were being exploited by the able-bodied poor who had no desire to earn an honest living. To prevent abuses, he recommended that trustworthy volunteers be recruited to undertake a thorough investigation of those seeking assistance; in this way, the home conditions, financial status and needs of mendicants and their families could be assessed properly. The application of his ideas to St John's Parish, Glasgow in the 1820s was not replicated elsewhere but influenced later philanthropists who advocated that reforms be made in the administration of charity.

The merits of private philanthropy were accepted more widely during the latter half of the nineteenth century and there was a substantial increase in the number and variety of charities in the United States, Britain and other European countries. In addition to the abuses which occurred in the workhouses, the charity movement benefited from the administrative inefficiencies and corrupt practices of Poor Law officials, and support for private philanthropy increased as these were publicised. In Britain, Bentham was one of the leading critics of corruption in Poor Law administration, and paradoxically many poor people were spared the rigours of less-eligibility because most of the local guardians were too inefficient to enforce the principles of 1834. But neither were the charities exempt from criticism; many

believed that they were sentimental about poverty, inefficient and
that they frequently duplicated each other's work. One vociferous
critic of the English charities at the time was Thomas Hawksley whose
celebrated address to the Association for the Prevention of Pauperism
and Crime in the Metropolis on the work of the charities of London
publicized what he described as 'some errors in their administration'.[3]
Hawksley's ideas and proposals for the reform of philanthropy attracted considerable attention and were influential in establishing the
Charity Organisation Society.

The Society, known originally as the Society for Organising
Charitable Relief and Repressing Mendicity, was founded in London
in 1869.[4] Apart from the writings of Chalmers and Hawksley, the
ideas of Octavia Hill, Canon Barnett and Charles Loch were
instrumental in defining its role. Organised charity was believed not
only to be a more efficient means of relieving distress but a method
of promoting a happy and self-reliant community. Some hoped that
the Society would bring about social reforms and Barnett argued that
organised charity could counteract the growing threat of socialism.

The ideas of Charles Loch, who was Secretary of the Society from
1875 until 1913, were the most influential and his views, which were
formulated in what he described as the 'principles of scientific charity',
soon governed the way the Society operated. Although the distinction
between the deserving and undeserving poor had been made
previously, Loch insisted that the charities and the Poor Law
authorities deal with different types of people; those who had fallen
into financial hardship because of events which they could not control
or experienced temporary difficulties should, he recommended, be
helped by philanthropy while the chronically poor should be referred
to the Poor Law officials. The primary objective of charitable relief
was to rehabilitate those who were temporarily destitute and to help
them to become self-reliant again; but all efforts should be made to
find alternative means of support before aid was given. Loch believed
that relief should not be given to those who could obtain assistance,
however meagre, from their relatives. Where no alternative sources
of help could be found, charity should be given as a last resort and
all means of persuasion should be used to encourage the recipient
to become financially independent.[5]

The administration of charity was entrusted to volunteer workers
who, as Chalmers had suggested earlier, made an investigation of the
background, circumstances and needs of each applicant. Interviews
were held first at the Society's office and detailed notes were taken;

these statements were verified subsequently by home visits and other enquiries. All applications were discussed by a special committee which decided whether or not help should be given. Those who received assistance were required to make repayments as this was believed to encourage provident habits. Applicants were referred often to other charities and because few had the resources to undertake individual enquiries, the Society's recommendations were respected.

The first American Charity Organisation Society was established in Buffalo in New York State in 1877 and in the early years, there was a great deal of contact between London and Buffalo. Since American and English ideas about self-reliance and the immorality of poverty were very similar, the two societies worked together closely and exchanged ideas and personnel. Other societies were established in a number of British and American cities and gradually, many other charities adopted the Society's procedures for dealing with those seeking poor relief. Volunteers were used increasingly to undertake social enquiries and, in time, many charities began to employ full-time, paid workers; it became apparent that these workers should be trained to undertake charity investigations.

By pioneering new techniques and procedures, the Charity Organisation Society laid the foundations for the emergence of professional social work. Procedures for interviewing clients, keeping records and making home visits are an integral part of the social worker's routine today. The Society's belief in temporary relief and the rehabilitation of the destitute expressed its adherence to liberal values and influenced the development of social work theory. Its attempts to replace indiscriminate charitable relief with decisions based on a careful investigation of the circumstances of applicants were incorporated into social work method. Above all, the decision to employ trained staff to deal with those seeking help led to the professionalisation of charity and the creation of the modern, professional social worker.

These activities were the bases for what was to become known subsequently as social casework. Although most charities were concerned with poor relief, others such as the youth clubs and the settlements had different aims. During the nineteenth century, numerous youth organisations, which attempted to cater for the needs of children and young people, were established; some became national or international movements while others were run locally as clubs sponsored by a variety of religious and secular organisations. Some, like the Sunday Schools and Ragged Schools, emphasised the educational aspects of youth work while others laid greater stress on organised recreation but all were concerned with the moral upliftment of the poor and the salvation of children from the vices of destitution. The settlements had similar objectives; in what must appear now to be a shockingly patronising definition, Queen described a settlement as: 'A colony of members of the upper classes, formed in a poor neighbourhood with the double purpose of getting to know local conditions of life from personal observation and helping where help is needed.'[6] In addition, the settlements wished to set an example; through direct contact with 'those who possess the means of higher life', as Canon Barnett put it, the poor could be encouraged to live soberly and better themselves. Barnett hoped also that settlements such as Toynbee Hall, which he founded in London in 1877, would promote social harmony between the classes for, through personal contact with slum dwellers, 'the sorrow and misery of class division and indifference could be alleviated'.[7] Many settlements had close links with universities and recruited adventurous students from middle-class homes to live and work in them as volunteers. The settlements provided a variety of group activities which, unlike the youth clubs, catered for adults as well as children. By providing organised leisure and educational services, they hoped to inculcate moral values and reform the habits of slum dwellers.

In addition to its poor relief activities, the Charity Organisation Society regarded itself as the leader of all philanthropic endeavour and attempted, as its name suggests, to co-ordinate the work of all the charities concerned with poor relief. One of its first efforts in this field was to establish a register of those in receipt of charity so that abuse and duplication could be prevented. In some American cities, where a local Charity Organisation Society had not been established, other organisations with similar aims came into being; the best known of these were the Social Service Exchanges. Based on an idea conceived by Tuckerman, the first Social Service Exchange was established in Boston in 1876 primarily to maintain a register of the different charities and their clients. But it was not used by all the charities and some resented the efforts of these organisations to co-ordinate their work. This led to acrimony: because of its clumsy approach the Charity Organisation Society in Britain succeeded in alienating several well respected charities.

These different fields of philanthropy were incorporated later into professional social work largely through the efforts of American social work professors, but initially, training for charity workers was designed to meet the needs of those who administered poor relief.

Youth work and other group activities and charity organisation were not regarded as topics for social work instruction until the 1920s and 1930s.

The Beginnings of Social Work Education in Britain and the United States

Specialised training for charity workers played a crucial role in the development of professional social work in Britain and America. It prepared students for employment, enhanced the status of the profession and provided opportunities for academic reflection and research which resulted in the formulation of theoretical ideas and principles. The Charity Organisation Society, the settlements and Octavia Hill were the founders of social work education in Britain. Octavia Hill, who delegated her rent collecting activities to volunteers, realised the need for training and instituted in-service courses. Margaret Sewell of the Women's University Settlement gave occasional lectures on charity work which were popular and Charles Loch, who believed that charity should be entrusted to what he described as 'social physicians', called for the proper training of workers. Under Loch's guidance, the Society took the lead and in 1896 established a training course for charity workers in London. Helen Bosanquet was responsible for these courses but her approach to social work education became the subject of controversy and was not resolved for many years.

Bosanquet believed that social workers should be taught the broad principles of social philosophy from which skills and techniques could be abstracted. However, there was considerable disagreement between those who believed in an academic education for social workers and those who thought that a vocational training was more suitable. Although the Charity Organisation Society's Committee on Social Education agreed that theoretical knowledge and practical skills were equally necessary, conflict over the proper combination of these two elements was not resolved easily. The inauguration of the School of Sociology in London in 1903 offered a compromise, which appeared to solve the problem temporarily. E. T. Urwick was instrumental in developing the course curriculum at the school which was based on a combination of theoretical education and supervised practical training. Also, it was recognised that different levels and types of training were required and, in addition to its full-time courses, the School provided part-time extension classes. The School of Sociology had a relatively brief independent life for in 1912, owing mainly to insufficient financial support, it amalgamated with the London School of Economics to become the Department of Social Science; Urwick was its first director. By 1915, the Charity Organisation Society felt that the teaching provided by the Department gave insufficient emphasis to practical training and did not meet the requirements of social workers fully. The Society approached Bedford College and succeeded in establishing a course which, in its view, paid more attention to the needs of practitioners. In time, social work courses were established at other British universities and institutions of higher learning.[8]

In the United States, Zilpha Smith of the Boston Associated Charities established one of the first in-service training classes for volunteers. Soon, the need for more extensive training was recognised and many agreed that the techniques of social work could not be acquired adequately through apprenticeship. In 1898, a summer school in philanthropy was launched by the New York Charity Organisation Society; this was a course of six weeks' duration, designed for graduates and others who had experience of charity work. Lectures and seminars were supplemented by supervised field work and students lived in settlements for the duration of the course. The summer school was a great success and it resulted in the creation of a one-year, full-time training programme which evolved subsequently into the prestigious New York School of Social Work at Columbia University.[9] Under the guidance of Abbott, Taylor and Breckenridge, the Chicago charities established the Institute of Social Science in 1901; later it became the School of Social Service Administration at the University of Chicago. Charities in other cities followed this lead and permanent schools of social work, which were subsequently incorporated into universities, were established in a variety of American cities in the early years of this century.

Originally, the schools of social work attempted to teach students to deal with specific social problems; courses in family and child welfare and medical and psychiatric social work were provided and field training in agencies which specialised in these fields of practice featured prominently. Some social workers, such as Edward Devine of the New York School of Social Work, opposed this emphasis on specialised technical training and argued that more attention should be paid to broader issues of social and economic inequality. Abbott, in Chicago, was also in favour of courses which taught broader issues of social welfare but most social work teachers supported attempts to formulate and refine social work's techniques and practical methods.[10] This was encouraged by Abraham Flexner's criticisms of social work;

in an address to the National Conference of Charities and Corrections in 1915, Flexner argued that social work could not claim to be a profession as it had failed to standardise its methods, had a poor academic reputation and did not possess an educationally communicable technique. Instead of applying professional knowledge and skills to deal with social problems, Flexner alleged that social workers did little more than refer their clients from one agency to another. Although these claims were dismissed by some social workers, Bruno suggested that Flexner's challenge was accepted at face value by many social work educators who concentrated their efforts on developing methods; this resulted in the neglect of the broader dimensions of social work education.[11]

Despite the rapid expansion of social work training in the United States, the professional schools could not satisfy the demand for social work education and many charities continued to train their workers on an apprenticeship basis. To foster the expansion of social work training facilities, the Association of Training Schools for Professional Social Work was founded in 1919. Variously renamed in later years, it encouraged the expansion of social work courses at American universities and sought to promote common standards. Admission requirements, curricula, course duration and other aspects of training were standardised and by the 1930s, the Association had achieved many of its aims.

In Britain, the content of social work education and the level at which it was provided varied greatly. Independent, professional schools were not established for many years and social work training at universities was provided within academic departments of sociology and social administration. A variety of different courses were also offered by different educational institutions and professional bodies; child care officers, almoners, psychiatric social workers and probation officers were trained at different levels of academic competence at universities, colleges and other training centres. Different approaches to social work education were adopted; some courses stressed the teaching of practical skills, others placed more emphasis on academic subjects and many believed in specialisation. The fragmentation of social work education in the United Kingdom persisted for many years. In America, on the other hand, there was a concerted effort to integrate social work training and to provide standardised courses which would equip students to practise in different settings. The need for standardised techniques and methods were discussed at numerous social work conferences before and after the First World War and subsequently, American social workers formulated a generic approach applicable to all forms of social work intervention. Although the principles of scientific charity were formulated originally in Britain, American social workers were far more innovative that their British colleagues and were responsible for social work's subsequent academic development.

The Diversification of Social Work Practice

Specialised teaching at schools of social work at the beginning of the century was prompted by the increasing specialisation of the charities. Even though the charities continued to work among the urban poor, they became less concerned with poor relief. While poverty remained central to their work and characterised their clients, the charities dealt increasingly with problems other than low income; neglected children, deserted wives, the aged, delinquents, the mentally ill and other poor people with special problems attracted their attention. Also, they attempted to treat these pathologies without providing financial aid. Social workers approved of these developments and many believed that the profession's interests would be well served if social workers were employed to treat the pathologies of the poor instead of being used to dispense charity to destitute families. In order to reflect their increasing specialisation, professionalisation and declining interest in poor relief, many charities changed their names; as a generic description, the term social agency was adopted widely in the United States while the term voluntary organisation was preferred in Britain.

On the other hand, the Charity Organisation Society not only retained its interest in poor relief but sought to influence government on this question. The Society's views on Poor Law administration in England were represented in the majority report of the Poor Law Commission in 1909 which recommended that the existing approach to public assistance be retained. Although it was hoped that the Society would be involved more closely in the administration of Poor Law funds, this and other recommendations of the Commission were opposed vigorously by the Webbs and the Fabian Society and were not fully implemented. In the United States, the Society and its branches were more successful and local charities in several American cities were able to persuade the authorities to abolish public assistance and to transfer their poor relief allocation to the charities instead. But with specialisation, many charities found that they had little in common with the Society and its continued concern for poor relief. Also, the

Society's relationships with several charities deteriorated as it sought to exert control over them, and its intemperate criticisms of those charities which did not conform to its views caused bitter dissension. Although it succeeded in suppressing bogus charities, its attacks on reputable voluntary organisations such as Dr Barnardo's and the National Society for the Prevention of Cruelty to Children (NSPCC) harmed its image in Britain. The campaigns waged against its philosophy by the Webbs and the Fabians contributed also to its demise as did the Liberal government's reforms which introduced a variety of social welfare measures before the First World War. As in Britain, rivalry between the Charity Organisation Society and the specialised agencies in America increased but whereas the Society contracted its role in the United Kingdom to become the Family Welfare Association, in the United States it was transformed gradually into a co-ordinating, planning and fund-raising body. This was fostered actively by the Russell Sage Foundation which encouraged the Society to concentrate on charity organisation instead of dealing directly with applications for poor relief. In Pittsburgh, the Society changed its name in 1908 to become the Council for Social Agencies and representatives of the various charities were appointed to its governing board. The Cleveland Charity Organisation Society adopted this name in 1913 and assumed fund raising responsibilities by establishing procedures through which public donations for social welfare were collected centrally.

Increasingly diverse opportunities for social work practice in different specialised charities were accompanied by the employment of social workers in new settings where they collaborated with professionals such as doctors, lawyers and psychiatrists; this collaboration aided social work's attempts to attract recognition and become established professionally. In the United States, recognition came first from the lower judiciary and the medical profession.

In the 1890s in Chicago, the social agencies petitioned the Chicago Bar Association and the State legislature to bring about changes in the way young offenders were dealt with in the criminal courts; they campaigned specifically for the creation of separate judicial procedures which would afford a greater measure of protection to children who had committed offences and deal with them more constructively than did the adult courts. These efforts resulted in the establishment of America's first juvenile court in Cook County, Chicago in 1899 and two social workers, paid by the local charities, were recruited to serve it. Julian Mack, the first judge to be appointed to the juvenile court bench, made extensive use of these workers and required them to prepare reports on the home circumstances of the children who appeared before him. Other members of the judiciary such as Benjamin Lindsay in Denver and Harvey Baker in Boston supported these reforms and they joined with the charities to campaign for the extension of juvenile courts; the Chicago example was replicated in numerous American cities and, in time, professional social workers became an integral part of juvenile justice in the United States.

Recognition from the medical profession was fostered through the employment of social workers in hospitals. Dr Richard Cabot, of the Massachusetts General Hospital, was one of the first to employ social workers to undertake investigations into the backgrounds of patients and to assist doctors in their treatment. Cabot believed that because medical practice had become dependent on hospital therapy, physicians were less well informed about the social circumstances of their patients and could do little to ensure that steps were taken to improve their home conditions; the need for these to be ameliorated was required especially in cases of malnutrition, tuberculosis and other diseases associated with urban poverty. Cabot began to employ social workers in 1905 and at the National Conference of Charities and Corrections in 1915, he reported that the experiment had been a great success. Another important proponent of the employment of social workers in medical practice was Dr Charles Emerson of the Johns Hopkins Medical School, who not only used social workers extensively but required medical students to work as volunteers at social agencies in Baltimore to gain a better understanding of the social aspects of illness.

Developments in psychiatry at the turn of the century were of great benefit to professional social work. Emerging from their earlier preoccupation with the custodial care of the insane, psychiatrists became more interested in the social causes of mental disease and some began to employ social workers. Among those who were well disposed towards social work at the time were Adolf Meyer, William Healy and Elmer Southard. Healy's paper on the role of psychology in social work practice to the National Conference of Charities and Corrections in 1917 was received with great enthusiasm and Meyer advised Mary Richmond on the formulation of her principles of social diagnosis. Southard promoted the view that social workers should be employed in mental hospitals and clinics to assist psychiatrists and together with Mary Jarrett, a social worker, he published an influential book on social psychiatry in 1922 which made extensive use of case histories prepared by social workers.[12] Closer collaboration between psychiatrists and social workers occurred during the First World War when a shortage of psychiatrists resulted in the frequent use of social workers to treat shell-shocked patients. After the war, psychiatric theories were incorporated into social work education in the United States and this development had profound implications. Also, psychiatrists were invited to give lectures at schools of social work on the causes of mental illness and to teach subjects which were not related directly to psychopathology such as child development and personality theory. In time, psychiatric social work became one of the most prestigious specialisations in social work.

Collaboration with the other professions was not as successful in Britain as it had been in the United States. Court missionaries had worked in the English magistrates' courts since the 1870s and with the enactment of the Probation of Offenders Act in 1907 it was recognised that social workers could make a useful contribution but it was not until the Criminal Justice Act of 1925 was passed that the probation service was properly established. Charles Loch was instrumental in creating opportunities for the employment of social workers in English hospitals. Known as almoners, they were required primarily to investigate the patient's ability to pay for treatment. Although they provided assistance to needy patients or referred them to the charities for aid, they were not used as extensively by medical doctors as they were in the United States.

At the turn of the century very few, if any, trained social workers were employed by local government authorities in Britain or the United States to administer poor relief or to undertake other welfare tasks. Inspired by the Charity Organisation Society, many charities regarded themselves as the rightful purveyors of social welfare and most resisted the extension of government services but, in spite of this, political and economic factors led to the expansion of public welfare services in both countries. The Liberal government's reforms after 1906 in Britain did not involve social workers but in America they were employed to administer state welfare provisions increasingly after the First World War. The first major discussion of the role of professional social workers in public welfare took place at the White House in 1909. Called by President Roosevelt, the Conference on the Care of Dependent Children was attended by delegates from the leading charities as well as Federal and State civil servants. Although the representatives of the charities argued that child welfare should be the responsibility of voluntary agencies supported financially by the state, this view was not accepted and with the enactment subsequently of child care legislation by the States and the creation of the Federal Children's Bureau in 1912, public child welfare provisions were established. While these developments were not in the interests of the private agencies, they were to benefit social work as they resulted in the employment of professional social workers in government on a substantial scale and boosted the profession's status considerably. The first director of the Children's Bureau was Julia Lathrop, a prominent social worker who had worked in the Hull House Settlement in Chicago.

Rising unemployment in the United States during the 1920s required the expansion of public assistance and increasingly, social workers were recruited to administer these measures. By the time of the Wall Street crisis in 1929, forty American cities employed social workers in their public welfare departments. Although President Hoover and his advisers believed that it was desirable that private agencies rather than public authorities should be responsible for the welfare of the unemployed and their families, the ensuing crisis revealed that the voluntary organisations and community chests could not deal with the problem; as their funds were depleted, the States were compelled to enact emergency legislation to provide for the unemployed. The first emergency administration was established in New York in 1932 under the directorship of Harry Hopkins, a professional social worker. Twenty-four States followed this lead in the same year and when Roosevelt took office in 1933, he appointed Hopkins to administer the Federal Emergency Relief Act. Hopkins required all States receiving federal aid to employ qualified social workers to deal with public assistance matters; this ensured the permanent employment of social workers in government social welfare services in America.

In Britain, the depression passed without the involvement of social workers in state services designed to maintain the unemployed. Although the implementation of the Beveridge proposals after the Second World War resulted in new employment opportunities for social workers in local authorities, they were not to participate in the administration of income maintenance services. The National Assistance Act of 1948 empowered local authorities to establish welfare departments which employed social workers to provide services to the elderly, disabled, homeless and other needy people. The Children's Act which was passed in the same year increased the recruitment of qualified social workers to local government service considerably by requiring local authorities to establish Children's Departments concerned with child care matters. But it was only after 1970, following the acceptance of the Seebohm Committee's recommendations and the enactment of the Local Authority Social Services Act, that British social workers achieved a degree of involvement comparable to that which had been enjoyed by their American colleagues for many years. This legislation consolidated local authority social work practice, increased the employment of social workers in local government considerably and has contributed enormously to the professional development of social work in the United Kingdom.

American Theoretical Innovations
Anxious to be respectable academically, the founders of social work education sought to increase the scientific content of their courses by providing instruction in the various social sciences; students were taught the principles of sociology, psychology, economics, social biology and eugenics. As there were no basic textbooks or general works which dealt with social work exclusively, teachers of social work made greater use of those social sciences which appeared to be most relevant to their needs. Close relationships with academic departments of sociology were fostered during the profession's early years and extensive teaching was given in what was known then as the sociology of social pathology. This subject dealt with the nature and causes of a large variety of social problems and since much social work practice at the time was specialised, this was thought to be appropriate. It was not until Mary Richmond published *Social Diagnosis* in 1917 that social workers had a textbook which dealt with the subject in its own right.[13]

The publication of this work had a profound influence on social work's professional development. Many thought that social work had reached maturity and it was believed that a general set of principles, which described the procedures which social workers should follow when dealing with their clients, had been expounded. But Richmond's book was concerned exclusively with social casework and it was of little benefit to social workers employed in the settlements or youth clubs. Later, Richmond was alarmed that casework had been elevated to such prominence through her writings and was quoted as having said: 'I have spent twenty-five years of my life in an attempt to get social casework accepted as a valid process of social work. I shall now spend the rest of my life trying to demonstrate to social caseworkers that there is more to social work that social casework.'[14] In this, she was not very successful.

Bruno reported that the term social casework first appeared in the profession's vocabulary at the National Conference of Charities and Corrections in 1897.[15] Between then and the First World War, numerous papers on the subject were read at social work gatherings and although efforts had been made to define the principles governing different forms of specialised casework practice, Richmond provided the profession with a methodology which integrated the different fields in which caseworkers were employed. She was commended also for distinguishing clearly between charity and professional social work; Richmond argued that social workers should not be responsible for the material needs of their clients by providing financial aid. The profession's primary responsibility was to develop the client's personality so that their clients could be helped to understand their problems, adapt to their circumstances and overcome their difficulties through their own efforts. In her view, social work comprised 'those processes which develop personality through adjustments consciously effected, individual by individual, between men and their social environments'.[16]

Because Richmond's book was concerned largely with the codification and clarification of methods and techniques, many felt that social work needed to embrace explanatory theories of human behaviour which would further strengthen the profession's theoretical content. Although sociology had influenced social work education considerably, its potential for providing a theoretical basis for social work practice was limited and it was soon replaced by the growing attraction social workers felt for psychology and psychiatry. This was fostered by the increasing collaboration between psychiatrists and social workers in the United States and social workers initially took an indiscriminate interest in new psychiatric theories and ideas. But what Woodroofe called the 'psychiatric deluge' came about in the mid-1920s as the work of Sigmund Freud became known more widely.[17] Freud first visited America in 1909 to lecture at Clark University in Worcester, Massachusetts but it was not until his writings had been translated by Abraham Brill and popularised that psychoanalysis gained widespread recognition in the United States. Soon, Freudian ideas were to dominate American psychiatry, to influence the development of psychology, sociology and anthroplogy and to have a profound impact on social work.[18] By the end of the 1920s, psychoanalysis was adopted eagerly and uncritically by schools of social work and within two decades of the publication of Richmond's work, social work theory was transformed.

Initially, a variety of psychoanalytic concepts were incorporated unsystematically into the profession's literature but these were refined and applied gradually to the formulation of a coherent psychoanalytic approach through the writings of Charlotte Towle, Gordon Hamilton, Annette Garrett and Florence Hollis. The Diagnostic School, as these writers became known, drew on Richmond's approach but applied Freudian ideas to reformulate social casework as a psychotherapeutic activity. Although few questioned the adoption of psychiatric approaches, some social workers opposed the adoption of Freudian psychoanalysis and a competing school of social casework emerged 'as a reaction against the excessive influence upon social work of what was felt by some social workers to be a deterministic and mechanistic view of man as embodied by Freudian psychology'.[19] This was the Functional School, which under the leadership of Virginia Robinson, Jessie Taft and others based its ideas on the work of Otto Rank. Critical of Freudian casework's concern with pathology, the Functional School viewed treatment as the client's capacity for development within the casework relationship and spoke of the psychology of growth instead of the psychology of illness which they believed characterised the Diagnostic School. Although the two differed in emphasis, both were indebted to psychiatric theories and this was reflected also in other writings on social casework which were not based explicitly on psychoanalytic concepts.

While the incorporation of psychiatric ideas into social work provided the profession with a substantial theoretical body of knowledge, it created difficulties. Academic training became more esoteric and divorced from the realities of social work practice. Students were taught to pay more attention to the childhood experiences and emotions of their clients than to their home conditions or material needs. Although the schools may have wished it, the financial circumstances of clients could not be disregarded and in public welfare agencies especially, these matters remained central to the social worker's task. The adoption of psychiatric approaches confirmed social work's primary concern for individuals and rephrased, in a more sophisticated way, the profession's nineteenth-century belief that social problems were the consequence of individual maladjustment. Also, by embracing psychiatry, social work undermined its capacity to bring about social reforms and to deal with social need on a wider scale. Instead, broader issues of social welfare were neglected and regarded as political problems which had no bearing on the profession's new, scientific role.

Psychiatric ideas strengthened the theory of social casework enormously and confirmed its position as the primary method of social work but some American social workers recognised that the activities of the youth clubs, Councils for Social Agencies and similar organisations should not be neglected and they began to write about these forms of social work practice. These efforts led to the formulation of the methods of social group work and community organisation.

As shown previously, the settlements and youth organisations made extensive use of group activities. Jane Addams, the founder of the Hull House Settlement in Chicago, was the first to write about group work; although she did not use the term and dealt exclusively with group activities for children she described basic principles and methods.[20] During the 1920s several American authors wrote about group work but it was not until the publication of Grace Coyle's *Social Progress in Organized Groups* in 1930 that the subject was dealt with comprehensively and some drew comparisons between this book and Richmond's *Social Diagnosis*, claiming that Coyle's work was as important to the development of group work as Richmond's had been to casework. Coyle defined group work as: 'An educational process aiming at the development and adjustment of individuals through voluntary group associations'.[21] She believed that group work could be used not only to achieve this objective but to improve social relationships between people and even to promote democracy. The best way to educate people to participate politically in democratic societies, she believed, was to teach them in small groups. In addition to describing these ambitious aims, Coyle's book dealt with a variety of topics such as the processes of group formation, behaviour in groups, leadership and the role of the professional worker.

Coyle's book and her subsequent writings on the subject helped to establish group work as a method of social work but disagreements about the definition, objectives and techniques of group work persisted for many years. These were resolved eventually as these issues were debated at social work conferences and meetings. The publication of standard textbooks on group work by authors such as H. B. Trecker and Gisella Konopka and their adoption by American schools of social work in the 1950s helped also to bring about consensus about the nature of group work intervention.

Although the foundations for community work practice were laid by the Charity Organisation Society and the Social Service Exchanges in the nineteenth century, community organisation agencies in the United States achieved a measure of success in the years after the First

World War. Many of the charismatic founders of the charities were no longer active and the jealousies and rivalries for status which characterised early philanthropy were replaced by a greater spirit of co-operation. As the Charity Organisation Society in the United States transformed itself to become Councils for Social Agencies, it collaborated more democratically with local charities and became more respected. The idea that these community welfare organisation should be responsible for fund raising was given greater impetus during the First World War when 'war chests', which collected public donations, were created. After the war, these became known as 'community chests' and since then have been an integral part of community organisation in the United States.

These developments permitted a more comprehensive description of community organisation in the 1920s and 30s. Norton's book on the co-operative movement in social work, Pearson's account of the Welfare Council of New York and Petit's case studies of community work agencies in the United States were all published in the 1920s and prompted the appointment of a special study group by the National Conference of Social Work in 1939 to formulate the principles of community organisation. The reports of this and subsequent study groups attempted to describe the principles of community welfare organisation and urged that it be recognised as a basic method of social work and taught at the professional schools.[22] Subsequent publications on the subject and especially the comprehensive textbooks published by American social workers such as Ross, Dunham and Harper in the 1950s contributed significantly to the development of community organisation methods.

The literature on community work, group work and casework dealt chiefly with each method in isolation and after the Second World War, the prospect of integrating the three methods was debated extensively. By the 1950s American social workers had articulated the generic principles. Professionalism, direct intervention, the development of interpersonal relationships, the application of knowledge and skills and the use of a variety of concepts such as individuation, self-determination and acceptance were identified as the essential features of social work practice irrespective of the settings or method used.

Social Work in Europe and Other Industrial Countries

The identification of the three methods, their codification and integration through the formulation of a unitary methodology reveals the profound contribution of American social workers to the profession's development. There were no comparable developments in Europe even though the origins of professional social work in these countries were similar to those in the United States. As in America, numerous philanthropic organisations were established in continental Europe in the nineteenth century to deal with the problems of urban destitution through voluntary effort. Many employed full-time workers to investigate the circumstances of needy families seeking charitable relief and, in time, training facilities which evolved into professional schools of social work were established to prepare them for philanthropic work. Unlike the United States, few European schools of social work were incorporated into universities and many adopted a vocational approach which was concerned primarily with inculcating practical social work skills. Although teaching in the social sciences and other academic disciplines was provided, these were regarded as ancillary subjects; philosophy, languages, law, economics and history were taught as a part of the student's general education and had little bearing on professional training.

Today, in countries such as West Germany, France, Sweden and the Netherlands, social workers are trained at non-university institutions of higher learning. In Italy, the great majority of schools of social work are non-university, tertiary institutions but some, such as the *Scuola per l'Assistenza Sociale* at the University of Sienna, which was established in 1956, are based at universities. Schools of social work in Sweden are separate from the universities but they have university status and are governed by regulations promulgated by the Ministry of Education. In West Germany and Holland, discussions have been held in recent years to consider ways of integrating social work education into the universities. In the Federal Republic, the *Fachohschule* or vocational schools of social work are run by a variety of organisations including religious bodies and the State governments and, as in many other European countries, these are supervised by public authorities. In the Netherlands, the Ministry of Education is responsible for the country's nineteen *academies*, as Dutch schools of social work are known. Schools of social work in France are controlled by the Ministry of Health and Social Security through a national body, the Joint Committee of French Schools of Social Service. Similarly, in Sweden, the country's six schools of social work are governed by the National Board of Social Work Education which is responsible for supervising their work, standardising their curricula and teaching and even for the selection of candidates seeking admission to the schools. In Italy, on the other hand, social work education is entirely free of state control and schools may structure their curricula as they wish; consequently there are considerable variations between the courses provided by the different Italian schools. In countries such as West Germany and France, social workers are awarded government qualifications. In the Federal Republic, the State governments award the *Staatlich anerkannte Sozialarbeiter*, which is the recognised professional qualification in the country while in France, social workers are awarded state diplomas of *Assistante Sociale*.

Social work training in different European countries has been associated with different fields of practice. In the Netherlands, the social academies offered courses originally which were comparable to social casework in the United States and Britain but, since then, they have broadened their interests to provide training in residential care, youth work, cultural work and personnel management as well. One of the oldest of the Dutch schools, which was established in Amsterdam in 1899 to train volunteers working in the local charities, was known as a school of social work until 1957 when it changed its name to reflect its teaching in these fields and it is known now as a social academy. Social work education in Sweden is linked to public administration and this is reflected in the curricula of the schools where subjects such as constitutional and administrative law, administrative methods and procedures and social legislation feature prominently. Also, the Swedish schools are responsible for training generalist civil servants for employment in local and central government and are known, therefore, as schools of social work and public administration. In West Germany, social work education is linked to the subject of social pedagogy and in France, social work has been associated with public health and medical care for many years. Although little is known about the training of social workers and their subsequent employment in East European countries, in Poland, social work education is linked also to health care. Polish schools of social work, such as the State Medical School for Social Workers in Warsaw, are located within para-medical training institutions which are run by the Ministry of Health and Social Welfare. In Yugoslavia, social work training is provided by specialised tertiary, training institutions, known as Higher Schools for Social Workers. There are five of these schools in the country and all provide a two year course of study leading to the award of a Diploma in Social Work. In 1972, a four-year course in social work and social welfare was established at the University of Zagreb to provide advanced training for senior welfare personnel.

Although different aspects of social work education are given emphasis in different European countries, social workers on the continent undertake similar tasks and, like British and American social workers, deal mostly with the problems of individuals and their families. For example, despite their traditional links with medical care, social workers in France find employment in juvenile courts, children's and old people's homes, drug rehabilitation centres, adoption agencies, social security and other governmental organisations. Because of this and because of a common desire to strengthen social work's academic content, social work education in Europe, as in other countries, has been receptive to American theories and ideas.

American social work theories have had the greatest impact on social work education in Britain. Originally, the majority of social work courses were pragmatic and vocational and only a few, such as the specialist psychiatric social work courses, made extensive use of American concepts. Also, British social work was not as professionalised and many, who were not trained in social work, found employment in occupations which were reserved for the professionally qualified in the United States. This was partly because of the emergence of social administration as an academic discipline in the United Kingdom and ambiguity about the respective roles of social administrators and social workers persisted for many years. Gradually, through the writings of Dame Eileen Younghusband, Noel Timms and others, the academic content of social work education in Britain was improved and after the enactment of the Local Authority Social Services Act in 1970, social work education adopted a more coherent approach. In recent years, social work training in Britain has expanded greatly and professorial chairs in the subject have been established throughout the country; this has raised the status of British social work education and it conforms more closely now to American approaches.

American theories have influenced social work education in English speaking countries such as Canada, Australia, New Zealand and South Africa as well. Canadian schools of social work conformed to the accreditation requirements of the American Council on Social Work Education until recently and there were few differences between the curricula of American and Canadian schools. However, unlike the United States, where undergraduate courses in social work were regarded as a pre-professional education, professional first degree courses have been established in Canada. Similar social work degrees of three or four years' duration have been offered at South African universities for many years. In spite of the country's ethnic and cultural heterogeneity and unique politics, these are based largely on American social work training practices and American textbooks are prescribed extensively. In Australia and New Zealand, vocational, non-degree courses, similar to those in Britain, were offered originally but during the 1960s efforts were made to provide a more professionally acceptable education in social work. Consequently, a number of first degree courses, which reflect the theoretical content of American social work education, have been established in the universities.

In Japan, one of the first schools of social work was established at Mejii Gakuin University in Tokyo in 1932. Since then, there has been a rapid growth in social work education and there are over twenty-five schools of social work in the country today, of which eleven are for post-graduates. Japanese social work training has adopted American standards and at the graduate schools especially, curricula have modelled on training practices in the United States.

With the exception of the French schools, which have remained tenaciously impervious to American social work theories, closer links between schools of social work in the United States and continental Europe have developed. As American textbooks were translated into European languages, American terms were used increasingly by the European schools. For obvious reasons, American ideas have not been adopted in Eastern Europe but it is interesting to note that the State Medical School for Social Workers in Warsaw stresses the need to teach its students 'to give assistance in an atmosphere of mutual confidence and respect', and to help their clients 'solve their difficult living problems independently and to improve their adjustment to new living conditions. (Help him so that he can help himself.)'[23] This statement conforms to American social work ideals so closely that it could have been taken from an American textbook!

Internationally, social work education expanded rapidly after the Second World War when many professional schools of social work were established in the newly independent developing countries. Social work training in these countries has been based on western approaches; as in Europe and other industrial nations, American theories of social work have had a considerable influence on schools of social work in the Third World.

3 Colonialism, Modernisation and Social Work

The export of western social work to the developing countries of the Third World reflects in a small way the complex processes which linked and continues to link these countries to the industrial West. These were established through centuries of colonialism and imperialism and have not been broken by the declarations which granted political independence to the former colonial territories after the Second World War. Although many retained their indigenous languages, religions and cultures, colonial rule permeated these societies to the extent that the economic systems, administrative structures, educational and other social institutions which were established during the colonial era survived after independence. Also, colonialism fostered the belief that western ideas and practices were superior and worthy of emulation. The replication of American and European social work theories and methods in the Third World is just one example of this attitude and together with other, more dramatic and significant manifestations of dependency, is rooted in the colonial experience.

Although few countries were colonised in the true sense of the word by white settlers, European imperialism dominated South America, Africa and Asia politically during the seventeenth, eighteenth and nineteenth centuries. Most countries which now comprise the Third World were ruled, at one time or another by the European powers and even those that were not, did not escape the effects of colonialism.[1]

Different Western European nations were more successful at subduing native people than others and some annexed larger territories but relatively few had no colonies in other continents. Different European nations were imperial powers at different times during the colonial centuries; when Britain and Holland were small trading nations, Spanish and Portuguese maritime supremacy had been established for many decades. Some concentrated their imperial ambitions in some regions of the globe while others gained colonies in Africa, Asia and South America. Although Portugal established small trading settlements which were scattered around the world and although Spain colonised the Philippine islands, Iberian imperialism was most successful in South America. The Dutch annexed territories in all three continents but like the Portuguese, established themselves originally in coastal areas where opportunities for maritime trade were most advantageous. Later, Portuguese and Dutch rule in Africa and the East was extended to incorporate larger areas. During the nineteenth century, as Spanish and Portuguese rule waned, Britain and France emerged as the great imperial powers. Previously, Britain and France had subverted Spanish control over the Caribbean and had extended their influence from island and coastal enclaves to annex inland territories. As a consequence of Britain's victories during the Napoleonic wars, many French and Dutch territories were ceded and came under British rule. In the latter half of the nineteenth century, Britain and France, together with Germany and Belgium, brought vast unexplored regions in Africa under their control. European competition to rule the hinterland of Africa began as late as the 1870s and it was not until after the First World War that colonial administrations were established effectively in these remote areas. Russia and the United States were latecomers and although both gained control over foreign people and their lands, their efforts were a pale imitation of the imperial achievements of countries such as Britain and France. This was true also of Japanese imperialism.

European domination of Africa, Asia and South America originated in the journeys of discovery and mercantile ventures of enterprising explorers such as Marco Polo, Bartholomew Diaz, Vasco de Gama and Christopher Columbus. Many of these expeditions were motivated and supported by commercial interests and they confirmed the vast trading potential of the unknown world. As a consequence of these travels, Western Europe began to import spices, cloth, jewellery and agricultural produce directly and reduced its overland trade through intermediaries in Southern and Eastern Europe; this was an important development for, through maritime trade, the Western European nations became great naval powers. Under the influence of Protestantism, capitalism emerged in countries such as Britain and Holland to give rise to independent trading companies such as the Vereenigde Oost-Indische Compagnie, the Levant Company and the British East India Company which pursued the exploration of the unknown world in search of new commercial opportunities.[2]

These companies and other European traders had little to offer the wealthy civilisations of the East with whom they wished to trade; often their goods were inferior and their ability to pay in gold was limited. Because they were unable to trade on equal terms with these kingdoms, the European traders relied increasingly on their military superiority to meet their requirements. In Latin America, the superior tactics and weapons of the conquistadors had annihilated the indigenous civilisations and subjugated their peoples. To reward the victors and attract new colonists, lands were granted and large agricultural estates, which enslaved the continent's native people in feudal serfdom, were established. While the kingdoms of the East were not subjugated to the same extent, European military supremacy initially threatened and later dominated their rulers; this permitted commerce on terms which were most favourable to the traders and merchant companies. European traders in Africa became wealthy through selling human beings, the continent's major resource. The Spanish colonists had decimated the native population of the New World and required more sturdy labourers to work on their estates. Slavery provided new commercial opportunities for the smaller mercantile nations; in order to finance the purchase of hides, sugar and other produce from the South American and Caribbean colonists, English sea captains such as John Hawkins obtained slaves in West Africa at little cost and sold them at great profit to the Spanish settlers.

Hawkins and others exploited what the Portuguese had begun earlier and soon the slave trade was extended to the English and French colonies of North America. Slavery not only brought wealth but contributed to the naval superiority of countries such as Britain and France. The English derived enormous benefit from the slave trade, improved their maritime skills and gained strategic control over the Atlantic. This was critically important during the wars with Spain and France and contributed enormously to Britain's subsequent rise as a world power.[3]

The mercantile character of early European colonialism gave way gradually to a more complex and comprehensive form of imperialism which was brought about by factors other than trade. Although trade remained an important feature of colonialism, other economic activities such as the direct exploitation of the natural resources of the colonies prompted the expansion of imperial rule. Unrestricted commerce had resulted in substantial imports of textiles, porcelain, jewellery and other goods which threatened Europe's industrial development. Consequently, protectionist policies, which favoured the importation of raw materials for the manufacturing industry in Europe were adopted. Prohibitive duties were imposed on imported goods in Britain and steps were taken to curb the powers of the merchant companies. Similar attempts to limit economic competition from the

North American colonies had failed but the previously powerful states of the East had been undermined and could do little to retaliate as the North American settlers had. Nor could they prevent the advent of plantation colonialism which acquired substantial areas of land to produce raw materials for export to the metropolitan countries on a large scale. New commercial enterprises came into existence to establish plantations in the colonies and to exploit the wealth of Africa and Asia through mining their mineral resources directly. The protection of these commercial interests and the security of their European managers and other personnel required the extension of colonial rule to remote areas. To finance colonial security, taxes were imposed on the native people of the colonies and this further increased the scope of colonial administration.

European imperial expansion was fostered also by diplomatic factors. Britain's policy of gunboat diplomacy and its frequent intervention in the affairs of local rulers extended British rule to territories from which it could derive little economic benefit. The extension of British colonial rule over African territories, which had little agricultural or mineral potential, was occasioned by its political rivalry with other European nations which were pursuing the same ambitions. Towards the end of the nineteenth century, European colonial possessions became symbols of military and diplomatic power as well as the means by which the imperial nations increased their wealth.

The expansion of imperial rule in the nineteenth century was prompted also by a commitment to 'civilise' the native peoples of the colonial lands. Although this was used often as a pretext to annex new territories, the missionaries pursued this objective with sincerity and zealous enthusiasm. Previously, proselytisation had been an integral part of Iberian colonialism in South America and during the nineteenth century there was a revival of missionary activity as members of different Christian denominations travelled to remote areas, especially in Africa, to bring the gospel and 'civilisation' to the indigenous people of what was known then as the 'dark continent'. Although there were frequent conflicts between the missionaries and colonial officials, the authorities were compelled to ensure their safety; as they established new mission schools, hospitals and settlements in the hinterland, the extension of colonial rule over these areas was inevitable.

As a consequence of these developments, colonial rule penetrated most of Africa and Asia during the nineteenth century and imposed on the peoples of these continents new systems of authority, languages, economic activities and social institutions. The effects of colonialism were even more dramatic in South America. By the time the Latin American colonies gained independence from Portugal and Spain, they had been permeated by European culture. Large numbers of the indigenous population had been exterminated and replaced by European colonists and African slaves, inter-marriage had blurred racial distinctions, Iberian languages and culture were adopted and the Christian religion was imposed. Although colonialism in Africa and Asia eroded traditional institutions, its effects were felt most strongly in the administrative capitals and other enclaves of European rule. Traditional values and beliefs continued to influence people in the rural areas and these were sanctioned by colonial governments, such as the British in Africa who recognised customary law. Provided that indigenous cultural practices did not challenge colonial authority or offend European morals too greatly, they were regarded often with indifference. However, traditionalism remained a serious obstacle to mobility and those who aspired to improve their position in the hierarchy of privilege created by colonialism did so by acquiring the benefits of western education and emulating their rulers in other ways. Although they did not achieve much status during colonial rule, they came to prominence at independence and as the new élite, ensured continuity between colonialism and independence during the years that followed it.

Those who had been educated by the missionaries or abroad in the metropolitan countries founded and steered the independence movements and while their populist nationalism drew support from the rural areas, their life styles and attitudes reflected the cultures of the former colonial powers rather than the traditional societies from which they came. When colonial rule ended in Africa, Asia and the Caribbean after the Second World War, English and French were adopted widely as the official languages of the newly independent nations and institutions based on administrative, judicial, economic, educational and other practices in the metropolitan countries were perpetuated through constitutional and legislative sanction.

Modernisation and Development

Although it was claimed, with justification, that the developing countries remained subject to neo-colonial and imperial influences after independence, frequently the new political élites encouraged the consolidation of colonial institutions and increased their dependence on the West by seeking consciously to emulate the industrial countries. By importing inappropriate technologies at considerable expense and encouraging foreign investment on a large scale they hoped to replicate, as quickly as possible, the economic achievements of the former colonial powers. These efforts were supported by the western countries who were anxious to prevent the spread of international communism and believed that economic prosperity was the best antidote against subversion. Western business enterprises encouraged these developments for they were eager to find new investment opportunities and to sell their technologies and industrial plant abroad. At the time, development was synonymous with industrialisation and 'modernisation', as 'westernisation' had become known euphemistically, was believed to be a prerequisite for economic and social progress.

American and European social scientists provided an intellectual basis for these beliefs which was formulated in the theory of modernisation. Modernisation theory attempted to apply to the developing countries, as recipes for their economic and social transformation, the processes of industrialisation and social change which the nations of Western Europe and North America had experienced in the nineteenth and early twentieth centuries. The modernisation school defined the objectives which it believed the newly independent countries should strive to attain and provided specific policy recommendations which it urged the governments of the Third World to implement. The ideas of modernisation theory had multidisciplinary application and were articulated with reference to the different interests of different academic subjects; these included economics, sociology, political science, demography and psychology. Modernisation theory was taught not only at the universities of the Western World where large numbers of students from the developing countries went to study and prepare themselves for senior positions in government, but at the universities of the Third World as well.

Economists made the theory of modernisation more respectable and plausible than did other social scientists. There could be little doubt that the industrial revolution had created wealth and raised levels of living in Europe and North America enormously. At the time, the Soviet Union and Japan, which had implemented policies designed to promote industrialisation, were developing rapidly. Marshall aid was demonstrating that international capital transfers and economic planning could revive the industrial prosperity of a war-ravaged Europe. Consequently, policies which advocated similar developments in the newly independent nations were most acceptable to their political leaders, and measures, which were intended to stimulate rapid economic growth through industrial investment and the application of western technology to production, were widely adopted.

The theory of economic modernisation was formulated by leading western economists in numerous publications in the 1950s and 60s. One of the first, by a group of experts appointed by the United Nations under the leadership of Professor W. A. Lewis, was published in 1951. The Lewis Report, as it became known, made numerous important recommendations and called especially for the implementation of economic policies which would foster the accumulation of capital for industrial development.[4] For example, it advocated that financial institutions, which would encourage savings be created and that capital aid should be provided by the rich nations on a large scale. In addition, other aspects of economic modernisation were analysed and other economists dealt with these in greater detail in subsequent publications. Many drew on the writings of Rosenstein-Rodan whose theory of the 'big push' towards industrialisation in Eastern and Southern Europe had special reference to the Third World.[5] The need for co-ordinated policies which led to balanced growth through simultaneous investments in infrastructure and different complementary industries was advocated by Nurske and others.[6] Econometric planning models, which specified the proportion of national income required for development, were formulated by economists like Harrod and Domar.[7] More than any other, Rostow's theory of the stages of growth expounded the theory of economic modernisation comprehensively and was acclaimed widely.[8]

Rostow's studies of European economic history led him to conceptualise development as an evolutionary process involving a series of stages in which progression from one stage to the next depended on whether or not certain preconditions had been met. For example, these included economic factors such as investment, which Rostow claimed must reach between 5 and 10 per cent of national income before a society could experience what he described as economic 'take off'. As capital accumulation increased, developing countries would progress to higher evolutionary levels until they reached the final stage of 'high mass consumption' when between 10 and 20 per cent of national income would be invested in productive enterprises. Rostow's work drew attention also to non-economic factors which he believed were preconditions for economic development. Rostow argued that entrepreneurial skills, a spirit of competitiveness and the work ethic were as important for the economic development of the Third World, as was the capital-savings ratio. These factors had been alluded to in the Lewis report and were dealt with in more detail in other economic publications but they provided most scope for sociologists and social psychologists.

These social scientists argued that measures designed to promote industrial development and economic growth in the Third World could succeed only if the traditional social institutions and values of the developing countries underwent radical social change. Traditionalism was thought to be inimical to development and numerous sociologists and social psychologists attempted to identify the cultural and social obstacles which they believed impeded economic and social progress.

Some, like William Goode, suggested that traditional family structures in developing countries were incompatible with the demands of modern economic life.[9] Family obligations and a large number of dependent kin in the extended family prevented labour mobility, inhibited savings and capital formation, suppressed initiative and individuality and maintained family members in traditional occupations which were incompatible with industrial development. Sociologists such as Hoselitz drew attention to the authoritarian systems of stratification in traditional societies which prevented social mobility and were a hindrance to the emergence of an achievement-orientated, open class system of stratification associated with industrial capitalism.[10] On a grander scale, Hoselitz applied the theoretical work of Talcott Parsons to analyse comprehensively, the traditional impediments to modernisation in developing countries.[11] Others such as Hagen concentrated on the psychological and attitudinal prerequisites of modernisation and Harvard psychologist, David McClelland expressed this in the concept of achievement motivation which he and others believed was lacking in traditional societies.[12] In a similar vein social psychologists Inkeles and Smith claimed that fundamental changes in human behaviour, which conformed to the western ideal of modern man, rational, motivated by self-interests, competitive and highly individualistic, were needed in the developing countries.[13]

Social scientists in other disciplines contributed to the theory of modernisation in a similar way. Political scientists claimed that political participation through liberal democratic institutions, such as those which existed in Europe and North America were necessary for development and demographers argued that with industrialisation, radical changes in population structure could be brought about. In the theory of demographic transition, they examined the processes which had transformed traditional patterns of population growth in the industrial countries and predicted that family size and fertility would decline as the effects of modernisation were felt.[14] Many described population growth in pessimistic, neo-Malthusian terms and believed that rapid population increases in the developing countries would negate the economic gains of development. Consequently, they advocated that population policies, which would accelerate fertility reductions, be implemented. Urbanologists regarded the migration of rural people to the capitals of the Third World as both desirable and inevitable.[15] Industrialisation in the West had been accompanied by a radical shift in the spatial location of the population from rural to urban and although some were alarmed at the pace of urbanisation and its social consequences in the Third World, these were believed to be temporary difficulties. It was believed that rapid urban growth would stabilise and that problems of urban squalor and inadequate housing would be resolved as rural migrants were absorbed into the modern, industrial economy and enjoyed higher levels of living.

Modernisation theory was based on the experience of industrialisation in the western countries and advocated explicitly that western values and institutions be diffused to the developing countries of the Third World. Social scientists recommended that steps should be taken to modify the traditional social structures of these countries so that they would conform closely to the western societies and particularly the United States which was regarded at the time as the ideal-typical advanced, industrial, capitalist state. As one American sociologist put it: 'What is involved in modernisation is a total transformation of a traditional society or pre-modern society into the types of technology and associated social organisation that characterise the advanced economically prosperous and relatively politically stable nations of the Western World.'[16]

Although sociologists and psychologists recommended that modernisation be promoted through social and attitudinal change, these were difficult to implement. While the recommendations of economists could be put into effect, proposals that changes in family structure, traditional authority, stratification and even attitudes and behaviour be brought about, could not. Apart from the practical difficulties, few recognised the political implications of attempting to modify established traditional institutions through legislative and administrative measures. Apart from anti-natalist population policies, which were adopted with dubious success in many developing countries, sociological proposals for planned social change were not implemented and the ideals of modernisation theory found practical expression primarily in the policy prescriptions of economists.

At the behest of the United Nations, the World Bank and western governments, centralised economic planning authorities were established in many developing countries. Often powerful and under the direct control of the head of state, these organisations attempted to direct the process of economic modernisation. Five-year development plans, which specified how investments and expenditures would be allocated, were prepared with technical advice from western economists. The economic policies contained in these plans directed capital resources towards infrastructure, manufacturing and heavy industry and many developing countries pursued the goals of economic modernisation on a grand scale. Steel foundries, cement mills, hydro-electric schemes and sophisticated transport and communication networks were built at great expense: many Third World countries are still indebted heavily to the foreign governments and financial institutions which provided the capital for these developments. Unfortunately, few reaped great benefit from these investments for, often, they were inappropriate to the needs of developing countries. Domestic markets could not consume the products of heavy industry and with few exceptions, developing countries could not compete internationally to export their cement, steel and other industrial surpluses profitably. Also, technical blunders, inefficiency and wastage characterised the efforts of many developing countries to industrialise. Coupled with widespread corruption, reserves were squandered on sophisticated technologies and symbols of national prestige which made little contribution to economic growth. Modern economic policies favoured the urban areas and although many Third World cities today show outward signs of prosperity, there is little indication that the incidence of subsistence poverty, squalor and deprivation has been reduced. Consumer goods, tall buildings, luxury hotels, traffic congestion and other manifestations of modernity are conspicuously evident in the capitals of the Third World but in the rural areas and the urban periphery, the majority of the people have been unaffected by these changes.

Foreign investments in manufacturing industry such as textiles and electronics produced spectacular results in some developing countries and high rates of economic growth were recorded in their national accounts. But, in spite of their efforts to become industrial states, most developing countries remain dependent on agriculture and earn foreign currency through the export of primary commodities for processing and manufacture in the industrial West. The vast majority of their populations continue to live in rural areas and derive their incomes from agricultural employment. Agriculture was neglected by the economic planners who believed that industrial development would draw the peasantry into the cities and into productive employment in industry; this would allow agriculture to become more efficient through mechanisation and commercial farming. Although this policy secured the interests of foreign owned agricultural enterprises such as the commercial plantations, rural populations have neither declined nor benefited from modern economic policies and they continue to live in subsistence agriculture in conditions of extreme poverty.

Today it is recognised that the causes of Third World poverty cannot be remedied through domestic economic policies alone. The modernisation school has been criticized by some social scientists who have provided very different explanations of the causes of under-development. Among the best known of these are Furtado, Frank and Baran who have argued that colonialism and imperialism were not discrete historical events but the foundations of a contemporary world economic order in which the developing countries are maintained in economic dependence on the rich industrial nations.[17] Although there are many aspects of the theory of dependency which are controversial, it has revealed the inadequacies of modernisation as an approach to development.[18]

Modernisation and Social Policy
Development policies in the post-independence years neglected social needs. Most national development plans, which were published in the 1950s made no reference to social welfare and were concerned exclusively with economic matters. The extent of poverty and deprivation was not recognised properly and in the rural areas, need was disguised; the traditional life styles of rural people were equated not with poverty but regarded as the simple and preferred ways of peasant farmers. At the time, expenditure on social welfare was thought to be a wasteful form of consumption which would detract from the efforts of developing countries to industrialise and promote rapid economic growth. Consequently, economists recommended that national resources should be allocated to development and that as little as possible be spent on the social services.

Implicit in these policies was the assumption that the transformation of the traditional economies of the developing countries would create wage employment, reduce the numbers of people engaged in subsistence agriculture and raise standards of living. Also, it was argued that, as personal incomes increased, social need would be reduced. With higher incomes, families could satisfy their own social needs, they could save and so prepare to meet the contingencies of old age, sickness or injury. They could subscribe to pension schemes or purchase insurance to protect themselves against the cessation or loss of earnings and could obtain health, education and housing in the private market through their own efforts. But it was recognised that public expenditure on social services and especially those dealing with social problems such as crime and delinquency, prostitution and begging, which were regarded as a nuisance, was inevitable and minimal resources were allocated for this purpose. Also, it was believed that, as national prosperity increased, governments would be able to raise greater revenues to provide for those needy sections of the population who were unable to care for themselves.

Previously, colonial administrations had been concerned about the growing problem of crime and vagrancy in the urban areas of the colonies and they took steps to deal with it. Although adult criminals were subject to the full rigour of colonial penal law, special provisions were made for young offenders. Following developments in the metropolitan countries, juvenile courts, remand homes and reformatories were built in the 1940s and in the British territories especially, probation services were established. Also, legislation was enacted to empower the colonial authorites to deal with beggars and the destitute and, in some territories, custodial institutions for the rehabilitation of beggars were built. The police were given powers to apprehend vagrants and to commit them to institutions or to repatriate them to the rural areas. In some colonies, limited public assistance measures were introduced to provide relief to the urban destitute. Punitive measures were introduced to curtail prostitution and often, in the Asian colonies, legislation prohibiting what was described as 'immoral traffic' was enacted; this legislation attempted also to protect children and young people from being recruited into prostitution or abducted for immoral purposes. More comprehensive child welfare legislation was enacted in many colonies before independence to deal with neglected or abandoned children. With urbanisation, groups of homeless and vagrant children, who earned their living through petty crime or begging, could be seen on the streets of the colonial capitals.

Originally, the authorities encouraged local voluntary welfare organisations to deal with them but as the problem became more acute, government child care services and children's homes were established. The colonial administrators believed that the problem of child neglect could be reduced if husbands or fathers were compelled statutorily to maintain their wives and children; legislation was enacted to empower the courts to order that men, who had deserted or failed to maintain their dependants, provide for them.

Social welfare services, which were established in the colonies before independence, were based on practices in the metropolitan countries. In the French territories, the social services of metropolitan France were replicated; family welfare and health were provided within an integrated administrative structure and, as in France, social security featured prominently. For example, in the French West Indies, social security was introduced before 1932 and although the benefits awarded were significantly lower, these income maintenance measures were identical to those in France. Social welfare legislation in the British territories was often based on the English statutes. Public assistance provisions, which were introduced in British colonies such as Jamaica and Ceylon, were modelled on the English Poor Laws and in many, the English Children's and Young Person's Act of 1933 was copied verbatim by officials responsible for drafting colonial laws.

To administer these services, social workers from the metropolitan countries were recruited into the colonial service and although they were allowed limited resources and were responsible often to indifferent superiors, gradually they were given greater autonomy and scope. For example, in some British colonies, these urban based social services were accompanied by activities directed at the rural areas. In West African territories such as Ghana, enterprising administrators, who were responsible for social welfare, initiated what were known as 'mass education' programmes which attempted, through the medium of literacy campaigns to improve social conditions in rural communities. Mass education workers were recruited, trained and sent to rural areas not only to teach local people to read and write but to improve their villages through self-help. Rural communities were shown how to upgrade their agricultural methods and to improve village sanitation and water supplies; they were encouraged to produce handicrafts, to build communal amenities such as roads, bridges and meeting places and to co-operate to improve their communities in other ways. These beginnings led to what became known later as community development, and programmes based on the West African experiments were begun in many other British territories. Previously, Indian leaders such as Gandhi and Tagore had initiated similar activities and, by the time independence was granted, community development had become an important feature of the Congress Party's political programme. In the 1950s, the Indian government established a national community development service which was designed to extend community development throughout the country's rural areas.

These colonial measures formed the basis of social welfare services in the newly independent countries. In many, these colonial services were consolidated and organised under the jurisdiction of Ministries of Social Welfare as they became known after independence. Metropolitan governments and international organisations such as the United Nations encouraged this development. The United Nations published numerous reports in the 1950s dealing with juvenile delinquency, physical handicap, prostitution and drug addiction in the developing countries and sent western experts to the Third World to advise on the improvement of services designed to deal with these problems. In spite of this and the provision of resources by colonial governments such as the British which would have permitted their extension, these ministries remained small and had little status and scope; in many cases, social welfare and community development expenditure, expressed as a proportion of government budgetary allocations, decreased. Social welfare was not to feature prominently in the public expenditure programmes of the developing countries and, in keeping with economic development priorities at the time, residual social welfare policies, which dealt with the most conspicuous manifestations of need at minimum cost, were adopted.

The residual social policies which characterised development thinking in the 1950s gave way gradually to attempts to provide more comprehensive social services, such as health and education in the developing countries. As it was recognised that the personal pathologies of the urban poor were only one aspect of the more pressing problems of poverty and deprivation in the Third World, the international development agencies called for the formulation and implementation of social policies and plans to deal with basic problems. But this realisation came gradually and initially, the social services in developing countries evolved incrementally to deal not with absolute need but to meet the growing demand for health, education and housing, especially in the urban areas.

The missionaries introduced western education, health and other social services into the colonies and, after independence, demand for their extension could not be ignored by political leaders. As in the colonial days, education was recognised to be an effective means for achieving social mobility and soon missionary education could not absorb the growing numbers who sought admission to the schools. Residual social policies, which advocated that social needs should be satisfied through private means, were untenable; self-financed private education was expensive and beyond the resources of most urban dwellers as well as an excessive burden on the emerging middle class of civil servants, professionals and businessmen. This was true especially of secondary and higher education. In order to meet demand and provide education at moderate cost, subsidies to private schools were increased and governments established public educational facilities rapidly. Higher education became a symbol of national prestige and in most developing countries, universities were created as a matter of priority. Economic planners were not averse to these developments for it was recognised that development required knowledge and skills which could be provided through formal education. Subsequently, they justified educational expenditure as an investment in 'human capital'.

Governments of developing countries also took steps to expand health services. Again, largely as a matter of prestige, medical schools were established to train doctors and other medical personnel locally. Relatively few had been able to study medicine abroad and during the colonial days, modern health services were provided almost exclusively by European physicians working for the missions, colonial governments and foreign companies. With the exception of the missions, western medical care catered primarily for Europeans and as demand for modern health services increased after independence, government hospitals and other health facilities were established in the urban areas.

The need for modern housing became apparent as the cities attracted greater numbers of rural migrants who established themselves in slums on vacant land or on the urban periphery. The former colonial capitals, many of which were laid out neatly, scenic and well served with amenities, became increasingly dilapidated as squatter settlements mushroomed. In an effort to restore the capitals to their former beauty, governments embarked on slum clearance and began to build public housing estates.

The provision of modern education, health and housing increased social expenditure but did little to meet the real social needs of the people of developing countries. The extension of these services especially favoured the urban minority and the urban élite. Public housing required substantial capital investments which were obtained through foreign borrowing and to repay these loans, rents above the means of slum dwellers were charged. Consequently, these supposedly low cost housing estates provided shelter not for the urban poor but for civil servants, school teachers and others in middle income occupations. The creation of universities and government subsidies to private education favoured the urban middle class. Although many governments now allocate more than 20 per cent of their revenues to education, rural education in most developing countries remains neglected. The provision of modern hospitals in the urban areas consumed the greater proportion of government health expenditure and inhibited the extension of medical care to the rural majority whose needs for basic services were more pressing. Physicians, who enjoyed the benefits of private practice in the cities, were not attracted to the rural areas where amenities and income opportunities were limited.

These services not only favoured the cities but, in keeping with the dictates of modernisation, were based on western practices. In education, the curricula of schools in the metropolitan countries were replicated and in the universities, academic departments, which taught subjects of no relevance to the Third World, were established. Western medicine, which was dependent on hospital treatment, modern drugs and sophisticated technologies, made little contribution to the eradication of fundamental health problems such as poor sanitation, polluted drinking water, malnutrition and the parasitic and epidemic diseases prevalent in most developing countries. Housing estates, which were based on housing standards in the West, were built without consideration of local needs or requirements. The importation of inappropriate western education had resulted in the widespread problem of graduate unemployment as the economies of many developing countries have not been able to absorb those with inappropriate qualifications. Western medical education has encouraged the migration of doctors from the Third World to Europe and North America on a large scale. Inappropriate housing policies and slum clearance programmes have exacerbated the housing problems of the Third World's cities. The result has been an expensive social policy which has maldistributed scarce resources and perpetuated the belief that western approaches were worthy of emulation.

This was also true of services established to deal with family welfare problems in developing countries. Ministries of Social Welfare in many countries catered only for a small proportion of needy people in the urban areas and were based on the welfare policies of the western nations. As in health, education and housing, where professional personnel such as doctors, teachers and lecturers, architects and town planners who had been trained to western standards were recruited, it was believed that professionals were needed to administer and provide social welfare services. It followed that professional social workers, skilled in the theory and practice of social work, as this was understood in the West, were required.

Modernisation and Social Work

Although some colonial welfare officials continued to serve to pro-vide the knowledge and skills required during the transition between colonial rule and self-government, steps were taken at the time of independence to accelerate the promotion of local people to assume full responsibility for the administration of social welfare services. Many were sent to Europe on scholarships provided by the former colonial governments during the 1950s to acquire the expertise for this task. Previously, many of these students had been employed in the colonial welfare service in subordinate positions but, as they returned to their countries with suitable qualifications, they were appointed to positions of responsibility and seniority. Although very few were sent abroad by the authorities during the colonial period, it was not uncommon for private families of means to send their children to study at schools or universities in Europe and North America and some, usually the daughters of wealthy families, studied social work. Many returned to their countries before independence but because career prospects for local people in public service were limited, few found employment in colonial administration. After independence, however, many became influential proponents of social work; some were appointed to ministerial or senior civil service positions in social welfare while others became professors of social work in the universities of their countries.

Because social welfare services in the newly independent countries were modelled on European approaches, those who went abroad studied the social policies of the western countries, learned how their social services were administered and were taught western theories and methods of social work. Although some teachers of social work, such as Marjorie Brown in Britain, argued that the training provided was inappropriate to the needs of these students, most disagreed, believing that social welfare services in the Third World would develop and conform eventually to western standards.[19] Because of this, the training needs of students in the industrial and developing countries would be identical. But it was recognised that training facilities should be established in the developing countries to train social welfare personnel locally.

Social welfare training was begun before independence in some countries. Community development training centres were built in several British colonies to provide short courses and in the French territories, similar educational institutions, which were concerned with public health or *animation rurale*, were established. But with a few exceptions, professional schools of social work comparable to those which existed in Britain and the United States, came into being after independence and this was due largely to the efforts of the international development agencies aided by private organisations and western schools of social work.

International development organisations played a significant role in the cross-cultural transfer of social policies after the Second World War. Although they were governed by their constituent member states, their activities were determined often by a professional bureaucracy of officials and experts. In the 1950s especially, these professionals, many of whom came from the industrial countries, were guided by conventional ideas and accepted that development involved the transfer of western technologies, skills and institutions to the developing countries. They endeavoured to expedite this process as efficiently as possible and did not question the assumptions which governed it.

Among the earliest activities of the United Nations in the field of social policy was an international survey of social work training, the findings of which were published in 1950.[20] The survey was designed to determine the extent of and need for social work education throughout the world and although it dealt also with the industrial countries, special attention was paid to the Third World. In 1951, following the publication of the survey, the United Nations Social Commission recognised social work as an international profession. When the fourth international survey of social work training was published in 1964, the United Nations reported that there had been a considerable expansion of professional social work education in the developing countries and that governments throughout the Third World had recognised the need for professionally qualified social workers.[21] The United Nations encouraged and, in many cases, sponsored the development of professional social work education in the developing countries and advocated that university schools, which provided an academic training of several years' duration, be established. Implict in this recommendation was the recognition of the contribution made to the professional development of social work by American schools and American training practices were used frequently as models for social work education in the Third World.

During the 1950s and 60s, various United Nations agencies sent teams of advisers to developing countries in Asia and Africa to formulate proposals for the creation of local social work training facilities and social work experts from schools of social work in the West and the United States especially were recruited for this purpose. For example, professional social work education in Pakistan began in the 1950s following the visit of a United Nations team of experts who had been asked to advise the government on social welfare policy. The advisers urged that priority be given to the creation of professional social work training courses and, as a result of this recommendation, the country's first school of social work was established at the University of the Punjab in Lahore in 1954. Through the Fulbright programme, American social work educators were recruited to teach at the school.[22] A social work training centre was established in Haiti in 1958 and in 1961 the school's curriculum was revised extensively by a United Nations team of experts. Before 1961, 'social work methods were offered in a very general fashion', but since then, following the recommendations of the experts, specialised teaching in subjects such as family casework, probation and psychiatric social work has been offered.[23] The Jordanian Institute of Social Work was founded in 1966 by the Ministry of Social Affairs on the recommendation of the United Nations Children's Fund. Previously, the Ministry's personnel obtained professional qualifications abroad or were given in-service training. UNICEF has supported the school financially since its inception.[24]

The creation of new schools of social work in the developing countries required additional teaching personnel and this need was met partially by appointing expatriate teachers and foreign trained, local social workers to the schools. Although scholarships were provided to train local social work educators abroad, expatriate teachers were required for many years and played a significant role in designing the curricula of the new schools. For example, in Indonesia, the government's School of Social Welfare was established in 1957 and until 1969 it was 'assisted in its curriculum development by five United Nations training advisers'.[25] The school has sent many of its staff abroad for training at graduate schools of social work in the West on scholarships provided by the United Nations, the United States Agency for International Development and the Colombo Plan. The Department of Social Work and Social Administration at Makerere University in Uganda was established in the early 1960s by UNICEF which 'carried' it until 1967 when it ceased to be responsible for the school's administration but continued to support the training of local staff abroad and 'supplemented funds for the expatriate teaching staff'.[26] The Teheran School of Social Work in Iran, which was founded in 1958, 'benefited greatly from international assistance in its early days ... channelled to the school through the UN Technical Assistance Programme and the US Fulbright programme'.[27]

Although the United Nations provided the initial impetus and gave considerable technical support, it did not have a monopoly over the diffusion of western social work to developing countries. In some cases, schools of social work were established by local organisations while in others, different western governments and schools of social work provided financial assistance and expertise. For example, the Delhi School of Social Work was founded by the Young Women's Christian Association of India, Burma and Ceylon in 1946 with donations from the United States. Located at Lucknow and known originally as the National YWCA School of Social Work, it moved to New Delhi in 1947. A year later it affiliated to the University of Delhi as a constituent college and in 1961, was integrated fully into the university. It was the first Indian school of social work to offer post-graduate courses.[28]

The international agencies made little contribution to the development of social work education in Latin America where many schools were founded by private organisations or governments without substantial technical assistance from abroad. In francophone Africa, social work training facilities were created with the help of experts from metropolitan France, and in English speaking African countries such as Zambia and the Sudan, British advisers and teachers were recruited. In some countries, foreign expertise and resources came from unusual sources. For example, social work training in Kenya was begun with the help of Israeli experts and funds provided by their government. The possibility of Israeli involvement was first discussed by Kenyan and Israeli delegates at a United Nations seminar in Addis Ababa in 1960 and some months later, a social work expert from Israel visited Kenya to assess the country's training needs and have discussions with local people. Although it was intended originally to establish courses for women rural development workers, the need for professional social work training was thought to be greater and in 1962, the Israeli government provided funds and personnel to establish a school of social work at Machakos near Nairobi. Because educational opportunities for women in Kenya were limited, the Kenya–Israeli School of Social Work, as it was called, admitted women only but by 1965 the regulations had been changed to allow men to register as well. A Certificate of Professional Social Work was awarded to successful students and this required two and a half years of full-time study. In 1965, the Kenyan government assumed full responsibility for the funding and administration of the school although Israel continued to finance the salaries of the expatriate Israeli staff. In 1968, the School became part of the Kenya Institute of Administration at Lower Kabete.[29]

Through the efforts of western social advisers, the international diffusion of social work to the Third World conformed to the ideals of modernisation. To promote 'modern' social work, western social work experts used as models the approaches to social work education, which had developed in their own countries. Motivated by the demands of modernisation, they designed curricula which replicated the content of western social work training, urged that social work courses be established in universities and recommended the adoption of western professional standards. In spite of economic, social and cultural differences between the industrial and developing countries, few questioned the relevance of these approaches to the Third World or attempted to provide courses which were suited to local needs or conditions.

4 Social Work Education in the Third World

In 1974, Katherine Kendall, Secretary-General of the International Association of Schools of Social Work compared the number of schools of social work in existence in 1973 with the number which were included in the first United Nations survey of social work training in 1950. The first survey, she reported, dealt with 373 schools in 46 countries. A subsequent directory, published by the United Nations in 1954, dealt with 422 schools in 50 countries. By 1973, the International Association had 459 member schools in 66 countries. As Kendall put it: 'A tremendous growth in and development of social work education since the Second World War can readily be seen.'[1] When the Association was founded in 1929, its membership consisted of a small number of schools located chiefly in Europe and North America; today it is 'the international spokesman for schools of social work in every geographic region'.[2] In 1973, the Association had 286 member schools in Europe and North America; the United States with 74 member schools had more than any other country. In the developing regions, the Association had 69 member schools in Asia, 64 in South America and the Caribbean, 25 in Africa and 9 in the Middle East. Of these 167 schools, 5 were in Israel and 16 in South Africa. However, there are many professional schools of social work in developing countries, and in Latin America especially, which are not members of the International Association of Schools of Social Work and the Association's membership must be regarded only as a crude indicator of the extent of social work education in the Third World.

The Association's directory reveals that the oldest school of social work in the Third World is the *Escuela de Trabajo Social* in Santiago, Chile, which was established by a private foundation in 1925. Originally, the school provided a two-year training course which led to the award of the professional title of 'social visitor' but subsequently this was increased to four years and its graduates are known now as 'social workers'. The school affiliated with the Catholic University of Chile in 1952 and became part of the School of Law and Social

Sciences. It merged with the School of Family Education in 1958 to become an autonomous school in the university.

In Asia, one of the oldest schools of social work was established in Bombay in 1936 by the wealthy Indian industrialists, the Tata family. Known originally as the Sir Dorabji Tata Graduate School of Social Work it was renamed the Tata Institute of Social Sciences in 1944. Originally, students who completed their studies satisfactorily were awarded a post-graduate Diploma in Social Service Administration but when the Institute was accorded university status by the government of India in 1964, this was replaced by a Master's degree in social work. Since it attained a university status, the Institute has diversified its courses and now provides a Master's degree in personnel management and labour welfare as well as a Ph.D. programme.

In Hong Kong, where the history of social work education has been well documented, courses in social work were begun at the University of Hong Kong in 1950 at the request of the government. After 1949, as a consequence of the civil war in mainland China, large numbers of refugees settled in the colony. Because of the influx of refugees, the population of Hong Kong increased from about 600,000 to more than two million by 1953 and large numbers of homeless and unemployed families had to be catered for. More than 300,000 refugees lived as squatters in shacks on the hillsides of the city and a substantial number slept on the streets. Problems of homelessness were compounded by malnutrition, illness, child neglect and an increasing incidence of crime, prostitution and begging. In an effort to cope with these problems, the government's mass relief programme, which provided emergency rations, temporary housing and other services, was begun in the early 1950s. The Social Welfare Office, which had been established as a sub-department of the Secretariat of Chinese Affairs in 1947, was given much of the responsibility for this task and soon it was recognised that many more qualified social workers were required to provide these services.[3]

The first social work training course was located within the Department of Economics but it was transferred to the Department of Social and Preventive Medicine in 1953. Only one lecturer was appointed and she was responsible for teaching, field work supervision and administration until 1959, when an assistant lecturer was recruited. At this time, the government recognised that additional resources for social work training were required and it approached the United Kingdom Committee for World Refugee Year which agreed to provide £137,500 for this purpose. In addition, a consultant from Britain was sent to Hong Kong to assess training needs and advise on the future of social work education in the colony. She recommended that the period of training at the university be lengthened and that changes in the curriculum be made; she proposed also that social work courses be created at post-secondary school colleges and that in-service training be provided by the government's Social Welfare Department.[4] In 1962, three more consultants were recruited and they urged that degree courses in social work be established, both at the University of Hong Kong and at the new Chinese University of Hong Kong.[5] As a consequence of these recommendations, an autonomous Department of Social Work was established at the University of Hong Kong in 1967 and a three-year degree course was inaugurated. In 1973, a Master's programme was introduced. A Department of Social Work was established at the Chinese University in 1964. In 1977, the Polytechnic of Hong Kong established a two-year diploma course for welfare assistants.

With the exception of Egypt and South Africa, where social work training was begun in the 1930s, most professional schools of social work in Africa were established in the 1960s. One school, which was established earlier is at the University of Ghana, where social work has been taught since 1956. In-service courses had been provided for government social welfare personnel since 1946 and in 1950, the government established the School of Social Welfare in Accra to provide a nine-month pre-service training course for new recruits. Although the Department of Social Welfare and Community Development sent a number of its staff to Britain to obtain academic qualifications in social work, it favoured the creation of local training facilities for its professional personnel and approached the university for this purpose. The Social Administration Unit was established in the Department of Sociology in 1956 with financial support from the government and today, it offers a two-year certificate course for non-graduates and a one-year diploma for graduates.[6]

Several schools of social work in Latin American countries were established before 1950. Uruguay's first school of social work was created by a religious organisation in 1937. Although the government supported the creation of a second school of social work, which became part of the University of Uruguay, the school has chosen to remain independent and obtains its revenues from private donations, subscriptions from graduates, student fees and periodic public appeals. Originally, a three-year course was provided but in 1959, this was lengthened to four years. The only school of social work in Costa

Rica was founded in 1942 by a group of voluntary welfare agencies which recognised the need for professional training in the country. A three-year course, which led to the award of a Bachelor of Social Work, was provided through evening classes. Two years later, the school was incorporated into the University of Costa Rica and became a Department in the Faculty of Economic and Social Science. In 1963, a Licentiate in Social Work, requiring five years of study was introduced.

Schools of social work at the University of Khartoum in Sudan and the Catholic University of the Dominican Republic are among the newer social work training institutions in the developing countries. Both were established in 1969. Social work training at the University of Khartoum was begun on the recommendation of the United Nations Regional Adviser on Social Work and Social Policy in Africa with professional advice from a British university; financial assistance was provided by the British Ministry of Overseas Development. The Catholic University of the Dominican Republic was founded in 1962 and seven years later, the first training course in social work was established; a Licentiate in Social Work is awarded on successful completion of four years of study. As in the Sudan, the university is the only centre for social work education in the country. One of the newest social work training courses in the Third World is offered at the University of Papua and New Guinea. The University was founded in 1965 and the first lecturer in social work was appointed in 1971; courses in social work and social welfare were begun in 1972.[7]

Patterns of Professional Social Work Education in the Third World

In the 1950s and 60s, the term social work was used loosely and there was disagreement about the proper designation of professional and non-professional training courses. Reference was made to a variety of training institutions in the United Nations fourth international survey of social work training, which would not be regarded as professional schools of social work by most European and North American social work educators. For example, the survey referred to a training centre for home demonstrators which was established in Colombia in the early 1960s; it described courses for rural health workers at the National School of Public Health in Tunisia and frequently mentioned community development training centres in African countries such as Kenya, Malawi, Sierra Leone and Nigeria. Although the survey did not propose a formal definition of professional social work education, it differentiated between the various training institutions for welfare personnel on the basis of admission requirements, the length of training and affiliation to universities. Courses which did not have stringent entrance requirements and were of short duration, were described in the survey as pre-professional or auxilliary training programmes while those offered at universities were designated as professional courses. In recognition of the non-professional courses, the most recent United Nations survey replaced the term social work in its title by the phrase: 'Training for Social Welfare'.[8]

The membership requirements of the International Association of Schools of Social Work give some indication of professional status in social welfare education in developing countries. The Association's Secretary-General revealed that the assessment of social work educational standards in different countries was a vexing problem not only because the level of training varied greatly, but also because the curricula of different schools reflected social and cultural differences between these different nations. Because the Association has 'no disposition to restrict membership,' its accreditation requirements are as flexible as possible and are designed to differentiate between professional and non-professional training institutions in general terms only.[9] Nevertheless, the Association has seven criteria for professional recognition: training institutions must have the objective of educating social workers for professional practice 'as social work is understood within the respective country', and their training courses must be of at least two years' duration. In addition, they must have full-time staff and students, combine theoretical study with practical work and have a library and other teaching resources.[10] Using these criteria, it is possible to gain some impressions of the degree of professionalisation and extent of professional social work education in different regions of the Third World.

Although many schools of social work were established by private organisations in Latin America, by 1964 about one half were affiliated to or incorporated into government universities and, of those under private auspices, the majority are attached to private universities.[11] There is a regional association of Latin American schools of social work and several countries, such as Argentina, Brazil, Chile, Colombia and Mexico have national associations of social work education. Social work training in several Latin American countries is governed by state regulations and in some, such as Brazil, Chile and Peru, legislation has been enacted which requires that specified social welfare tasks may be undertaken only by qualified social workers. Although these factors give some indication of the considerable degree of professionalisation in the region, there are significant discrepancies between the standards of different Latin American schools of social work and marked variations in the extent to which they conform to government accreditation requirements. In addition, the length of training and qualifications awarded by different schools are not standardised.

The standardisation of qualifications and professional titles is a major task for the Latin American professional associations. While some schools award the professional title of *Assistente Social*, others prefer the title *Trabajadora Social* even though both may be regarded as full professional social work qualifications. In some countries, the two have different status, while in others, professional titles are awarded together with university degrees to reflect the superior qualifications of graduates. Professional titles are regarded as superfluous in other countries and academic qualifications are awarded only. Although the *Licenciado* is used to designate a first degree in social work in most Latin American countries, in some a *Bachiller* or *Doctorado* is awarded.

In Mexico, only nine of the country's thirty-seven social work training institutions have university status and the remainder are regarded as vocational, pre-professional training centres by the National Mexican Association of Schools of Social Work. In Argentina, schools of social work are governed by Decree No. 2761 of 1969 which requires that, to qualify for the award of the title *Assistente Social*, students must be trained for a minimum of four years. However, because a subsequent decree of 1970 permitted non-university training institutions to award the same professional title, numerous universities changed their qualifications to *Licenciado* or *Doctorado* in social work and very few comply now with the provisions of the original decree. Although Argentina has about forty social work training centres, only twenty are accorded professional status by the Argentinean Association of Schools of Social Work.

In some countries, such as Brazil, Peru and Chile, a greater measure of standardisation has been achieved. There are thirty-seven professional schools of social work in Brazil and all are university institutions. The great majority are within the Federal universities and all are governed by regulations promulgated by the central government. These require a four-year training programme and stipulate that basic social science and related academic subjects as well as professional practical instruction be provided. Nine of Peru's eleven schools of social work are located within universities and all provide a five-year professional training which leads to the award of a Licentiate in Social Work. Of the remaining two institutions, one offers a four-year training leading to the award of the title *Assistente Social*, while the other awards the title of *Trabajadora Social* which requires the same period of academic study. Chile's twelve schools of social work are affiliated to the Chilean Association of Academic Institutions for the Teaching of Social Work which accredits training institutions and sets broad standards; since 1973, following the military coup, social work education in the country has been subject to stringent government control.

Although there are a substantial number of institutions providing a basic training in social welfare in Africa, the United Nations reported that there were 'a relatively small number of independent or university based schools of social work', and that most African social welfare personnel were 'without advanced education or professional qualifications'.[12] Although the International Association of Schools of Social Work has twenty-five member schools in Africa, sixteen are in South Africa. The regional body, the Association for Social Work Education in Africa admits rural community development and other non-professional training centres as well as university schools to membership; its recent directory included a list of eighty-two institutions in thirty-six African countries of which only seven were university schools.[13] These exist chiefly in British Commonwealth countries such as Ghana, Zambia, Uganda and Sudan. With the exception of Zaire, there are no professional schools of social work within universities in the French speaking countries. Apart from South Africa and Zimbabwe, other countries with university schools of social work are Egypt and Ethiopia.

In Ethiopia a two-year diploma in social work was established by the Ministries of Education and Public Health with assistance from the United Nations; this course was taken over by the University in 1961 when a separate department of social work was established in the Faculty of Arts. In 1966, the Department became an autonomous school of the university.[14] In Egypt, professional social work training has been provided by specialised institutions, which have university status, for many years. For example, the Higher Institute for Social Work in Cairo, which was established in 1946 by the Ministry of Education, offers a four-year Bachelor's degree and it also has a Master's and Doctoral programme. More recently, some universities, such as the Assuit University in Menya, have established departments of social work.

Very few anglophone African universities have autonomous academic departments of social work; at the University of Mauritius, social work is taught within the School of Administration and at the Universities of Khartoum and Ibadan, diploma courses in social work are provided by the Departments of Extramural Studies and Adult Education respectively. At the University of Ghana, social work is taught within the Department of Sociology; this was true also of Makerere University in Uganda, where social work courses were located within the sociology department until 1968, when an independent department of social work was created. In Zambia, social work was taught originally by the Oppenheimer School of Social Service which was founded in 1961; it became an independent department of the University of Zambia in 1965.[15]

In many francophone African countries, social work training was provided originally by schools of nursing. For example, courses in social work were inaugurated at the School of Nursing in Mali in 1961. In common with many other French speaking African countries, students who wished to become *Aides Sociales* or *Assistantes Sociales*, shared a basic first-year training in health subjects and practical nursing with student nurses and, in the second year, attended special lectures in social welfare. These courses were open to women exclusively and many who qualified found employment subsequently in health fields. In some francophone countries such as Senegal and Upper Volta, courses in rural development or *animation rurale*, were established. These placed far less emphasis on public health and, like community development training centres in English speaking countries, subjects such as agricultural extension, adult literacy, handicrafts and home economics were taught.

Several training institutions in francophone Africa have attempted to improve their professional status; training courses have been extended to three years and at some schools, men have been admitted for training. The Higher Institute for Social Studies at Bakavu in Zaire now offers a three-year course which leads to the award of the title *Assistante Sociale* and it is the only French speaking school which is affiliated to a university. The School of Social Service in Tananarive in Madagascar has also lengthened its training to three years and the course leads to the award of the State Certificate in Social Work. Although subjects such as sociology, psychology, statistics and jurisprudence are taught, emphasis is given still to medical subjects and the school's enrolment is restricted to women. In spite of these efforts to set higher professional standards, no francophone training schools in Africa are members of the International Association of Schools of Social Work even though the Association has forty-four member schools in metropolitan France.

Schools of social work in many Asian countries are located within, or affiliated to, universities; others have been granted university status by the authorities. The United Nations reported: 'The dominant pattern and trend among Asian countries is for schools of social work to be incorporated within the university system generally at the under-graduate level.'[16] Although a regional professional association has been established only recently, social work training in Asia is more standardised than in Africa or Latin America and most schools offer a three-year Bachelor's degree or a two-year Master's degree in social work.

The major exception is Indonesia, where social work is offered not only at universities but at academies and secondary schools. Like those in the Netherlands, the academies are post-secondary school institu-tions and most provide a course of two years' duration. Also, the government's Department of Social Affairs has its own school of social work in Bandung which has university status; a three-year Bachelor's degree and a two-year post-graduate *Doctorandus* is offered. Social work courses are offered at several universities and, as is common in Indonesia, most students aspire to complete the *Doctorandus*. In recent years, the government has introduced social work education at secondary school level to train social work assistants for field level positions. There are sixteen of these schools in the country today which are controlled by the Ministry of Education; four years of study are required. The government's policy is to encourage the universities to take greater responsibility for professional training and to abolish the academies, so that social welfare personnel will be trained at universities and secondary schools only.

Professional social work education in India is well developed and training is provided at a higher level than in many European countries. There are thirty-four professional schools of social work in India and the great majority provide a basic training in social work at the Master's level. Of the thirty-four, only ten offer an undergraduate programme and of these, four provide a Master's degree as well. Eleven Indian schools have doctoral courses and only two offer diplomas in social work; both are for graduates.[17]

Indian schools of social work were founded by a variety of organisations and individuals. Some, like the Department of Social Work at Vidyalaya Arts College in Tamil Nadu, which was founded by the Sri Ramakrishna Mission, came into existence through the efforts of religious organisations. Others, such as the College of Social Work in Hyderabad, which was founded by the Indian Council for Social Service in 1966, were established by voluntary agencies. Some, like the Tata Institute and the Department of Social Work at PSG Arts College were created by charitable foundations owned by wealthy families. Others evolved from rural development training centres into professional schools of social work.

The most notable of these are the Departments of Social Work at the Gujarat Vidyapith University in Ahmedabad and the Visva-Bharati University in West Bengal. The Gujarat Vidyapith was founded by Gandhi in 1920 to train workers who would promote 'rural construction'. Social work training courses were begun in 1947 and in 1970, six years after the Vidyapith became a university, a Master's degree in social work was introduced. The Visva-Bharati had a similar history; it evolved from the work of Tagore, who like Gandhi, believed passionately in rural development. Visva-Bharati became a university by a special Act of Parliament in 1951 and the Department of Social Work was established in 1963.

As in India, social work education in the Philippines has achieved a high degree of professionalisation. Social work training in the country is governed by legislation enacted in 1965 and the Schools of Social Work Association of the Philippines has differentiated clearly between professional and non-professional training courses. To qualify for membership, schools must be recognised by the Ministry of Education and provide a Bachelor's or Master's degree in social work.

While several Asian countries, such as India, Korea, the Philippines and even Hong Kong, which has three schools of social work, provide extensive training facilities, others with large populations have only one professional school. In Iran, which has a population of some thirty-two million people, the Teheran School of Social Work was the only professional training institution in the country before the revolution. It was founded in 1958 and was accorded university status in 1961 but it has now ceased to operate. Until recently, the Department of Social Work at Thammasat University in Bangkok was the only professional school of social work in Thailand; the country has a population of forty-two million. In Malaysia, with a population of twelve million, professional social work courses are provided at the University Sains Malaysia in Penang only and the Malaysian government continues to send students to Britain for professional training.

Although Sri Lanka has a population of approximately fourteen million people and a federal university with four main campuses, it has no university school of social work. The country's only school is run by the Ministry of Social Services and provides a three-year diploma in the subject.

In the remaining regions of the developing world, facilities for professional social work training are very limited. With the exception of Israel, schools of social work in Middle Eastern countries such as Jordan and Lebanon are not affiliated to universities. However, social work courses have been recently established within the Department of Sociology at the University of Riyadh in Saudi Arabia. In the Caribbean, non-university training centres have been created in francophone countries such as Haiti, but the only university school is at the University of the West Indies in Jamaica. Here, social work is taught both within the Department of Sociology and the Department of Extramural Studies. In Oceania, professional social work courses are offered only at the University of Papua New Guinea. Little is known about the situation in socialist developing countries such as China, Vietnam and Cuba and while these countries undoubtedly employ personnel in the field of social welfare, their training is likely to be very different from the professional approach adopted in many other developing countries.

American Influences on Social Work Education in the Third World

The professionalisation of social welfare training in the Third World resulted in longer training courses, the provision of social work education at universities and the adoption of curricula which reflect the influence of western and American approaches especially. It is not surprising that American standards were emulated in many developing countries. In the 1950s, American schools of social work were regarded as the most prestigious in the world; they had been established in universities of renown and were staffed by social workers who held professorial positions. Unlike the European schools, American universities offered post-graduate, professional training courses and even awarded doctoral degrees in the subject. Many students, who wished to study social work abroad, were attracted by the reputation of the American schools and the opportunity of taking degrees in social work rather than diplomas. After the Second World War, American influences in the Third World grew rapidly and generous scholarships were provided to train students from the developing countries in the United States.

American social work professors were held in esteem and accorded much status abroad; they produced textbooks and journals, which were disseminated internationally, and they took a leading part in international conferences and meetings. Consequently, they were used frequently by the international development agencies to advise on the creation of social work training courses in developing countries and many taught at the new schools. In countries such as Iran and Pakistan, American teachers of social work, provided through the Fulbright programme, were used extensively. This was true also of the Philippines, where the first social work courses were established by Filipino social workers who had been trained in the United States.[18] In India, the first director of the Tata Institute was an American; similarly, the Delhi School of Social Work was established with funds from the United States and 'again, its founder-director was an American'.[19] Degree courses in Hong Kong were established on the recommendation of three consultants, of whom two were professors of social work at North American universities in Pittsburgh and Toronto.

Studies of the curricula of schools of social work in developing countries, which were published in the 1960s, revealed that the content of social work training in these countries conformed closely to American approaches. Although a wide variety of qualifications, ranging from certificates to doctorates were offered, the curricula of these schools had many features in common with those in the United States and conformed to American standards, such as those laid down by the Council on Social Work Education. As in the United States, teaching in basic social science subjects and social welfare was provided. Supervised field work in specialised social work agencies was regarded as an essential element of instruction. Professional teaching in social work methods, which was based explicitly on American techniques and theories of casework, group work and community organisation was offered and a generic approach, which integrated the methods within a unitary methodology, was widely adopted.[20]

There were exceptions and in different countries and regions of the Third World, social work education remained subject to different academic traditions and influences. As shown previously, social work training in francophone Africa has been linked to nursing and public health and although some schools have achieved a greater measure of professionalisation, socio-medical subjects still feature prominently in their curricula. In schools where emphasis is given to *animation rurale*, the syllabus has nothing in common with social work education in western countries. But it is interesting to note that, although the *Ecole de Service Sociale* in Madagascar does not use the term 'casework', it provides teaching in what is described as 'individualised social service'; students are taught to 'individualise the help, encourage the expression of feelings ... to accept, not judge, respect the client' and to 'respect professional secrecy'.[21]

Subjects such as community development and social administration are taught at English speaking schools of social work in Africa and these reflect British rather than American influence. Although writers such as Shawkey recognised that community development had become popular at African schools of social work, he claimed that these schools gave more emphasis to casework than community development training. Shawkey was critical of this for he believed that it reflected the western concept of curative welfare which had little relevance to the needs of Africa. As he put it: 'With all the major social problems facing Africa, social work cannot continue to fiddle with minor problems.'[22] Shawkey reported also that most African schools were dependent on western social work literature and that few efforts had been made to develop indigenous teaching materials. Similarly, while several anglophone African schools of social work teach social administration, the United Nations reported that very few schools are able to prepare students for practice in this field in a coherent and systematic way. Describing curriculum developments at the University of Zambia, Brown reported that efforts had been made to foster a generic approach to social work education; so that students could be trained adequately in all three methods of social work, the teaching had been 'integrated'.[23] Subsequently, Dunning showed that because of this and other factors, Zambian social work education differed in few respects from social work training in America and Britain; these approaches, he believed, were of little relevance to Zambian requirements.[24]

Latin American schools of social work differ from those in North America and Britain by providing more instruction in basic academic subjects; in addition to psychology and sociology, a great variety of subjects such as history, law, languages, biology, philosophy, mathematics and economics of development are taught.[25] Portuguese is obligatory at Brazilian schools and in other countries, social work students are required to study Spanish. Tuition in philosophy is given prominence and some Latin American schools provide ·advanced teaching in the subject. This broader approach reflects European and Iberian educational traditions; as Jones put it: 'Since the Latin American countries have looked to Europe for educational leadership, it was natural that experts called to help establish the first schools of social work should come from Europe and that the first students to go abroad, should go there.'[26] But after the Second World War, increasing contacts with schools of social work in the United States were established. In spite of the differences between social work training in Latin and North America, there was a clear trend in the 1950s and 60s 'to bring the curriculum structure closer to that of US schools with emphasis on the methods of social work'.[27] As Paraiso showed, Latin American schools adopted American theories and methods but made no attempt to adapt these training practices to the needs of Latin American countries or to 'develop original conceptual formulations and to identify the mainsprings of a truly Latin American social work philosophy'.[28]

There are few differences between the curricula of most Asian schools of social work and those in the United States. Although the United Nations claimed that there 'is a close association of social work with community development in the Asian region,' increasing professionalisation at Asian schools of social work has resulted in a decreasing interest in community development teaching.[29] As Nagpaul showed, Indian schools have developed courses in a variety of specialised fields and now provide more teaching in family casework, psychiatric social work and medical social work than they do in community development.[30] At the University of Hong Kong, where community development is given emphasis, teaching in this subject is integrated with other social work methods. On the other hand, students of social work and community development are trained separately at the Institute of Social Work and Community Development at the University of the Philippines.

A unique characteristic of Indian social work is labour welfare. The Factories Act of 1948 required industries to employ qualified social workers as labour welfare officers and this legislation has resulted in the inclusion of subjects such as industrial relations, personnel management and industrial welfare in the curricula of many Indian schools. Some, such as the Tata Institute offer post-graduate degrees in this field but, in others, labour welfare is no longer given prominence, and at several schools it is offered as an optional subject only.

Although social policy and administration is taught at some Asian schools of social work, a major study of the curricula of schools in the Asian and Pacific region, which was published in 1972, found that teaching in social policy was given little priority. Commissioned by two United Nations agencies, the study examined the relationship between social work education and what was described as 'national development goals' in the region. Eighty-eight social work teachers were asked to report on the emphasis they gave to different aspects of social work education in their schools. While subjects such as social work methods had an important place in the curriculum, social policy and planning were given little emphasis. Drucker, the consultant to the study, recommended that teaching in these subjects, which would be more relevant to national development, be expanded.[31]

Social work curricula in many Asian countries were based explicitly on American approaches; as Thomas reported: 'The main currents of inspiration for social work training in India have come and continues to come from America.'[32] This is reflected not only in the structure of the courses but, as he put it: 'Conformity to the American pattern is discernable even more in the basic attitudes, concepts and vocabulary of social work . . .'[33] Herbert Aptekar, a respected American social work professor, who led a United Nations social work mission to India in the early 1960s, revealed: 'Many outstanding social workers from India have been to the United States for special preparation and the Team of Consultants to Indian schools of social work has brought a great deal of American orientation to Indian social work.'[34] In Hong Kong, the consultants' recommendations for the re-organisation of social work education in the colony were based explicitly on American curricula. Describing the concepts and principles to be acquired by social work students, the consultants used Bernice Madison's book on undergraduate social welfare education in the United States and, in designing courses in human growth and development, adopted the guidelines of the American Council on Social Work Education.[35] Teachers of social work at the Department of Social Work at EHWA Women's University in Seoul, Korea were distressed to find that their courses gave insufficient emphasis to social work methods. After attending a United Nations seminar on social work education in 1963, they realised that their teaching would be improved by 'emphasising more social work methods courses'. Consequently, steps were taken to remedy this deficiency and 'the number of class hours for casework, group work and community organisation were increased, and this has continued to the present'.[36]

As in Africa and Latin America, where Spanish translations of American textbooks are used, Asian schools of social work rely extensively on western social work literature. Much of this comes from the United States and is unsuitable since, as Nagpaul put it: 'they have been written with an American audience in mind'.[37] The Director of the Teheran School of Social Work reported: 'The teaching material printed in the Persian language is meagre. The student must, by necessity, draw upon western literature on the subject which is not quite suitable since it does not take into account the socio-economic problems of Iran.'[38] Reviewing the bibliographies of Indian schools of social work in some detail, Nagpaul claimed that Indian government and other local publications were prescribed infrequently. As long ago as 1952, when an important conference on social work education was held in Madras, Indian social work educators spoke about the desirability of promoting indigenous literature. In 1972, Nagpaul revealed: 'Not a single textbook exists on Indian social work which takes into consideration indigenous social, economic and political conditions on the one hand, and the contribution of Indian social scientists on the other.'[39]

Although schools of social work in developing countries differ from each other and from schools of social work in the West, these differences are not substantial. As American standards, theories and methods have been adopted, these differences have become less marked and, as many critics have shown, the content of social work education in the Third World is very similar to that in the United States.

Some social workers have claimed that the common features of social work training in the developing and industrial countries are desirable because this has fostered a common professional identity. The international professionalisation of social work is dependent on what Jane Hoey described as the recognition of 'universal problems and common goals'.[40] Consequently, it is argued that social work in different countries should be based on the same concepts, principles and theories. Addressing a seminar on social welfare in India, Aptekar thought that it was laudable that Indian social work textbooks should be produced but, he pointed out that these would be 'quite similar in essence to American literature,' since the principles and methods of social work should be the same in all societies.[41]

Other social workers believe that the problem of western influence has been overstated and dramatised excessively and that social work in the Third World is not as dependent on American approaches as many have claimed. Others feel that the topic has been discussed so exhaustively that it is no longer of interest. As the editor of one journal exclaimed, with some exasperation: 'We have had quite a spate of contributions lately deploring the influence of American models of social work ... that this theme is now threadbare and no further articles on it will be welcome.'[42]

Some social workers believe that schools of social work in developing countries are now not only aware of the need to relate their courses to local conditions but also that they are promoting indigenous social work education actively. The Secretary-General of the International Association of Schools of Social Work argued that, although there was an uncritical acceptance of western ideas previously, the situation had changed considerably by 1973. As she put it: 'Schools of social work in Asia, Africa and Latin America are staffed by their own qualified faculty members and are no longer dependent on western assistance. Indigenisation has become a cause as well as a means to make schools of social work significantly more relevant to the society they serve.'[43] Although it is true that: 'It is now widely recognised that traditional models of social work training do not fit the needs of the newer societies for whom new models must be designed', an awareness of the problem does not imply that solutions have been found.[44] As Nagpaul showed, Indian teachers of social work have been talking about indigenising social work training since the Madras conference in 1952 but they have done little, if anything, about it.

Current Trends in Social Work Education – A Recent Study

To examine the extent to which the curricula and other aspects of social work education in the Third World have been adapted and modified to be more relevant to the social, economic and cultural realities of developing countries, thirty-two schools of social work in Latin America, Africa and Asia were approached and requested to provide information about their courses. All were professional schools; community development and other non-professional training institutions were excluded. Twenty-two schools responded; of these, seven were in Africa, seven in Latin America and eight in Asia.

The twenty-two schools offered forty-three professional training courses which permitted graduates to practise as professional social workers in their countries. These courses varied considerably in academic status and level; they ranged from certificates for non-graduates to post-graduate degrees. Post-graduate qualifications were offered most frequently by the Asian schools which participated in the study; none of the Latin American schools offered post-graduate courses and only three of the sixteen qualifications provided by the African schools were for graduates.

Although these twenty-two schools do not constitute a random sample of professional social work training institutions in the Third World, they are a fair cross section and give some indication of current training practices. Because the study has limitations, it is not possible to reach final or absolutely valid conclusions about social work education in developing countries, although clear trends emerge.

Information about the content of the courses offered at these schools was examined in some detail. The classroom instruction provided may be categorised into social science and other general academic subjects on the one hand, and social work theory and methods courses on the other. All the schools provided tuition in the behavioural sciences and the most popular of these were psychology and sociology. Psychology and sociology were given approximately the same emphasis at most schools and although other social science subjects, such as anthropology, economics and social administration were taught, psychology and sociology comprised the largest element and common ingredient of basic social science instruction. The study confirmed that Latin American schools of social work offer a broader range of background courses than Asian or African schools and that many of these subjects were of a general nature having little direct bearing on the student's professional training.

At most schools, courses in psychology emphasised subjects such as human growth and behaviour, personality theory and clinical psychology. Psychology was given more prominence at Latin American schools than in Asia or Africa but at all the schools, teaching in psychology was based extensively on western theories; there was no indication that use was made of cross-cultural psychology or that courses had been devised which were relevant to local cultural conditions.

Sociology curricula provided more evidence of indigenisation. At some Latin American schools, teaching in dependency theory, which reflects the contribution of Latin American social scientists to the sociology of development, was given. Courses in the sociology of African societies were taught at African schools of social work in Ghana, Uganda and the Sudan. At the University of the West Indies, seminars on Caribbean social structure were offered. In addition, standard sociology courses included subjects such as social change, rural sociology and the sociology of development, and at several Latin American and African schools, anthropology was taught. In spite of this, the approach adopted by teachers of sociology utilised the concepts and theories of western sociology and often, courses which were relevant to local conditions comprised only a small part of their instruction.

Social administration and social policy courses were offered at several African and some Asian schools included in the study. Although many provided courses dealing with local social welfare procedures and social legislation, this was seldom referred to as social administration. Instead, teaching described as social administration by many schools dealt with British social policy and the administration of the social services in the United Kingdom; instruction in the broader issues of social policy relevant to developing countries, was neglected.

Teaching in social work theory and methods was provided universally. Although the greater part of classroom instruction was devoted to social science and other academic subjects, social work theory and methods comprised the largest single component of the curriculum at most schools. About one third of all teaching was devoted to social work subjects at Asian and African schools; because they offered more general academic courses, this proportion was somewhat lower at Latin American schools where it comprised approximately 20 per cent of classroom teaching.

Many schools offered introductory courses in the history of social work, its philosophy, values and basic principles. Most of this was based on American sources and at many schools, where the history of social work was taught, students learned about the Charity Organisation Society and the philanthropic movement in Europe and North America; very few schools taught the history of social work with reference to their own countries. One exception was Hong Kong, where a course on the history of social work and social welfare in the colony was offered.

Although the majority of schools provided instruction in all three methods of social work, casework techniques were given the greatest emphasis. At most schools, students were instructed first in casework methods, while group and community work was taught usually in subsequent years together with advanced casework. With one or two exceptions, casework tuition was based entirely on American theories and many schools gave advanced teaching in specialised fields of casework such as child care, medical and psychiatric social work, family casework and marital guidance. Group work and community work were neglected at most schools. The handbook of one school participating in the study states: 'Casework is the primary method of practice but students are also introduced to group and community work methods.' Group work and community work courses were offered as optional subjects at some schools and omitted from the curriculum at others but these were in a small minority and most accepted the need for a generic approach, at least in principle. Many schools used American sources exclusively when teaching group work and community work; several used the term community organisation and gave instruction in establishing and running a typically American, urban community organisation agency.

African schools were the major exception; here, American approaches to community work were ignored and instruction in community development was provided instead. These courses were orientated almost exclusively to rural development in Africa and at some schools, extensive teaching in the subject was provided. Nevertheless, this teaching was not given as much prominence as casework and field placements in rural settings were not used widely. Some schools offered courses in urban community development which were concerned with the needs of slum dwellers and other urban communities. At the University of Hong Kong, courses of this kind featured prominently and at Thammasat University in Bangkok, more emphasis has been given to teaching in this field in recent years.[45]

Some schools offered courses in social work which were related specifically to local conditions. At the Department of Social Work and Social Administration at Makerere University in Uganda, courses in social casework with African clients have been devised. Some Asian schools offered courses on social work and traditional values; a course on the relationship between social work and the religions of the country was provided at the Sri Lanka School of Social Work and at Thammasat University, a course dealing with social work and Thai culture was taught. At the School of Social Work at the Catholic University of Chile at the time of the Allende government, a radical approach to social work education, directed at the needs of working people in the country, was adopted. During this period teaching was highly politicised and close links between the school and 'popular organisations' were established. The training provided was regarded by staff and students alike as highly relevant to the country's needs and circumstances. Courses in unusual or highly specialised fields of social work were offered at some schools; one provided a course on social work with minority groups and, as may be expected, an Indian school participating in the study provided a specialised course in industrial welfare and personnel management.

In addition to analysing the content of the curricula of these schools, attention was paid to the reading materials prescribed. With the exception of the Latin American schools, most schools participating in the study relied extensively on English language textbooks and journals which were published in the United States and Britain. Many required their students to be proficient in English in order, as one prospectus put it: 'to benefit from the professional literature and from the lectures given by foreign consultants'. Many African and Asian schools reported that they had received donations of books from the international development agencies and western governments and that most of these were published in Britain or the United States. The bibliographies of the Latin American schools referred frequently to textbooks which had been written in Spanish. Some social science and other general books, which were prescribed reading, were written by Latin American authors but many were standard American textbooks which had been translated into Spanish.

The most popular social work textbook on the reading lists was Friedlander's *Concepts and Methods of Social Work*. For social casework teaching, textbooks by well known American authors such as Biestek, Hollis, Perlman and Hamilton and one British author, Timms, were prescribed by the great majority of the schools. For social group work, the most popular book referred to in the reading lists was by Konopka, followed closely by Trecker's introductory work on the subject; both are American authors. Generally, schools which provided teaching in community organisation recommended textbooks by American authors such as Dunham, Ross and Harper. These books are so specific to the organisation of local voluntary and public welfare agencies in the United States that it is difficult to imagine that students in developing countries gain anything from them at all. This was true also of the few books on social administration which were recommended at some schools; most were by British authors and dealt with the British social services. At several African schools, where community development was an integral part of the curriculum, textbooks on community development in Africa were used frequently. Although written by foreign authors such as Batten and Du Sautoy, they were highly relevant to community development practice in these countries.

Various social work journals were recommended also. Two American journals, *Social Work* and *Social Casework* were prescribed almost universally. Next in popularity were the British magazine, *Social Work Today* and the American *Social Service Review*. The *British Journal of Social Work* and the *Journal of Education in Social Work*, which is published in the United States, were also recommended.

With some exceptions, local teaching materials were referred to infrequently. Some schools prescribed government publications and statutes but these formed a small part of the reading lists. Indian schools of social work prescribed reading materials published locally more frequently than schools of social work in other countries. Although this suggests that Nagpaul may have been too severe in his criticisms of Indian social work's lack of indigenous literature, local reading materials comprised a small proportion of the reading lists at the Indian schools included in the study. At one Indian school, only six out of one hundred and seven titles on the reading list dealt with social work in India. Although several books on community development in India have been published, only one out of a list of seventy-nine textbooks on community work was written by an Indian author. In Hong Kong, community work publications dealing with community work in the colony by authors such as Hodge, Spergel and Rich, were listed. In Hong Kong and India, local social work journals have been produced and these were prescribed but articles from these journals were not mentioned frequently. It is surprising that the journal *International Social Work*, which publishes many articles about social work in developing countries was not prescribed at the majority of schools included in the study. Equally surprising was the omission of Clifford's *A Primer of Social Casework in Africa* from the bibliographies of all but one African school participating in the study.

Because field work placements used by schools of social work reflect the content of the teaching they provide and the emphasis they place on different methods of social work, information about practical instruction was obtained from all the schools which participated in the study. In all schools, field work included visits of observation to various welfare agencies and more substantial, subsequent placements. A variety of governmental and voluntary welfare organisations were used for this purpose but most schools made greatest use of social casework agencies, specialising in child and family welfare. Medical settings, residential institutions for children, the aged and disabled and psychiatric hospitals were next in popularity. Residential placements were used widely and in one country. These included: 'homes for children, approved schools for young offenders and homes for the aged and chronically ill'. Students were placed in the prison and probation services in Africa and Asia but in Latin America, only one school employed correctional agencies for this purpose. Specialised placements in fields such as marital guidance and alcohol and drug rehabilitation agencies were used less frequently. Even less common were placements in educational social work; only one school made use of placements of this kind. Field work in labour welfare was arranged only by one Indian school participating in this study.

Practical instruction in group and community work was neglected at many schools and where placements of this kind were provided they were of short duration and of secondary importance to field work in casework agencies. In some countries, students were placed with women's and youth clubs for short periods but many schools provided no field work in group work at all. Community work placements were arranged by very few schools of social work in Asia and Latin America and even in Africa, community development placements were not used frequently. Some schools have attempted to provide placements in community work which are more relevant to the needs of developing countries. For example, the Department of Social Work at Thammasat University sponsored a community work project in a squatter settlement on the outskirts of Bangkok known as Klong Toey. This project was described in the School's handbook as its 'training site for social work students and faculty members in the area of social research, urban community development and integrated social work process in a development programme for social welfare'. Also, more extensive placements for social work students have been arranged in the government's village development programme by the University of Zambia.[46] But placements of this kind were in a minority and most schools used conventional field work placements which confirmed the dominant position of casework tuition in the curriculum. It is surprising, in view of a new interest in family planning among social work educators in the Third World, that only two schools of social work sent their students to family planning agencies for practical work.

Since it is natural, although not inevitable, that teachers of social work who have been trained in western countries should impart what they have been taught to their students, the educational backgrounds of social work educators at the schools were examined. Although some schools did not supply this information, it appears that a substantial number of teachers of social work were trained overseas, chiefly in Britain and the United States. More than one half of the teaching staff at the Asian and African schools had foreign social work qualifications; about one third had been trained abroad exclusively. At Latin American schools, this proportion was about 25 per cent.

Foreign qualifications in social work were not distributed evenly among the staff. About one half of the lecturers and instructors had foreign qualifications but 90 per cent of the professors and heads of schools had obtained social work qualifications in western countries. Although some had studied in continental European schools, more than 80 per cent of those with foreign qualifications had obtained them in the United States, Britain and, to a lesser extent, Canada. The most popular schools of social work in these countries were at the Universities of Columbia, Chicago, London, Swansea College and McGill. There is every indication that social work educators are continuing to study abroad; a number of the staff of the schools participating in the study were on study leave abroad during the academic session when the research was undertaken.

The study revealed also that schools of social work in the Third World continue to employ expatriate teachers and that few require them to have special knowledge of developing countries. In a recent article, Clarkson, a British social work teacher, who has considerable experience of developing countries, had no hesitation in advising British social workers to teach in the Third World; she prescribed no special qualifications for this task except 'a spirit of adventure' and 'a willingness to learn as well as teach'.[47] Similarly, the western schools of social work at which students from developing countries study, provide no special courses which are appropriate to their needs. As with expatriate teachers, who have no special training, they actively facilitate and encourage the transfer of inappropriate theories and methods to the Third World.

The findings of this study provide little evidence that schools of social work in the Third World have modified their curricula substantially in recent years to provide a professional education in social work which is appropriate to developing countries. The training which students of social work in the Third World receive is dominated by theories and methods which have been imported from the United States; this teaching and the field work placements which accompany it are designed primarily to train professional social workers for casework practice and few schools have experimented with new and more relevant forms of social work intervention. Where appropriate courses in community development and other, more relevant subjects are provided, these comprise a small part of the curriculum. Although it has been claimed that schools of social work in developing countries today are more aware of the need to indigenise their training, there is little evidence to show that this has been achieved.

5 Social Work Practice and the Problem of Cultural Diversity

As was shown previously, students of social work in developing countries, as in the West, are trained to deal with social problems by applying the methods of individualised intervention; they are taught the techniques of interviewing, of establishing meaningful relationships with their clients and of strengthening their inner capacities to solve their own problems. They are taught theories of human behaviour which, derived from clinical psychology, provide explanations of the causes of maladjustment. They learn the generic principles of individuation, self-help, self-determination, acceptance and controlled emotional expression and are trained to apply these concepts in professional practice.

This methodology has been influenced considerably by the cultural milieux in which it evolved. The model of man which has been incorporated into social work theory, and which emphasises ideal-typical traits such as individuality, rationality, self-reliance and ambition conforms to the image of man which is widely accepted in the industrial, capitalist nations of the West. The principles of social work as well as the profession's ethics embody the values of western, industrial society.

It is not necessary to cite anthropological evidence to support the obvious contention that the peoples of Third World countries differ greatly from each other and from those in the West in their attitudes and values. Undoubtedly, modernisation and the spread of western education and technology has had an impact on traditionalism, and although traditional values were eroded by colonialism, the lives of hundreds of millions of people in developing countries today are still governed by traditional customs and beliefs. In spite of these differences, social work education in the Third World has taken little account of the problem of cultural diversity. Although short courses on local religion and culture are offered at some schools of social work in developing countries, these have not displaced the western values inherent in social work's methodology. One reason for this is the belief that the values of western social work are shared universally. As will be shown, some social workers have argued that, because human beings in all societies share a common concern for the welfare of others, social work's humanitarian ideals are relevant to all cultures.

The Value Content of Western Social Work

Social work emerged in nineteenth-century Europe and North America and was greatly influenced by the social and political ethos of the time, a value milieux which many writers have loosely called 'liberalism'. Espoused by the ruling élite and the middle classes of these societies, liberalism manifested itself in different forms and was given different designations. In economic affairs, liberal ideas were form-ulated in the theory of capitalism. In political matters, the *laissez-faire* principle dictated that government intervention should be kept to a minimum. Philosophers argued that rationality and utilitarianism governed human nature; men were born free to choose between different courses of action. They taught that the principles of pleasure and pain determined behaviour and that human beings behaved consistently in ways which increased their well-being and avoided situations which were to their disadvantage. Also, the social philos-ophy of liberalism extolled individualism; individuals had rights, duties and obligations and were held responsible for their happiness and welfare and for their errors, failures and inadequacies.[1]

It is easy to caricature a culture and to exaggerate the degree to which these beliefs pervaded European and North American societies. Certainly, there were disagreements among leading social thinkers at the time; also, collectivist doctrines were not only being expounded but were exerting increasing influence. But liberalism undoubtedly had a profound impact on social attitudes and government social policies. For example, in the nineteenth century, traditional approaches to criminal justice were transformed through the adoption of liberal ideas and its precepts were employed to devise new methods of dealing with the poor.

As was shown previously, liberal ideas about the nature of poverty had a considerable influence on the development of social work. Like others of their class, the founders of social work believed that because men were born free and equal and were capable of the same ambitions and efforts, differences between the rich and the poor could be explained in terms of individual morality. But their strong views on the virtues of work, sobriety, self-reliance and responsibility were tem-pered by a humanitarian concern for those who were poor through no fault of their own. Although they believed that the able-bodied poor preferred idleness and vice and should be coerced to work and mend their ways, they were compassionate towards those who could not be held responsible for their predicament such as the aged, widowed, handicapped and orphaned. This was, as Bruce argued, consistent with the ideals of liberalism which provided, what he called 'a philosophical and schematic unity to the reforming surge of the age'.[2] The philanthropic movement gave expression to these humanitarian concerns and nineteenth-century charity workers put them into practice.

Soon, liberal values and beliefs were incorporated formally into social work. Loch's principles of scientific charity exude classical liberal ethics and charity workers who implemented them were required, for example, to make every effort to restore the individual to self-reliance; it was for this reason that charitable relief was said to be temporary. The value of self-reliance featured prominently in sub-sequent social work publications. Richmond argued that the social worker's primary task was to help individuals to find solutions to their own problems rather than dispensing charitable relief, and case-workers in the 1920s and 30s combined this belief with the value of freedom or self-determination, arguing that treatment should never be imposed but that clients should be helped to take their own decisions. Liberalism also influenced social work's conception of the causes of social problems. Although the crude explanations of poverty which governed social work practice originally were replaced by scientific theories of psychological maladjustment, social work retained its original approach to the understanding of human need. These theories are sophisticated reformulations of earlier nineteenth-century ideas. The individualism embodied in these explanations has been a major source of controversy between social workers and students of social policy who tend instead to favour sociological explanations. But there are indications that the issue of individual versus social-structural causation has become a matter of controversy within the profession also.

The formal incorporation of these and other liberal beliefs into social work was fostered most vigorously by American social workers. Although this may not have been recognised explicitly in the early development of American social work theory, the formulation of the generic principles relied extensively on liberalism and revealed the profession's dependence on its values. In his widely read introduction to social work, Friedlander pointed out that social work's generic principles are derived from liberal, democratic, American values such as equality of opportunity, freedom, independence and individual development; social work, he said 'is directed toward their realisation'.[3] The adoption of these values by American social work was hardly surprising; in the United States, liberal values shaped the cultural milieux and were accepted widely. Free from the devastation of war, significant working class militancy and the growing European trend towards increased state intervention and welfarism, the ideals of capitalism, freedom, democracy and individualism personified the popular culture; amalgamated with frontier values, the result was an even more robust form of liberalism than that which had emerged in Europe. Immigrants, farmers, steel workers and middle-class suburbanites were said to share the American Dream and an unshakable belief in the virtues of the open society and its opportunities. Suspicion of 'big government' impeded the spread of state intervention and enshrined individual autonomy as an unalienable right; citizens were believed to be free to decide how they wished to live and bring up their children, what to believe and how to be governed.[4]

Obviously, the tenets of classical liberalism are no longer as dominant in western industrial society as they were in the nineteenth century. In Western Europe welfarism and the growth of working class movements have modified the culture of liberalism. But liberal ideals are by no means obsolete; conservative political parties in these countries score regular election successes by the simple expedient of extolling the virtues of economic and social policies which are highly congruent with classical liberalism. Nor do the authors of most social work textbooks appear to be greatly influenced by the changes which have taken place. References to values in most standard works reveal the profession's commitment to western liberal ethics. Similarly, systematic studies of the values of social work, such as those undertaken by Muriel Pumphreys, show that the profession's values have been shaped by the ethics of liberalism.[5] Values such as humanitarianism, individualism, freedom, self-determination, equality and participation are of fundamental importance to social work.

Many authors of social work textbooks regard humanitarianism as the most important value of social work and the literature is full of references to social work's altruism. Gisella Konopka argued that social work method is 'rooted in religious and humanistic values',[6] and Dame Eileen Younghusband described the profession as 'the embodiment of the social conscience'.[7] Biestek's account of the social worker's role takes this belief to the extremes of romanticism: 'With the motive of love, he strives for skill in the use of the wisdom of science to help his brother in need. The caseworker hopes that he is, in some small way, an instrument of divine providence'.[8]

Indeed, many social workers are motivated by altruism and a genuine concern for human suffering; although there can be little disagreement with their view of themselves as members of a helping profession, social workers are required to behave sometimes in ways which cannot be described as humanitarian. Social workers are used often by the authorities as instruments of social control rather than love. It is not humanitarian, as Briar and Miller point out, for social workers to arrange that their elderly clients be institutionalised in old age homes and geriatric hospitals that are 'beyond description in terms of their deterioration and sadistic administration'.[9] In Britain, social work's humanitarian ideals were the subject of unfavourable editorial comment in several national newspapers recently because of a protracted strike by social workers in several local authorities which resulted in the withdrawal of services to deprived children, old people and others in need.

The value of individual worth is believed to be of fundamental importance to social work. As Friedlander argued: 'the ideal of the worth and dignity of the individual remains pivotal'.[10] But Briar and Miller have castigated American social workers who profess a commitment to this value while condoning acts which contradict this belief. Does the concept of individual worth have any meaning in a society that, as they put it: 'proceeds to electrocute its murderers, discriminate against its Black citizens or starve its out-of-wedlock children?'[11] The profession, they allege, is guilty of shameful hypocrisy; social workers extol the value of individual dignity and then agree to spy on women recipients of social security to determine whether they are cohabiting or not.

The profession's adherance to the value of individualism requires, in practical terms, that social workers encourage their clients to become self-reliant and self-sufficient. This was a cardinal principle of nineteenth-century charity and as Stein showed, its veneration by social workers in the United States and adoption as a generic principle, was occasioned and reinforced by their belief in the American pioneer spirit. American views of themselves as independent and self-sufficient, capable of standing on their own feet and facing their problems with resolute determination, spring from the westward migration of settlers who were compelled to be self-reliant in the face of difficult odds.[12]

Social work believes also in the liberal values of freedom and democracy and it gives expression to these values in the generic principle of self-determination. Describing how social workers translate this ideal into practice, Friedlander argued that social workers should not intervene until their clients request help and express a desire for self-improvement; they never impose remedies but encourage their clients to find solutions to their own problems. Those who seek the help of social workers, as he put it, have 'a human civil right' to decide what their problems are and how they should be solved.[13]

There are, of course, innumerable practical problems facing social workers who seek to apply this value to their professional dealings with their clients. Social workers are required frequently to bring pressure to bear on individuals who do not wish to co-operate and they work with clients, such as those who are subject to judicial orders, who do not choose freely to be the recipients of social work intervention.

The liberal value of rationality is applied also to social work practice through the generic principle of self-determination. Social workers believe that their clients are capable of making rational decisions and of being able to find rational solutions to their problems. Although they accept that those in difficulty face emotional problems, which impede their capacity for rational action, they retain an optimistic belief that self-confidence and clear-headed reasoning can be restored through social work intervention. But social work publications dealing with the profession's values make no mention of the contradiction between the ideal of rationality and the incorporation of psychological determinism into social work theory. It is difficult to see how social workers who have been schooled in psychoanalysis can accept that their troubled clients, who are subject to irrational psychological forces, are capable of dealing with their problems rationally and of exercising free will to find suitable remedies.

Stein showed that other, typically American values such as work, progress and family life, which reflect the country's historical experience, have found expression in the profession's philosophy. Early Americans were imbued with strong utopian ideals believing that the land in which they had settled held the promise of freedom and unlimited opportunity and that, through hard work and determination, human capacities for self-betterment could be realised. The puritan ethic, which embodied these values, was regarded not only as a means to an end but as a matter of pride and self-respect. The colonists and settlers established new kinship patterns; marriages could be dissolved, the mobility of offspring was permitted and the rigidity of family structure was modified. More emphasis was placed on immediate kin relationships than on distant obligations and, gradually the nuclear family emerged as the desired kinship unit. This change was compatible with prevailing values; controlled emotional relationships between spouses and between parents and children created a climate for socialisation in which individualism, achievement and autonomy were permitted to flourish.

Stein argued that these and other values were absorbed into American social work; the value of progress is given expression in the profession's claim that it is helping to bring about a better world, and the value of work reinforced the belief that individual effort and self-reliance should be encouraged. The ideal of the nuclear family is referred to frequently in the profession's literature and the treatment of needy families and the reintegration of their members is a prime goal of casework practice.

In describing these values and their relevance to social work practice in western societies, an attempt has been made to show that the issue of values in social work is extremely complex. As Briar and Miller demonstrated, many of the profession's values are inconsistent with the demands of social work practice. This is not to deny their intrinsic worth; there is nothing wrong or bogus about the profession's commitment to values such as humanitarianism, progress and freedom. But to idealise their application to professional practice, as some social workers have done, is to grossly oversimplify the issue and ignore the very real practical difficulties which hinder their realisation. It is because of the superficiality of these accounts that many social workers sympathise with the view that descriptions of the profession's values amount to little more than 'a futile parade of harmless platitudes and postulates'.[14]

Of course, it cannot be claimed that there is consensus among western social workers about these values; for example, the recent writings of Marxist social workers show that liberal values are not endorsed universally. It is obvious also that the status accorded to these values has varied at different times and between social workers in different societies. But there can be little doubt, as many social work textbooks reveal, that the methodology of social work has been infused with the values of the culture in which it emerged.

The relevance of these values to non-western cultures is highly questionable. Although social work students in other cultures are reared on western textbooks and taught the profession's western methodology and its liberal ethics, it is doubtful that they readily accept and internalise these values. As Huang, a lecturer in social work at the University of Hong Kong pointed out, students from non-western cultures who study at schools of social work in the West experience cultural conflicts. He reported how, as a Chinese student of social work in the United States, the alien concepts and ideas of social work caused him and other students from the Third World a great deal of tribulation. Of the four students from developing countries who were on his course, two could not sustain the process of 'cultural footbinding' and terminated their studies.[15]

The Search For Cross-Cultural Universality

Because it has been recognised that the values of social work are an expression of European and North American liberal ideals, the proponents of international social work have been pressed to justify the profession's cross-cultural diffusion to non-western societies. In response to this, there has been some discussion about the relevance of social work's values to different countries and several social workers have attempted to demonstrate that the profession's ethics and its principles are compatible with the values of the world's non-western religions and cultures.[16] Although much of this discussion has been superficial, it has sought to substantiate the claim that the diffusion of western social work to the Third World is legitimate and desirable.

Publications on this topic have been concerned largely with the belief that humanitarianism is prevalent in most cultures; several social workers have argued that because all societies applaud altruism, they are amenable to western social work. Aptekar claimed that 'much ethnographic evidence could be cited to show that precursors of modern social work did exist in primitive societies'.[17] These are the institutions of mutual aid and reciprocal obligations which characterise many traditional communities and which, he suggested, exist even among animals; human altruism, he claimed, is probably an expression of an instinctive 'bio-morality'.

Several teachers of social work in Asia agreed with Aptekar's views. Desai argued that Zoroastrianism teaches a way of life which is compatible with social work's humanitarian values. The religion stresses 'the qualities of character that one would expect from a good social worker – good thoughts, good words, good deeds'.[18] Writing about Islam and social work, Rashid pointed out that the religion 'seeks to and does make ample provision for the beneficent regulation of all aspects of human conduct'.[19] Its humanitarianism finds expression in many ways but especially in the institution of *zakaat*, which is a religiously prescribed tax designed to benefit the poor and needy. In addition, Muslims are required to be clean in body and spirit, just and truthful, sympathetic and compassionate and must possess 'high morality'. These features of Islam, she claimed, are very similar to the ideals of social work. Hasegawa drew similar parallels between the virtues of social work and Zen Buddhism. The fundamental tenets of Zen are to help others, to contemplate one's true self and to practise *jihi*, or compassion. These are not only ideals but practical prescriptions for living. Social workers and Buddhists share the same ideals and commit themselves to a life of service. To substantiate his argument, Hasegawa related how Zen Buddhist disciples and young social work students co-operated to build a place of recreation and 'social welfare' on the slopes of Mount Fuji. Motivated by the same humanitarianism, they worked long hours to cut down trees, level the ground, provide a water supply and living quarters. The project was not only a great success but demonstrated how social workers and Buddhists made sacrifices to benefit others; as he put it: 'It was the fruit of the sweat and passion of young people who challenged the slopes of Mount Fuji' that established a place which others could enjoy.[20]

These studies, if they can be described as such, reached the same conclusions but were based solely on impressionistic evidence and were remarkably idealistic. A more rigorous attempt to research into the cross-cultural application of social work values was Yasas' study of the relationship between social work's humanitarian ideals and the philosophy of Mahatma Gandhi. Initially, Yasas compared Gandhi's moral beliefs, as portrayed in Fischer's biography, with Pumphreys' description of the values of social work. She found that the humanitarian values described by Pumphreys were highly congruent with Fischer's account of Gandhi's philosophy and especially with his 'predominant concern for the dignity of man and the fight for his rights'.[21] Satisfied that this initial exploration supported her hypothesis, Yasas embarked on a more detailed analysis in which Gandhi's autobiography was compared with the values of social work. Using content analysis techniques, Yasas found overwhelming evidence that the two value systems were compatible. For example, Pumphreys' first value, which states that 'each human being should be regarded as an object of infinite worth', was identified in the Mahatma's writings no less than 265 occasions. But Yasas sounded a cautionary note; her work was concerned primarily with Gandhi's humanitarianism and there were other aspects of his moral philosophy which were not compatible with social work's values. For example, she found that the Gandhian concept of *ahimsa* is not, as many Indian social workers believe, identical to social work's generic principle of acceptance.

Muzumdar reviewed and confirmed Yasas' findings but went further to suggest that Gandhian ideals 'prepared the ground work for the establishment of professional social work in India'.[22] Clearly, Gandhi recognised the need for social welfare services and his work inspired much of India's progressive social legislation on the status of women, the welfare of the scheduled castes and community development. But Gandhi's conception of social welfare was very different from that of individualised social work and whether he would have accorded the same status to casework as some Indian social workers have is doubtful. Nehru, his disciple and successor, when addressing a seminar on social welfare in India, apologised to the participants for straying from 'the narrower aspects of social welfare in which you are interested', and spoke instead of the need to secure the basic necessities of life for India's citizens and to bring about significant social development.[23]

Aptekar's view that modern, professional social work is comparable to traditional kinship obligations and rural communalism, takes the argument beyond the bounds of credibility. Mutual aid in traditional societies has specific limitations and traditional communities are not the utopian havens of benevolence they are sometimes thought to be. Although these institutions may be compared to modern systems of social welfare and social security, they are not remotely akin to social work.[24] While the medicine men, herbalists and charmers of traditional societies may be likened to modern doctors, pharmacists and psychiatrists, these cultures have not produced traditional social workers.

Those who have argued that social work's western humanitarian values have counterparts in traditional culture, are guilty of what Wijewardena, a Sri Lankian anthropologist, described as 'myth building'. For example, he pointed out that idealised descriptions by social workers of the Indian *panchayats* as traditional institutions which dispense justice with equity are erroneous; the *panchayats* are more concerned with the maintenance of caste privilege than social justice and cannot be described as humanitarian.[25] Humanitarian values are not indigenous to Asia but were imported, together with other secular humanist values, from the West. In spite of what social workers have written about him, Wijewardena claimed that Gandhi personified the diffusion of western humanism to the East;

his humanitarianism 'showed a very western concern for making this life worth living for India's poor'.[26] Gandhi's moral values were incompatible with the traditional culture of India for he campaigned, in the face of entrenched opposition, to abolish indigenous caste privileges and to correct the belief that suffering is the price paid for past sins and that individuals must bear their sufferings fatalistically.

Few social workers who have written on the subject of the cross-cultural universality of social work values have approached the issue with the same critical attitude. Instead, some have taken the argument even further and have claimed that, in addition to humanitarianism, other values of social work, such as individualism, democracy and rationality are compatible with traditional cultures as well. For example, Liyanage argued that many values of social work are complimentary to the theology of Buddhism. Social work extols the virtue of democracy and this is equally important in Buddhism for the Buddha taught 'democracy as a way of life'. Social workers believe that individuals have a basic human right to self-determination and that they should never impose their views on their clients; similarly, Buddhists believe that the beliefs of others should be respected. When asked by his followers how they should respond to the many other religious teachings which were being expounded at the time, the Buddha did not insist that his teachings be accepted uncritically and he urged his followers to examine critically what he had taught them. This, he claimed, reveals the Buddhist value of rationality which, as in social work, can be developed through reflection and self-awareness. Self-awareness or *sama ditthi* is an important Buddhist ideal for it is one of the most important steps in the Noble Eightfold Path to the cessation of suffering. Liyanage believed that the equivalent of *sama ditthi* in social work is the technique of helping clients to gain insights into their problems and behaviour. These and other teachings of Buddhism and social work are so identical that, as he put it: 'One is inclined to come to the conclusion that a good social worker is a good Buddhist and that a good Buddhist is a good social worker.'[27]

Other social workers have echoed Liyanage's findings and conclusions about the relevance of other social work values to non-western cultures. Desai argued that the right to exercise free choice is as fundamental in Zoroastrianism as it is in social work; the religion's theology is characterised by dichotomies of choice and on moral issues, Parsees are taught to reach their own conclusions. Rashid attempted also to draw further parallels between the ideals of social work and those of Islam; she claimed that Islam also extols values such as rationality, freedom and self-determination. While it may be true that the world's religions teach tolerance, freedom of choice and other desirable values which are similar to those of social work, history has shown that, often, the realities are very different. Nor are these abstract theological precepts necessarily reflected in the traditional customs and attitudes of ordinary people. Idealised accounts of the similarities between social work's values and the theologies of Eastern religions have not been accompanied by accounts of how values such as democracy, rationality, self-reliance and progress find practical expression in traditional culture. Although several social workers have argued that the different world religions venerate rationalism, it is not difficult to demonstrate that traditional cultures have many non-rational traits, at least in the western sense. In their efforts to draw analogies between social work and traditional values, many social workers have overlooked these issues and some have not noticed that they contradict themselves. For example, Desai argued, on the one hand, that the Parsee community is very cohesive but also, on the other, that the 'Parsee is very individualistic'.[28]

The criticisms which writers such as Briar and Miller have levelled at social workers in the West for hypocritically professing to believe in humanitarianism while condoning inhuman practices applies equally to social workers in the Third World. Residential institutions to which the elderly and mentally ill in some developing countries are confined are worse than they are in the United States. In some countries probation officers recommend that juvenile court magistrates should sentence young offenders to be whipped. In others, social workers are responsible for incarcerating beggars, vagrants and other homeless people in penal work camps. Similarly, those who extol the humanitarian values of non-western cultures have failed to account for non-humanitarian practices in certain cultures such as the harsh penalties imposed on adulterous wives, the painful mutilation of children during initiation ceremonies and the practice of untouchability. Moreover, social workers in developing countries have not been vociferous critics of these practices.

This raises the difficult issue of social work's ethical position on customs such as arranged marriages, child labour, the seclusion of women and the cruel punishments prescribed under the criminal law in some cultures. Should social workers in the Third World challenge and seek to change these practices or should they accommodate them because they form a part of the traditional culture? Obviously, there is no simple answer to this question but it is a pity that it has not been debated adequately in the literature on the relevance of social work's liberal values to other cultures. Social workers have not examined the issue of the cross-cultural universality of social work in sufficient depth or with an attitude of scholarly scepticism and, on the flimsiest evidence have concluded that, as Aptekar put it: 'Social work is not a western institution. In Eastern countries it is not simply an import, grafted on, as it were, on the indigenous Eastern tree.'[29]

One exception was a seminar of forty-two social workers and social scientists which was held at the East–West Centre in Hawaii in 1966. Organised by the American Council on Social Work Education the seminar was attended by participants from ten countries and they included some of the best known figures in social work in the Third World. Although some of the papers presented to the seminar were insubstantial, the discussion which followed served, as the organisers recorded: 'to shake up some of our most preciously held preconceptions'.[30] The delegates found that there were significant differences between the values and beliefs of the different societies represented and that many accepted ideas about the universal relevance of social work were based on misconceptions; they found even that the basic terminology of western social work and social science was not acceptable in all cultures. The term 'adjustment' had negative connotations in India and the sociological concept 'system maintenance' was unacceptable to the Japanese. In spite of the fact that western social work textbooks use the concept of 'human rights' freely, the participants struggled to define and apply it to their own societies. Wijewardena argued, in a refreshingly iconoclastic way, that the concept had little relevance to most developing countries in view of their social and political characteristics. It made little sense, he claimed, to suggest that in the Third World, 'society has a responsibility to the individual – a responsibility for the protection of certain rights'.[31] In many developing countries, the notion of rights has the same particularistic connotation as it had in feudal Europe; individuals had rights because they had power, wealth and influence and because they were born of certain parents. The idea of natural rights was completely alien, and in many countries still is; even in the western democracies, the concept of rights is associated with wealth and the ownership of property.

Practical Problems of the Cross-Cultural Application of Social Work

Social work educators in developing countries have taken little account of these very complex issues. Instead, the image of man and the values which are embodied in western social work are transmitted through social work education to social work practice in the Third World. Schooled in western theories and equipped with the profession's culturally determined methodology, social workers in developing countries are expected to treat their clients as individuals who have the same needs, emotional reactions, attitudes and potential for personality growth as do the recipients of social work in the West; also, they are expected to treat them as if they were amenable to becoming self-reliant, independent, rational, insightful, caring and coping individuals.

Because of marked cultural differences, these objectives of western social work are unattainable in the Third World; people in developing countries do not share the American Dream or the liberals' belief in rationality or the individualism which is so prized in the West. Nor are the techniques used by social workers in the West relevant when dealing with clients who are different culturally; people in developing countries may find it difficult to express their emotions openly or understand the concept of self-determination or accept the need for confidentiality. The application of social work's culturally specific principles to non-western societies is fraught with practical difficulties.

Many social workers would disagree with this interpretation; indeed, many have claimed that social work methods are highly effective when dealing with the problems of people in non-western cultures. To examine this belief, case histories, which describe social work practice in two different developing countries have been selected for discussion; both purport to show that social workers in the Third World implement the profession's principles more or less as the textbooks prescribe and that they do so without experiencing undue difficulties or cultural impediments.

The first case history comes from Bangladesh; it was published by Clarkson and Halim and is based on a report written by a student of social work at the University of Rajshahi.[32] During a field placement at a local hospital, the student was asked to see a thirty year old man who was being treated for typhoid and dry gangrene of a leg, which required amputation. The patient was in a state of great distress, refusing to co-operate with the doctors and nurses, and refusing also to agree to amputation, without which his life would be in jeopardy. The student realised that the man's lack of co-operation was due to deeper emotional difficulties and with patience, sympathy and understanding he attempted to diagnose the patient's problems. Using his skills, he was able to establish a relationship with the man and having secured his confidence, discovered the real cause of his distress.

The patient came from a poor, low caste, Hindu family who farmed a small plot and were dependent on subsistence agriculture for their livelihood. His father had married twice and the patient did not get on with his step-brothers, whom he believed had an intense dislike for him. After his father's death, he left home and spent eight years as a disciple of a holy man, but bored with this life he returned home. His family did not welcome him and, at the instigation of the step-brothers, made things difficult for him. His arranged marriage to a very young girl aggravated the situation for he believed that by compelling him to marry against his will, his family were demonstrating their contempt of him. He admitted that his marriage was unhappy and that he had been involved in extra-marital relationships to spite his family. At the time of his illness and hospitalisation, the family appeared to be disinterested and he was convinced that they were relieved that he was out of the way.

The student social worker recognised that the patient's unhappy home circumstances and unsatisfactory relationships with his family had caused him to be hostile and depressed and that his medical problem had aggravated the situation; his refusal to co-operate with the medical personnel was a symptom of his underlying social problem. In an effort to deal with this problem, the social work student wrote to the man's family explaining that he was distressed and anxious and that he needed their support. Also, he wrote to some of the man's friends, asking them to help. To the patient's surprise and delight, the step-brothers responded positively, as did his friends, promising to care for him after his discharge. This news appeared to encourage him enormously for he soon became less withdrawn and depressed. The student attempted now to deal with the medical problem; he pointed out to the patient that despite his loss of a leg, he could still be useful to his family. His younger brothers looked to him for guidance and he had a responsibility towards them; if he was not there to encourage them, they would probably lose heart, leave school and sink into destitution and this would be worse than the amputation of a leg. As a consequence of these efforts, the patient agreed to give consent to the operation and he began to make constructive plans, considering ways in which he could contribute to the family's income.

The social work student maintained a close relationship with the patient throughout his stay in hospital and was able to give practical help in the form of crutches after the operation. After the man's discharge, the student received news that he was doing well and that he had been reintegrated into his family successfully.

The second case history comes from Zambia in Central Africa; it is taken from a book on social casework in Africa written by William Clifford who was formerly Principal of the Oppenheimer College of Social Service in Lusaka.[33] To illustrate how social workers in Africa use their skills and theoretical knowledge, Clifford examined a case taken from the files of the Zambian government's Department of Social Welfare; it relates how a well-dressed woman, obviously in emotional turmoil, burst into the social worker's office weeping and complaining angrily about the treatment she had received from a doctor at a local hospital. Although the social worker was extremely busy, she did not interrupt the woman's outburst but waited patiently for her to finish, paying sympathetic attention to what she said. Eventually, the woman calmed down and began to talk about the real problems she was facing. She came from a rural background and was married to a labourer; now she was pregnant and her husband insisted that she have the baby delivered at the local hospital. The doctor examined her and explained that because her confinement was unlikely to be complicated, she could not be admitted to the maternity ward; demand for places was great and only those with potentially difficult pregnancies could be hospitalised. The doctor assured her that she could deliver the child safely at home.

The woman told the social worker that this was not possible. She had no relatives in the city who could help her and she did not have the funds to meet the travel costs of returning to her village to have the child there. Also, she was reluctant to leave her husband because he was likely to squander his earnings on drink in her absence. Although she asked the social worker to help her financially so that she could travel to the village, she seemed to be very uncertain about leaving her husband. The best solution, she believed, was to have the baby delivered at the hospital and she had set her heart on this.

The social worker realised that the woman's desire to have her child at the maternity hospital was not really at her husband's insistence, but she allowed her to finish and then intervened, explaining kindly but firmly that her wish to be admitted to the hospital was unreasonable and unfair; the hospital was overcrowded already and if she were given a bed, another more deserving expectant mother would suffer. Although the social worker offered to see the husband to explain the problem to him, it was clear that the woman had responded to the social worker's kindly admonition and patient efforts to help her gain insights into her behaviour; she began to discuss ways in which she could facilitate her confinement and said eventually that she would inform her husband that the baby could be born at home. Again, the social worker listened sympathetically, interjecting only to give constructive advice. Also, she attempted to strengthen the woman's self-confidence, assuring her that she was a mature and capable person who would be able to cope. Subsequent enquiries revealed that the woman gave birth to a healthy baby at her home and that she had solved the problem capably.

These two case histories are very similar; both are optimistic, claiming that social work methods can be used effectively to deal with the psychological and emotional problems of people in distress in very different cultures. The social worker in Zambia and the student in Bangladesh employed similar techniques. Both delved into the backgrounds of their clients to discover the real causes of their problems and they were not content to deal only with the immediate complaint which was presented to them. To discover the underlying causes of people's problems, as Clifford argued, requires considerable skill. As he put it: 'A skilful professional social worker uses the interview purposefully to uncover conflicting emotions and attitudes ... and to probe the fundamental individual problems which might otherwise remain untouched.'[34] Both social workers treated their clients as persons worthy of dignity and respect, listened sympathetically and permitted them to vent their emotions. The student social worker in Bangladesh allowed his client to express his feelings of bitterness at being rejected by his family and although this belief was unfounded, the student remained tolerant and understanding. The social worker in Zambia was under great pressure of work but did not regard the client's problem as trivial and listened sympathetically. This not only allowed the woman to release her pent-up emotions and calm down but prepared the way for establishing an effective relationship with her. Both social workers approached their clients' problems in a rational way and they were responsive to this. The student in Bangladesh helped his client to see that his refusal to consent to surgery was unrealistic and the social worker in Zambia demonstrated to the woman that her wants were illogical and unreasonable. Both applied the principles of social work to help their clients come to a better understanding of their problems and to ease their confused state of mind. Finally, neither social worker prescribed solutions; by giving constructive advice and clarifying the consequences of different courses of action, their clients were able to resolve their own difficulties.

Both case histories are typical of the literature about social work practice in developing countries. Testimonials to the success of social work intervention, the problems and difficulties of professional practice in developing countries are mentioned rarely in publications of this kind. But, while Clarkson, Halim and Clifford agreed that the principles of western social work can be applied to deal with social problems in disparate cultures, they conceded that cultural differences do impinge on social work practice. For example, Clifford recognised that Africans in rural areas especially, remain ignorant of the benefits of social work and that they see no need for social work assistance 'in their traditional scheme of thinking'.[35] Because they are dependent on the extended family and tribal affiliations, they are not always amenable to individualised treatment. Clarkson and Halim recognised also that cultural practices, such as arranged marriages, complicate social work intervention. But neither study gave more than superficial consideration to these problems and Clifford was optimistic that these difficulties would be overcome as people in developing countries are exposed to modern ideas and begin to understand and appreciate the role of social workers in society.

A more critical account of the problems of social work intervention in non-western cultures, which reached very different conclusions, is Almazor's description of the effects of traditional culture on social work practice in the Philippines.[36] Although she admitted that it is difficult to describe a 'modal' or basic value system in a society which has marked religious, linguistic and regional differences, Almazor believed that Filipinos share certain common cultural characteristics. The most dominant trait of Filipino culture is the belief in *bahalana na*, or fate. People in the Philippines believe that an individual's future is decided at birth and that events can be explained best in terms of predestination. Astrology is popular and it is thought to be better to discern the future through astrology than resist fate. Also, Filipino culture is characterised by authoritarianism; the elderly and those with status in the community are not only respected but obeyed. Filipinos accord great status to those in positions of authority and expect to be led and follow their directions. Another feature of the culture of the Philippines is social acceptability; Filipinos go to great lengths to be approved of and will behave frequently in ways which conform excessively to the expectations of others. To avoid conflict and maintain good relationships, or *pakikisama*, with others, they seek to please those with whom they interact. This is coupled with the phenomenon of 'face saving'; situations which challenge or diminish individual worth are avoided and Filipinos under stress seldom admit that they have problems, for to do so would involve a diminution of status and loss of respect. Family life and kinship ties are valued highly and extended family obligations are maintained; kin members are consulted whenever decisions are made, even if these do not concern relatives directly. The family's good name and reputation is regarded as being of paramount importance and is always defended.

Almazor pointed out that because of these institutionalised cultural values, social workers face insuperable difficulties when seeking to apply the principles of western social work in their dealings with Filipino clients. Because of their belief in predestination, most Filipinos bear their troubles with resignation and the social work concept of self-betterment through individual effort has little meaning. Similarly, unless they are in dire material need, few Filipinos are likely to seek the assistance of social workers, believing that their problems are pre-ordained. Also, asking help of a social worker is regarded as degrading for it involves 'loss of face' and an admission of personal inadequacy. Those who do are unlikely to express their true feelings or emotions and will attempt to present their problems in the best possible light. 'Opening up,' said Almazor, 'is a slow and long process because of fear of losing face.'[37] Expression of feeling is inhibited because of *pakikisama*; Filipino clients wish at all times to maintain polite and mutually respectful relationships and would be greatly troubled and confused by the social worker's efforts to encourage them to release their pent-up emotions. Also, they would be unlikely to respond positively to any implied criticisms of their behaviour, no matter how gentle or subtle these might be. Because of institutionalised authoritarianism, Filipinos view social workers as people who have status in the community and will expect to be told how to solve their problems; they will find it very difficult to understand that they must find their own solutions. Similarly, the western concept of self-determination is almost impossible to apply in Filipino society where decisions are taken not by individuals but by families collectively. Because of extended family ties, the western social work principle of confidentiality is unworkable; it has little relevance to a culture where family members expect to be fully informed and to share each other's troubles.

Almazor's description of the problems of social work practice in the Philippines is a far more realistic and searching account than the idealised case histories of the successes of social work which pervade the literature. Her analysis of the cultural obstacles which hinder the application of the principles of social work to non-western societies, applies not only to the Philippines but to many other countries where social work's clients differ in their attitudes and values. Teachers of social work in developing countries have been so anxious to receive recognition and approval from western schools of social work and the international professional fraternity, that they have not realised to what extent they are promoting the diffusion of western values to non-western cultures; nor have they considered its deeper implications. If they had they might have justified their actions on the grounds of inevitability or may have argued that to promote progressive social change and modify traditional culture, the diffusion of western liberal ideas is desirable. Instead, they have claimed that social work is no more than a formalised, modern expression of traditional values.

The myth of social work's cross-cultural universality can have credence no longer. Social workers who attempt to apply the profession's theories and principles to non-western societies will find, as Almazor showed, that they are unworkable. Also, because they were designed to treat the emotional and personal maladjustments of individuals, these theories and principles are irrelevant to the pressing problems of mass poverty and deprivation in developing countries which demand urgent solutions and more appropriate forms of intervention.

6 Social Work Practice and the Problem of Underdevelopment

Cultural diversity is only one problem facing social workers in developing countries; another concerns the profession's ability to contribute to the amelioration of the pressing problems of poverty and deprivation in the Third World. The methodology of social work not only embodies specific cultural values but is a specific approach to the amelioration of social problems. As shown previously, social problems are conceptualised in social work as individual maladjustments and it is the social worker's primary function to treat these emotional difficulties and problems by interpersonal relationships. By applying their knowledge and skills, social workers foster a desire for self-improvement in their clients and help them to cope with their problems independently. This is the explicit purpose of social case-work, which is the primary method of social work instruction and practice in both the industrial and developing countries. Even in those countries, where American theories of casework do not dominate the curriculum, students are trained primarily to work with individuals who have personal problems and most social work graduates are employed subsequently in this capacity.

The case histories of social work practice in the Third World described previously, accord fundamental importance to this role. In their portrayal of social work practice in Zambia and Bangladesh, Clifford, Clarkson and Halim emphasised the social workers' attempts to deal with the emotional problems of their clients; neither appeared to be much concerned with problems of material need and deprivation. Clifford made little reference to problems of this kind and he argued that social workers should not be concerned primarily with the provision of material aid; this is the least important aspect of social work practice. Helping clients to obtain financial assistance or find employment or meeting their material needs in other ways is only an expedient for, as he put it: 'We are dealing not merely with problems but with the people within these problems.'[1] Instead, social workers should seek to develop their clients' personalities and encourage them to deal with these problems themselves.

The patient described in Clarkson and Halim's case history came from a poor, low caste family.[2] In spite of the obvious fact that the amputation of the client's leg would have aggravated his impoverished material circumstances, the case history paid little attention to this, stressing instead the student's efforts to deal with the patient's personal problems. Apart from providing crutches, the student was concerned primarily with improving the unsatisfactory relationship between the client and his family. It may be argued that there was little else that the student social worker could do but his conclusion that the problem had been resolved satisfactorily, seemed naive. Although the family indicated their willingness to care for the man after his discharge from hospital, the outlook for the handicapped poor is bleak in a country where survival is a daily struggle. Familial affection cannot feed or clothe a disabled man and where relationships have been strained in the past, an additional burden on a poor family's income is likely to resurrect them. In spite of his handicap, the man hoped that he could be productive and make a financial contribution to the family. But, in view of the economic and social circumstances of Bangladesh, where the labour force is growing rapidly and where unemployment is a serious problem, this is unlikely. Begging, rather than productive employment, would have been a more likely source of income.

The Bangladesh case history is especially poignant in view of the country's extreme poverty. A relatively small country geographically, Bangladesh's population of eighty million people is growing at a per cent rate of 2.5 per annum and is expected to reach 140 million by the end of this century. Per capita income, which is among the lowest in the world, declined from $100 in 1974 to $90 in 1976. This was due not only to rapid population increase; since 1960, the country has had a negative rate of economic growth. War, domestic violence and a history of recurrent natural disasters has hampered development. For example, in 1974, the worst floods for two decades submerged more than two thirds of the cultivated land and almost all standing crops were destroyed. This disaster exacerbated the appalling conditions of poverty and malnutrition in which the majority of the population live, and many died of hunger. The country's statistics provide further evidence of the immense social problems it faces; in 1975, life expectancy at birth was only 42 years and of every thousand children born during that year, 140 died within twelve months. Forty-four per cent of the population have no access to safe drinking water and approximately 31 per cent of all rural families are landless. Less than a quarter of the adult population can read or write a simple sentence and more than a third of the children do not go to school.[3] Faced with social problems of this magnitude, social work's concern with emotional maladjustments seems trivial and superfluous.

The Social Problems of Underdevelopment

When schools of social work were established in developing countries, little evaluative research into the efficacy of social work intervention had been undertaken and it was accepted that professional social work was a modern and effective method of dealing with social problems. This belief was supported by the narrow and erroneous definition of social problems which was accepted at the time. Sociological textbooks on the subject dealt largely with problems such as crime, mental illness, alcoholism, family disorganisation and other forms of deviant behaviour, and reflected the view that social problems were manifestations of individual pathology. Although it was believed that these problems were common to both the industrial and developing countries, it was recognised that there were certain differences. The incidence of some social pathologies was thought to be greater in the industrial countries: crime, alcoholism, divorce and mental illness were believed to occur more frequently in the West, and it was thought that these problems were symptomatic of alienation and the disintegration of moral values in the industrial world. Other social problems such as begging, child neglect and homelessness were thought to be more common in the newly independent, developing countries. But it was accepted that the processes of development and modernisation would weaken traditional institutions in the Third World, such as the extended family, and that this would lead to an increase in deviant behaviour.

Indeed, social problems such as crime, alcoholism and mental illness do exist in the developing countries and as far as statistics and other sources of information may be regarded as reliable, the incidence of these forms of deviant behaviour has increased over the years. Problems of vagrancy and begging have become more common also, especially in the urban areas and are perceived often as a nuisance by the authorities. In the capitals of the Third World, the élite and the middle class view these problems in the same way as did their colonial predecessors: begging, squatting, public drunkenness and delinquency are believed to have adverse effects on tourism and are regarded as a threat to the stability and well-being of the urban community.

Consequently, governments in the Third World confirmed the approach to social welfare introduced during the colonial era; social problems were equated with individual deviance and social workers, capable of treating the pathologies of the urban poor, were recruited to deal with them.

The problems of individual pathology, serious though they may be, are of insignificant proportions when compared to the problems of poverty and deprivation in developing countries; hunger, disease, underemployment and unemployment, inadequate shelter and land-lessness, illiteracy and ignorance comprise a way of life for hundreds of millions of people in the Third World today. Originally, these were not regarded as social problems at all and even social workers took little notice of them, except when they were intrinsic to the individual cases they dealt with. Today, the enormity of the problem of absolute poverty in the Third World is recognised and social workers cannot remain ignorant of it.

Economic data, such as those which provide information about the gross national product or per capita incomes of developing countries are crude indicators of poverty in the Third World, but they give some insights into the extent of the problem, both in absolute and relative terms. In 1976, twenty-nine countries had per capita incomes of less than $200 and in some of these, per capita incomes were below $100. With the exception of small, capital surplus oil producing nations such as Kuwait, Bahrain, Qatar and the United Arab Emirates, which had per capita incomes in excess of $10,000, the richest countries in the world were concentrated in Europe and North America. Countries such as Sweden, Canada, West Germany, Switzerland, Norway and the United States had per capita incomes of more than $7,000 in 1976. Japan, Australia, New Zealand and most other Western European countries had per capita incomes in excess of $4,000. In the socialist countries of Eastern Europe, per capita income in 1976 averaged approximately $2,700. At the other end of the scale, countries such as Zaire, Afghanistan, Mozambique, India, Vietnam and Pakistan had per capita incomes of less than $200. The six poorest countries in the world, Bangladesh, Ethiopia, Mali, Laos, Upper Volta and Bhutan, with a combined population of some 124 million people, had per capita incomes of $100 or less in that year. Although these statistics are unreliable, they give some indication of the enormous differences in living standards between people in the rich and poor countries of the world.[4]

Many economists believe that these differentials will be reduced when the developing countries experience rapid economic growth. Some have argued that the problem of relative poverty between the developing and industrial countries is a temporary phenomenon; as the economies of the Third World industrialise, the gap between the rich and poor nations will narrow. Indeed, national growth rates reveal that the economies of many developing countries have been growing steadily, and in some cases, rapidly. The World Bank reported that economic growth rates in the developing countries in the 1950s and 60s, exceeded the rates experienced by western countries in the early stages of their industrialisation. Moreover, economic growth exceeded population growth in most countries.[5] The United Nations revealed that annual average rates of growth of gross domestic product in developing countries in the 1960s increased by 5 per cent; a rate exceeded marginally by the western capitalist nations which grew at an average annual rate of 5.2 per cent. By the 1970s, the situation had been reversed; gross domestic product in the developing countries grew at an annual rate of 6.2 per cent in the western economies, it was only 4.8 per cent.[6] Excluding the oil exporting countries, some Third World nations such as Brazil, South Korea, Hong Kong, Singapore and Kenya adopted open economic policies and experienced even more rapid economic growth in the 1960s and early 1970s.

In spite of these achievements and of what the World Bank described as an 'impressive' record of economic development during the last two decades, per capita growth rates in the developing countries are still below the rates experienced in the industrial West. Between 1968 and 1973, when the economies of many developing countries grew rapidly, per capita incomes in the Third World increased at an annual average rate of 3.4 per cent. In the industrial nations, however, per capita incomes increased by 3.7 per cent annually.[7] As a recent United Nations publication put it: 'in recent years, there has been no significant reduction in income inequality among countries at the global level, in spite of the increased rates of growth achieved by many developing countries'.[8] The prospects of 'catching up', as Donaldson called it, is so slight that it is a meaningless possibility for most developing countries. For example, he argued that it would require at least 1760 years for Pakistan to close the gap between itself and the United States if it maintained the rates of growth it achieved during the late 1960s.[9] Since then, the energy crisis, world currency instability and economic recession in the West have affected the economies of Third World countries negatively. As the cost of imported petroleum products have risen, the developing countries have experienced serious economic problems; 'their foreign exchange reserves dwindled and their balance of payments deteriorated'.[10] The adoption of protectionist policies in the West and the higher prices of their manufactured goods exacerbated the problem. Today, the external debts of many developing countries are of staggering proportions and in many, over 20 per cent of export earnings are used to service foreign borrowings. Official foreign capital inflows on a concessional basis from the industrial countries have not reached the United Nations First Development Decade target of 0.7 per cent of gross national product and even if they did, would make a negligible impact on the problem of international inequality.

In addition, current levels of economic growth are not likely to bring about a significant reduction in the incidence of absolute poverty in the Third World in the near future. In 1976, the World Bank estimated that no less than 800 million people in developing countries were in absolute poverty earning less than the equivalent of $50 per year. The great majority of the poor live in South Asia and Sub-Saharan Africa and in these countries, which contain more than one half of the world's population, economic growth rates have been small and the incomes and consumption levels of the poor have stagnated or even declined. In spite of its optimism, the World Bank admitted that even if the economies of the developing countries continue to grow 'absolute poverty will continue to be a problem of immense dimensions'.[11] Using sophisticated forecasting techniques, the Bank projected a decline in the numbers of people living in absolute poverty in the next twenty years. Although its forecasts showed that there could be about 600 million people in absolute poverty by the end of the century if population growth declined and economic development proceeded, it concluded that this prediction was 'somewhat optimistic'.

International differentials in levels of living are reflected domestically in many developing countries where inequalities of income and wealth are more marked than they are in the industrial capitalist world. Even in developing countries which have experienced rapid economic growth in recent years, income distribution has worsened. Studies in income patterns in countries such as Brazil, Mexico, Kenya and the Philippines have shown that the benefits of high growth do not accrue to the poor; in fact, much of it is transferred to the rich industrial countries. As Myrdal demonstrated, capital flows from Latin America to the United States in the 1960s were four times as great as were flows in the other direction.[12] Inequalities of income and wealth exacerbate the problem of poverty; inequalities in living standards between the cities and the rural areas, industrial workers and peasant farmers, land owners and landless labourers, between the rich and the poor and the very poor are fundamental obstacles to progress and social development. In most developing countries, the richest 5 per cent of the population own approximately 30 per cent of the nation's wealth and income while the poorest 20 per cent own less than 15 per cent of national income and wealth.[13]

Inequality and poverty are linked and manifest themselves in different ways; ill health, malnutrition, squalor, homelessness, illiteracy and landlessness are harsh expressions of deprivation and inequality which have not been abolished through economic growth. Nor do the growth rates recorded in the national accounts of the developing countries have any meaning to the poor who do not feel the effects or share the benefits of prosperity. Describing the realities of poverty in the Third World, as the poor experience them, Donaldson wrote: 'One of the first problems of being born poor is how to survive infancy . . . being born poor the chances are that you will spend the rest of your life being rather hungry.'[14] Disease and malnutrition are perhaps the most common manifestations of poverty in the Third World today. A report on the children of the Third World, published by the United Nations in 1970, showed that of every one hundred children born in the developing countries, twenty die within one year. Of the eighty who survive the first year of life, sixty will have no access to medical care during their childhood and more will die before the age of five. Of those who survive, many will experience malnutrition which may leave them physically or mentally retarded.[15] A report of the World Food Congress recorded that more than 50 per cent of the world's population are underfed. It was estimated that in India alone, fifty million children die of malnutrition every decade.[16] Infectious diseases, which are endemic in the developing countries, have not been eradicated in spite of considerable advances in medical knowledge and technology. In the developing countries, about 380 million people are still exposed to malaria and approximately ten million suffer from leprosy. Schistosomiasis, a chronic parasitic infection, threatens some two hundred million people in the Third World. 'Approximately one third of the world's population suffers from ill health in one form or another and in many areas, half the children die before the age of five largely as a result of malnutrition.'[17]

Although it has been assumed often that these forms of ill health persist because of shortages of physicians and other medical personnel in the Third World, a primary reason for the perpetuation of these diseases is poverty and deprivation. Nevertheless, the lack of trained medical staff and the maldistribution of services are serious problems. Health statistics published by the World Bank showed that there are very few doctors and nurses in many developing countries in relation to their populations. For example, in countries such as Ethiopia and Upper Volta, which have very few physicians, there are about 60,000 inhabitants for every doctor. Although these ratios have improved significantly in many countries since 1960, there were in 1974, 33,000 people for every doctor in Mali, 53,000 in Rwanda, 36,000 in Nepal and 26,000 in Yemen. There were 75,000 people for every nurse in Bangladesh, 36,000 in Nepal and 28,000 in Afghanistan. In the United States, on the other hand, there were 610 inhabitants for every physician and 160 for every nurse. Countries such as Austria, Czechoslovakia and the Soviet Union have even better ratios than these. In some countries such as Dahomey, Gambia, Liberia and Swaziland, there are 'no more than five dentists each, if that many, for the dental care of their total population'.[18]

Living conditions, standards of housing and sanitation in developing countries bear little comparison to the conditions of luxury in which the majority of people in the industrial countries live. Even though it is recognised that much housing in the industrial nations is inadequate and below acceptable standards, poor housing and inadequate shelter are accepted norms in the Third World. In the 1960s, the United Nations estimated that three quarters of the world's population live in substandard housing and that no less than 400 million housing units were required to meet their needs for minimum standards of shelter.[19] But the prospect of housing the Third World's population, even in conditions which would be regarded as barely adequate in the industrial countries, is so remote that it has been abandoned. Housing norms are meaningless when the majority of people in the Third World do not have access to safe drinking water or to basic sanitary services. Another United Nations report noted that: 'Health cannot be taken for granted when about 75% of the world's inhabitants are without an adequate and safe supply of water, when 85% depend on the most primitive methods for the disposal of excreta and refuse.'[20]

Poor educational standards, limited opportunities and the paucity of educational facilities in many Third World countries is another characteristic of underdevelopment. A UNESCO report estimated that there were 740 million people in the world who could not read or write; that was in 1960 and by 1970 this figure had increased by a further 80 million people. The same report revealed that 45 per cent of the world's children are not exposed to any form of schooling.[21] Although recent school enrolment statistics suggest that more children in the developing countries are now in school than ever before, estimates indicate that some 275 million children of school going age do not receive any formal education and that 'the drop-out rate in the first four years of primary education was almost 50% in parts of Africa, Asia and Latin America'.[22] Educational facilities are concentrated in urban areas and most of those who have no access to education are the children of the rural poor. As the United Nations put it: 'The unevenness of the distribution of educational benefits among the population is widely recognised.'[23]

Another social problem which is of immense proportions in the developing countries is unemployment and underemployment. Unproductive agriculture, migration and limited employment opportunities in industry and service occupations have resulted in serious problems of unemployment in the Third World. Official data, which reveal high levels of unemployment in many developing countries, provide no indication of the extent of underemployment among agricultural labourers, seasonal workers and others who comprise what has been described as the non-formal labour sector. Although the concept of unemployment is derived from western economics and is of limited usefulness in the Third World, the sad phenomenon of secondary school and graduate unemployment is revealed in the official statistics. The problem of the educated unemployed is largely the result of the adoption of inappropriate educational policies from the West, with the result that many who acquire an expensive education in non-technical fields, find that there is no work for them.

Rapid population growth and population pressure is widely regarded as another social problem of underdevelopment. Many countries now record annual population increases of over 2 per cent; between 1970 and 1975, the average annual rate of increase of the population of developing countries was 2.3 per cent while the corresponding rate in industrial countries was only 0.8 per cent.[24] Although much of the literature on this subject is coloured by gloomy neo-Malthusian sentiments, many agree that rapid population growth is a serious problem. More problematic is the question of how population growth can be regulated; there is today much disillusionment with approaches which have advocated the delivery of contraceptives without considering the issue of population growth in cultural, economic and political terms. The argument that population stabilisation will occur only when the basic problems of mass poverty and underdevelopment are dealt with has much credence.

The problems of Third World agriculture are basic causes of poverty in developing countries. The World Bank reported that approximately 87 per cent of the population of the poorest developing countries live in rural areas, 85 per cent of the labour force engaged in agriculture; but landholdings are small and agricultural production and productivity is low. In India, for example, 30 per cent of rural households subsist on plots of less than half a hectare in size. In many countries, land fragmentation has exacerbated the problem. In the Indonesian islands of Java and Bali, average farm size has declined over the years to only 0.6 hectare and many rural families are dependent on non-agricultural employment to meet their basic needs. Also, vagaries of weather and natural disasters aggravate the precarious existence of many rural families whose agricultural output is low already.[25] Many of these families have no land of their own and work as tenants, sharecroppers or labourers. Most of the landless labourers find irregular employment, usually on a seasonal basis; with very small incomes they are among the poorest of the poor. The International Labour Organisation estimated that there were about 75 million landless workers, comprising 30–35 per cent of the agricultural labour force, in the Third World. In some countries of Latin America, this proportion was as high as 66 per cent of the agricultural labour force.[26] Agrarian reform is regarded by many as a prerequisite for agricultural development and the alleviation of rural poverty. Although many developing countries now have land reform provisions, 'Ways of evading land reform legislation have not been difficult to find particularly when land owners have realised that governments have been more concerned with paper revolution than with real change.'[27]

The poverty of rural people in developing countries is aggravated by the concentration of public services in urban areas. In spite of rapid urbanisation, the rural population has not declined but continues to grow at about 2 per cent per annum while their access to health, education, clean water, sanitation and other public services is restricted. In Asia, 94 per cent of primary schools in urban areas give a comprehensive education in all primary grades; only 54 per cent of rural schools offer instruction in all primary grades. Similarly, while urban people have ready access to medical services, rural populations are poorly served. For example, there were 3700 urban dwellers per physician in Pakistan in 1970; in the rural areas the ratio was 24,000 per physician.[28]

The Challenge to Social Work

Poverty, deprivation, inequality and their various manifestations are the real social problems of developing countries; the pathologies of individual maladjustment may require amelioration but they are not the most serious or urgent social problems of the Third World. Today, more social workers realise that the social problems of underdevelopment pose a challenge to the profession and some have advocated that social work should contribute to their amelioration. Lochhead summarised the need for this involvement succinctly: 'At a purely material level of argument, low income countries cannot afford the luxury of casework services for the few. There are more urgent tasks to ensure the survival of the many.'[29] Thomas took a similar view arguing that while social workers would still be required to treat the personal problems of individuals, they must pay more attention to the problems of mass poverty; to single out individual problems of maladjustment 'in a setting that closely resembles the clinical, is comparable to winning battles but losing the war'.[30]

In spite of these forcible arguments, not all social workers are agreed that the profession should be concerned with the problems of underdevelopment. Gore regarded the issue as controversial, pointing out that Indian social workers are undecided about whether or not the profession should adopt this role.[31] Other social workers believe that these problems are the legitimate concern of politicans, economists and development planners. They argue that social workers have not been trained to deal with these problems; because the social problems of underdevelopment can be solved only through political action and economic measures, social workers have little to contribute. Instead, social workers should concentrate their skills on those they are capable of helping.

Other social workers claim that the profession is making an impact on the problems of poverty and deprivation already and that its methodology does not require reformulation to deal with them. Professor Gore explained that because 'a mass problem is nothing but a problem of a mass of individuals and that there is no other way of tackling problems except by working with individuals', social work's approach was appropriate. Although he conceded that social work would have to treat large numbers of individuals, this problem could

be overcome by treating them in groups.[32] Rashid argued that social
work was meeting the needs of the poor and socially vulnerable in
Pakistan, where it had succeeded to 'put these people back on their feet
through well devised rehabilitation and training programmes'.[33]
Writing about social work practice in Iran, Farman-Farmaian
claimed that: 'Social work, a relatively new profession in this part of
the world, attempts to define answers to the overwhelming problems of
mass poverty, disease and ignorance ... through control and preventive measures.'[34] In addition to casework, social workers used
group and community work methods to facilitate social change and
bring about social reform; in this way they were improving the welfare
of the community and contributing to the nation's development.

It is difficult to accept that social work's conventional approach can
be applied effectively to deal with the problems of mass poverty in the
Third World. The problems of underdevelopment have their roots in
political, economic and social factors and not in the minds of
individuals or in their maladjustments. Helping the poor to gain
insights into their problems or make a healthy adjustment to their
social circumstances does not meet their basic needs for food, shelter,
health, education or income; the principles of social work are intended
to govern the way social workers deal with those who have personal
problems, they are not prescriptions for development.

In support of the argument that social workers are contributing to
the development of the Third World, some have claimed that social
workers are not employed as caseworkers only but that they work in a
variety of fields, such as community development and family planning,
which are relevant to development and directed at the amelioration of
basic social problems. But, as was shown previously, there is little
indication that social work education in developing countries prepares
students adequately for these tasks. Also, there is little evidence to
substantiate the claim that social workers are employed extensively in
occupations which are concerned with development.

A follow-up study of 426 graduates of social work of the Teheran
School of Social Work found that only a small proportion worked in
fields which were related to development. For example, in 1974, only
8 per cent of the School's graduates were employed by the Ministry
of Co-operation and Rural Affairs, and only 4 per cent worked in
family planning clinics. The study showed that the majority had found
employment in voluntary welfare organisations, family welfare centres
and government agencies which were responsible for conventional
social welfare activities.[35]

Weisner's study of graduates of the Kenya School of Social Work found that the majority were employed as caseworkers. Of eighty four former students, 81 per cent worked primarily as caseworkers; twenty-three (27 per cent) were engaged exclusively in casework while the remaining forty-five (54 per cent) had additional responsibilities in other fields of social work such as group work or community development as well. Only two graduates worked exclusively in community development. The remainder were employed as school welfare officers, administrators, supervisors or research workers. Weisner reported that many social workers trained at the school had been absorbed into child welfare, medical social work, correctional welfare work and educational social work. He noted that the training these graduates had received in 'counselling, interviewing and casework techniques plus their insights into human behaviour and rapport with clients were of great value in each of these field settings'.[36] Also, he reported that the employment of social workers in government correctional institutions and the probation service had increased significantly and that the Ministry of Home Affairs would be an important source of employment for social workers in the future.

Some studies have shown not only that social workers in developing countries are employed in fields which have no bearing on development but that they face serious administrative obstacles and resource constraints which impede their conventional professional functions and limit their potential for assuming new responsibilities. Jagannadham argued that, although it was desirable that social workers involve themselves in developmental activities, 'the complexities of the problems and the meagreness of resources place severe limitations upon the fulfilment of this role by social workers'.[37] Resource problems are so serious that social workers in many developing countries are unable to assist even those who come to them for help. A graduate of the Kenya School of Social Work reported that she had no resources to help the many families in dire need of material assistance who had come to her; she admitted that she had helped a few very desperate cases by giving them money which had been allocated for office stationery.[38]

Social workers in all countries cannot function in isolation and are dependent on services provided by governmental or voluntary agencies to which they can refer their clients in need of specialised assistance or material aid. These services are very limited indeed in developing countries. Public agencies do not have adequate funds to provide for the many cases of financial distress which social workers deal with and voluntary organisations are few in number and equally impecunious. Often, psychiatric, social security and other referral services are unavailable. Although India has a well established system of public welfare services and many more voluntary organisations than most other developing countries, the large number of destitute families seeking temporary relief cannot be provided for. The Central Social Welfare Board, which supervises voluntary welfare organisations gave subsidies to more than 3000 agencies in 1974–5 but, simultaneously, the Union Ministry of Education and Social Welfare announced cuts in its welfare expenditures.[39] In Ghana, the Department of Social Welfare and Community Development has made a concerted effort to identify and assist disabled people in the community. Although it estimated that there were not less than one hundred thousand physically handicapped people in the country, only thirteen thousand were on the Department's register and it had insufficient resources to help all of them.[40]

In spite of a rapid expansion of social work training facilities in the Third World, personnel shortages limit the effectiveness of social work intervention. Because social workers in most developing countries have very large caseloads, they are unable to practise effectively. A government study team on social welfare in India recommended in 1959 that at least 7500 qualified social workers be recruited to administer the government's social welfare services. By 1965, only 2000 social workers had been trained at all the Indian schools of social work and a large proportion of these graduates were not employed in government but in industry as labour welfare officers.[41] The shortages of trained personnel in the rural areas especially limits the profession's capacity for contributing to the amelioration of the social problems of underdevelopment. For example, Lochhead reported that of his former students employed in rural community work in Africa, 'many served communities stretching over hundreds of miles and numbering from one hundred thousand to a quarter of a million'.[12] In many countries, social workers are reluctant to work in rural areas; this is true especially of those who have been trained at university schools of social work in countries where employment opportunities for graduates are good. A professional training at university enhances status and raises expectations; few graduates would readily relinquish their urban comforts and prospects of promotion to higher levels of administration for a harder and less prestigious role in rural development.

In addition to personnel shortages, social workers in many countries are inadequately paid, subject to poor conditions of service and promotion prospects and are accorded little status. In some countries, government social welfare personnel are ranked low in the civil service hierarchy and it is not uncommon for social workers, who are in public employment, to seek to be transferred to other government departments. Also, in some countries, government social workers are paid less than those in comparable civil service ranks elsewhere and in others, senior social welfare administrators are not qualified social workers. Obviously, these factors and the demoralising effects they have on social workers detract from their ability to be effective in the field.

These and other practical problems impede social work's intention to contribute to ameliorating the problems of poverty and deprivation in the Third World; shortages of resources and manpower, poor salaries and conditions of service as well as inappropriate training not only limit the profession's ability to assume new, developmental responsibilities but contradict the optimistic case studies which purport to show that social workers in the Third World deal effectively with the problems of their clients.

The Problems of Social Work Practice – A Recent Study

To gain further insights into the problems of social work practice in developing countries, forty-one social workers who had been trained at the University of Ghana agreed to participate in a study of their experiences as practising social workers. Ghana was chosen as a setting for this study not only because social work is well established in the country but because government social welfare services, among the first in Africa, have been provided since 1943. Social work training courses have been offered since 1950 and, at university level, since 1956. Also, community development in Ghana is extensive and is integrated with social welfare services; both are administered by one government department. Much emphasis is given to community development in social work training in the country. Because of their involvement in community development, it was hoped that the Ghanaian social workers would provide some insights into the problems of formulating appropriate roles for social work in the Third World.

Those participating in the study were interviewed in depth and many issues relating to social work practice were discussed with each respondent. These included resource constraints, conditions of work, the needs of clients, the usefulness of social work's principles and theories to the demands of practice, the profession's contribution to development and several other matters. The majority of those interviewed were trained between 1970 and 1972; all were professionally qualified and five had post-graduate diplomas in social work. All had extensive experience both before and after their professional training; all were employed as field workers by the Department of Social Welfare and Community Development before enrolling at the university and, on average, they had worked for six years in this capacity. Of the forty-one, thirty-three were still employed by the Department at the time the study was undertaken. Four were working in another field of social welfare: two were employed by voluntary agencies, the Society for Mentally Retarded Children and the Christian Mothers Association. The other two worked in statutory organisations: the National Youth Council and the Social Security and National Insurance Trust. The remaining four were no longer in social work and had found employment in private enterprise or another branch of government administration. Of the forty-one, thirty-two or 78 per cent were men; the average age of the respondents was forty-one years.

Of those who were employed as social workers at the time the study was undertaken, 27 per cent were responsible primarily for administration or supervision, but most reported that they were active simultaneously as practising social workers. Sixty-one per cent of those interviewed were engaged in social casework, 15 per cent were involved in residential work and only 12 per cent were employed in community development. The rest worked primarily in adult education or group work. Of those practising as social caseworkers, about 22 per cent worked with the physically handicapped and 20 per cent were employed as probation officers dealing both with adult and juvenile offenders. A small proportion worked as medical social workers in hospitals and one dealt with the problems of lepers. The remainder were responsible chiefly for family welfare services and were concerned mostly with problems of child neglect and the non-maintenance of dependants.

The respondents were asked what they thought the major problems facing social workers in Ghana were. The majority felt that these were administrative and financial in character; many reported that they had insufficient resources to do their work properly; equipment, stationery and other materials were in short supply and transport facilities were inadequate. Those working in the rural areas reported that they found it difficult to carry out their duties because of inadequate transport. Often, they were unable to reach the villages and even in the towns it was difficult to undertake home visits. Only one respondent did not complain about the shortages of resources but added that he was aware that his circumstances were exceptional. Those working in community development reported that it was difficult to undertake village development projects because of the shortage of materials. Some respondents thought that the resource problem had become more serious in recent years. One argued that social welfare services in the country survived only because of grants from international development agencies and this was particularly frustrating as Ghanaian social workers felt that available government revenues were being spent on projects which had little bearing on the social needs of the people.

Several thought that there was a serious shortage of social workers in the country; consequently, they were overworked and had insufficient time to deal properly with their cases. Others believed that the quality of social work practice was poor. Because the best qualified staff were usually engaged in administration and supervision, there were too few trained social workers in the field. Similar shortages of professional personnel in related fields such as child guidance, psychiatry and remedial education made it difficult for social workers to refer their clients to specialised agencies.

Problems of co-ordinating and administering social welfare programmes were mentioned also. Social workers employed in community development thought that they had relatively little status and that rivalries between different divisions of the Department of Social Welfare and Community Development did little to improve matters. Others felt that there was insufficient co-operation between social workers in the field and their superiors; they believed that decision making was centralised excessively and that field workers were controlled too stringently by distant administrators. Some indicated that social welfare and other government services were poorly co-ordinated and some thought that this problem could be attributed to their low status in the civil service.

Respondents were asked to comment on this issue in general. Did they feel that social workers were accorded status in the community and paid salaries commensurate with their training and skills? Most of those interviewed felt that social workers were respected often as individuals by other government officials, other professionals and the community as a whole but they believed that most people had little understanding of the social worker's role and function. However, many believed that as social work became more established, social workers would gain greater status and respect. Others were less optimistic; nearly one third of those interviewed thought that their profession had very little status. Officials in other government departments treated social workers as if they were poorly educated and they tended to disregard their opinions. Doctors and teachers were equally disparaging; teachers thought that they were capable of dealing with the social problems of their pupils and regarded school social welfare officers as intruders. Doctors 'looked down' on social workers and often required medical social workers to perform menial tasks. Some respondents commented that the profession's status depended on its ability to solve the problems of its clients and that it had failed to do this. One social worker believed that the community would lose all respect for social workers when they realised how ineffective they were.

There was a general feeling among those interviewed that social workers were paid badly and that their conditions of service were poor. There was some acknowledgement of recent salary improvements but still 78 per cent of those interviewed thought that social workers in Ghana were underpaid. Only a small minority were satisfied with their present salaries while the remainder thought that their salaries would be acceptable if promotion prospects and conditions of service improved. Promotion prospects were believed to be poor particularly for those without higher academic qualifications, but even those with university degrees and post-graduate diplomas had limited prospects when compared with civil servants in other government departments. Some argued that this was a major reason for the shortage of graduates in social work. Those who had left the profession and found employment in private enterprise or another field of government administration stated that they had changed careers because of the low salaries and poor promotion prospects. It is worth noting that all four were graduates who had obtained the post-graduate diploma in social work at the university.

These findings, which are not unique to the profession in Ghana, show that social workers are greatly frustrated by poor conditions of service, inadequate resources, low salaries and limited promotion prospects. Although they regard themselves as academically trained professionals, they are not treated as such by their employers, the government or by other officials, members of other professions and the community as a whole. These problems are serious constraints which limit the effectiveness of social workers in the field. To gauge the extent of their frustration, those interviewed were asked whether they had ever contemplated leaving social work to seek employment elsewhere. More than one half of those interviewed stated that they had thought seriously of leaving social work, and some had done so already; less than one third reported that they had no intention of leaving the profession. Although the majority had contemplated changing career, few had taken concrete steps to find employment in another field. A few reported that they had attempted to find alternative employment but had been unsuccessful, changed their minds at the last minute or had been persuaded to remain in social work. Several respondents indicated that their frustrations arose out of the poor conditions of service and other problems associated with government employment; some said that they were keen to find employment in voluntary welfare agencies rather than leave the profession altogether. However, the interviews revealed that many were dedicated to their work; in spite of inadequate resources and administrative constraints and although frustrated and dissatisfied, many were prepared to carry on as best they could.

Another topic discussed during the interviews concerned the relevance of social work's theories and principles to the social problems of people in developing countries such as Ghana. Respondents were asked several specific questions which dealt with this issue and were asked then to comment on it in general. First, they were asked to indicate which aspects of their training they had found most useful in social work practice. Although some had difficulty in answering this question, believing that all that they had been taught was equally useful, the majority reported that basic social science subjects such as sociology, social administration and psychology were the most relevant. These subjects had given them a broader understanding of human behaviour and society had helped them to practise more effectively. Others thought that practical subjects which were related to development, such as community development, agriculture, adult education and health administration were the most useful but added that more instruction in these topics was required. The minority, only 24 per cent of those interviewed, believed that social casework instruction had been the most useful aspect of their training and a very small proportion, only 4 per cent, thought that group work had been the most relevant.

With further reference to this issue, those interviewed were asked whether they could be justifiably criticised for being too concerned with remedial welfare work. Did they think that social workers in Ghana were contributing to the amelioration of basic social problems such as poverty and deprivation, and were they promoting the development of their country? The majority agreed that social workers were concerned excessively with the remedial aspects of social welfare but some pointed out that social workers in Ghana were involved also in rural community development and that this could not be construed as a remedial activity. Others argued that, because there was a serious shortage of social workers, they were compelled to deal with the most pressing cases of need; invariably, this implied that remedial intervention was required. The majority of those interviewed thought that, with the exception of those involved in community development, social workers were making little, if any, contribution to the development of the country. Most felt that social work needed to involve itself more actively in preventive work and to seek to contribute to the amelioration of underdevelopment.

Respondents were asked whether they thought that social work was a product of western society, unsuited to the needs of developing countries such as Ghana. Although the majority disagreed with this interpretation, many felt that social work's principles and methods needed to be adapted to local cultural and social conditions to be of value to developing countries. Only four of those interviewed believed that social work was a western invention which was unsuited totally to developing countries. One respondent stated that social work was based on western values and a capitalist ideology and that it was of no use to the Third World.

Those interviewed were asked to indicate in which ways they thought social work could contribute to development and the eradication of poverty in the Third World. About one third of those interviewed felt that social workers could contribute best to the solution of social problems in developing countries through adult education; in this way people could be helped to understand their rights and could also be encouraged to change their traditional attitudes. Some thought that adult education could increase popular participation in development and one respondent believed that it would inspire patriotic attitudes in people. Twenty per cent believed that social work could solve society's problems through community development; through rural development projects, self-help, co-operatives, home industries and agricultural extension, village incomes could be increased and social conditions improved. Some felt that social work could contribute to development best through participating in the formulation of social policies and through social planning but they pointed out that social workers in Ghana had little influence on government welfare policy and were unlikely to become involved in these activities. A very small minority believed that conventional social work methods such as casework and group work could deal with basic social need. Although 61 per cent of those interviewed reported that they were working as caseworkers, very few thought that this was an appropriate way of dealing with the social problems of developing countries.

Although the majority of those interviewed thought that social workers could contribute to development and the amelioration of the social problems of underdevelopment, it was surprising that no less than 30 per cent believed social work was incapable of solving these social problems; they felt that the profession's achievements were negligible and that resources were grossly inadequate. Social work was so impotent that, to quote one respondent, 'it was not taken seriously by anyone'. Another said that social work was not only ineffective but dangerous as it tended to raise hopes and expectations which it could not fulfil. Others took a less extreme view; conceding that social work had made little impact on the social problems of Ghanaian society, they believed that the profession had much to contribute if it had more resources and involved itself more positively in developmental tasks.

In view of the constraints of inadequate resources, those interviewed were asked to indicate how effective they thought they were when dealing with the problems of their clients. Their replies to this question were generally pessimistic; the majority indicated that although providing help in individual cases, they were doing little to deal with the root causes of the problems of their clients, nor were they able to meet their basic needs. However, social workers in different specialised fields varied in their assessment of the effectiveness of social work intervention. Those concerned with the rehabilitation of the disabled were more optimistic than other social workers, pointing out that they were encouraging families to accept that they had a responsibility for the maintenance of their handicapped dependants and, in this way, were ensuring that the disabled remained in the community and participated in community life. On the other hand, those responsible for probation and family welfare work were negative about their ability to deal effectively with the needs of their clients; they said that while they were attempting to treat the immediate problem, there was little they could do to deal with underlying causes.

Many of those interviewed said that the problems of their clients could be attributed to factors which they, as social workers, were unable to remedy. For example, those working in the field of probation indicated that most of their clients came from deprived backgrounds and they believed that many had committed crimes, such as petty theft, because they were poor. Similarly, those engaged in family welfare reported that the majority of their clients came from the poorest sections of the community; they had very low incomes, were badly housed, poorly educated, employed sporadically and often in poor health and malnourished. Medical social workers reported that many of the problems they were required to deal with could be attributed to poverty; many of their clients suffered from diseases which were associated with low levels of living and many could not afford to pay for treatment and drugs. Some social workers concerned with child care and youth work conceptualised the problems of their clients in a different way, tending to blame the parents whom they thought were responsible for many cases of incorrigibility. These social workers referred to the 'generation gap' which they believed explained the origin of the problem, but one youth worker felt that the problems of delinquency and misbehaviour among young people could be attributed to the poor state of the economy which had resulted in a lack of employment opportunities for youth in the country.

The findings of this study contrast sharply with the idealised accounts of social work practice in developing countries which pervade the profession's literature. The Ghanaian social workers admitted frankly that they were not solving the basic social problems of their country and even, that they were unable to deal adequately with the problems presented to them; they had insufficient resources and many felt that these problems were symptomatic of more fundamental problems of poverty and deprivation which they were unable to ameliorate. Although as many as 30 per cent of those interviewed believed that social work was of limited usefulness to the amelioration of these problems, the majority took the view that social work was potentially useful provided that more resources were made available and that it involved itself more actively in fields which were relevant to the country's needs.

It is interesting that the Ghanaian social workers expressed such strong views; unlike most developing countries, social workers in Ghana are engaged in developmental activities such as community development and adult education and their training is more relevant than most. Clearly, this is not enough; the Ghanaian social workers recognised that to be effective in the field and contribute to the development of their country, substantially more resources and more appropriate forms of training were required. Those who claim that social work is contributing to the eradication of poverty and deprivation in the Third World, would find it instructive to take note of the views of these social workers. Also, those who propose that the profession assume responsibilities for developmental tasks, should recognise the constraints which hinder social work practice and the implementation of new professional roles.

7 Development Roles for Social Work in the Third World

Although it is not a new issue, the question of social work's involvement in activities which are designed to promote development has been discussed more widely in recent years. Today, more social workers recognise that conventional social work is incapable of contributing to the eradication of poverty and deprivation in the Third World, and it has been recommended that new developmental roles for social work be identified. A few proposals have been made; these vary in the extent to which changes in the profession's character are envisaged. While some recommendations require little more than a change in emphasis in the curriculum of social work education, others propose that the profession assume entirely new responsibilities. Also, while some are directed specifically at the problems of Third World poverty, others are concerned with activities which are associated either with development in general terms or with the social and cultural conditions of developing countries.

The debate on social work's proper role in developing countries has revolved largely around the term 'indigenisation'. The fifth United Nations international survey of social work training used it in 1971 with reference to the disillusionment felt by Latin American social workers about the inappropriateness of American social work theories to their societies; it reported that ten years earlier in Costa Rica, participants at the Fourth Pan American Congress of Social Work expressed doubts about the relevance of western theories of social work to Latin America. Although they believed that the profession's basic approach and philosophy was useful, some concepts required modification if the profession was to be of relevance to the values, social organisation and needs of Latin American countries. The report noted: 'Since such thinking began, associations of schools of social work and faculty have been seriously applying themselves to the challenge of evolving an indigenous philosophy and approach to the problems of social intervention in the Latin American region.'[1]

Since then, indigenisation has become a popular term among social workers. Numerous articles on the subject have appeared in social work journals and it has been debated at several conferences. Indigenisation was a major theme at the Sixteenth Congress Schools of Social Work which was held at The Hague in 1972. Reporting on the conference, Herman Stein said: 'We have entered the era of indigenisation, of indigenous development based on the needs of the cultural, political and economic landscape of each society.'[2] These developments have been supported by the international agencies; for example, the debate on indigenisation was given much impetus by the International Conference of Ministers Responsible for Social Welfare which was held in New York in 1968. The ministers were concerned with broader issues than social work but their recommendation that social welfare programmes in developing countries should 'maximise the contribution of social welfare to meeting the tasks of development and the achievement of national goals', had implications for social work and carried much weight.[3] The First Asian Conference of Ministers Responsible for Social Welfare which was held in Manila in 1970, discussed social work education at length and concluded that: 'Curricula for social work training should be geared towards national development goals while being constantly examined, reviewed and evaluated in the light of the changing needs of a society.'[4] An expert group of social work educators, meeting under the auspices of the United Nations Economic and Social Commission for Asia and the Pacific in 1974 noted that there was 'growing international concern' about social work's limited and inappropriate role in the Third World and it urged the profession to adopt new approaches which 'would more directly contribute to national development goals'.[5]

The concept of indigenisation has become popular among social workers in developing countries because it recognises the uniqueness of culture and the right to self-determination. Although its use in contemporary social work has intrinsic appeal, it is not without problems. Although speakers at international social welfare meetings and social work conferences have used the term with monotonous frequency, it is still defined imprecisely and social workers continue to use it to mean different things. Some have used it to describe alternative fields of practice for social work in the Third World, arguing that the profession should become involved in adult education, community development or family planning. Others have used it to emphasise the concept's cultural connotations; they believe that social workers should recognise cultural differences between societies and refrain from acting in ways which affect local cultural practices and traditions negatively. However, most use it superficially; while their knowledge of the term demonstrates a recognition of the need for social work to be involved in development, they are unable to define it adequately or suggest ways in which the profession can realise this objective. In this sense, the term has become little more than a cliché in the vocabulary of contemporary social work, for its usage has not been accompanied by many successful attempts to clarify its meaning or debate some of the more difficult issues attending its use.

Some social workers have shown, through their writings, that the term raises very difficult issues indeed. For example, Lasan's article on the need for indigenisation on the Philippines demonstrates that the popular use of a new term often obscures complex problems. Lasan, a Filipino social work professor described the apprehension felt by many at the declaration of martial law in her country in 1972. Many social workers believed that the new political order challenged the profession's commitment to democratic principles and values. The shift towards centralisation, rule by presidential decree and the invocation of stringent security powers seemed to many social workers to violate their professional beliefs. But Lasan argued that, because these social workers were trained to accept western social work principles, they failed to realise that the new political system was an indigenous development which was highly compatible with traditional Filipino culture. Their western democratic values were an alien acquisition which had no relevance to the Philippines where authoritarianism is institutionalised and where firm government is respected.

In view of a more widely shared sensitivity to allegations of cultural imperialism, western social workers may be inclined to respect the view that professional practice in different countries should accommodate cultural differences. But Lasan calls on social workers to adapt their principles not only to cultural but political practices in different societies. As she put it: 'The time has come when social work as it evolved in the West has to adapt not only to existing socio-cultural patterns but to political realities.'[6] Many social workers would find this interpretation of the term problematic. To urge social workers to recognise totalitarian regimes because they are indigenous is to repudiate the profession's values entirely and to call on them to deny whatever commitment to social change, democracy or social justice they may have. It is more than a call for indigenisation; it is a formula for total ethical detachment and professional conservatism and ultimately, for the legitimation of political repression. Lasan's provocative challenge to social work and her controversial interpretation of the concept attracted little comment from the profession. Although she illustrated how difficult new ideas can be, few social workers who now use the term have considered its deeper implications.

Proposals for the indigenisation of social work have not been concerned with these ethical issues but have attempted to identify alternative practical roles for social work in the Third World. Although several suggestions have been made, they have not enjoyed unequivocal support and their feasibility and relevance to all developing countries is questionable.

Social Work and the Problems of Modernisation

Several social workers have argued that the profession can make a particularly appropriate contribution to developing countries by dealing with the problems of social disruption, dislocation and disorganisation produced by rapid social change; they believe that social work's most useful role in developing countries is its ability to deal with the harmful consequences of modernisation. Clifford has written about social work's potential involvement in this field of service at some length. Drawing on sociological literature about the modernisation of developing countries, he argued that because of social change, the previously well-integrated peasant community had become less cohesive and less able to deal with the social problems of its members. Traditionally, the rural family was self-sufficient, functioning as an integrated social and economic unit; each individual had clearly defined duties and obligations towards the family, community and tribe and, conversely, these groups were responsible for the welfare of the individual.

Clifford argued that as modernisation came to Africa, the pace of social change increased rapidly, resulting in the erosion of traditional life styles and systems of social welfare. This has been accelerated by the associated phenomenon of urbanisation. The modern cities of Africa exerted a powerful influence over the rural areas and attracted peasants to the urban centres. The promise of urban prosperity had great appeal to the young and as young people have migrated to the cities, rural communities have been denuded of their most valuable assets. This resulted in a serious shortage of labour and a decline in agricultural production; as a result, older people have been left without adequate support. In the urban areas, migrants have faced unforeseen problems. They have experienced difficulties in finding employment and adequate housing. Many have been compelled to live as squatters in unhygenic and overcrowded conditions and many have had to work for low wages, often on a temporary basis. The problems of urban poverty have been exacerbated by psychological maladjustments; for example, the loss of tribal identity brought about by inter-tribal marriages and the disintegration of tribal customs has been especially disruptive. The social anomie caused by rapid urbanisation has been accompanied by an anomie of the mind which has left many Africans bewildered, without moral roots and a sense of folk obligation. As Clifford put it: 'In the towns we are faced not only with amorphous populations, shapeless, normless and often suspended between two ways of life, but also with the psychological effects of this hiatus.'[7] These psychological maladjustments, he believed, manifest themselves in different ways; crime, mental illness, divorce, alcohol abuse and a disregard for the welfare of children, old people and the handicapped are just some examples of the pathological consequences of modernisation.

Social workers in other developing countries have identified similar problems in their societies. Writing about the effects of modernisation in Iran, Farman-Farmaian stated: 'The individual finds the old structure crumbling around him and feels ill-equipped to adapt himself to new modes of living.'[8] This has resulted in serious psychological tensions and a disruption of traditional relationships between the young and the old, husbands and wives, workers and employers. Also, modernisation has brought about a rapid increase in the incidence of social problems such as juvenile delinquency, prostitution, psychiatric illness and corruption. Bulsara argued, in a similar vein, that social change had weakened traditional institutions in India; although modernisation had given people more freedom, it had made them more insecure and vulnerable.[9]

These authors believe, that by concentrating on the problems of modernisation, social work has a unique opportunity to increase its relevance to the Third World. Clifford argued that this required that social work education be adapted to suit African conditions; African social workers should be trained locally and not abroad so that they can be made more aware of these problems. They should be given a sound education in anthropology in order to understand the social problems caused by the disintegration of tribal communities. It is a mistake, he argued, to imagine that Africans have an instinctive grasp of tribal life. Just as European students of social work are taught to understand their societies, Africans must be given insights into their traditional cultures and taught about the effects of social change on tribal institutions. Apart from this, Clifford did not propose that the principles or techniques of western social work be modified to treat these problems; the skills required to deal with the harmful consequences of modernisation in Africa are the same as those used by social workers in the West. Others who have written on this subject have argued also that the social pathologies of social change require individualised casework treatment. Because of the weakening of traditional institutions in India, Bulsara claimed that 'the individual needs guidance and support to meet the demands made upon him. Social work today aims at this support'.[10] From her observations of social change in developing countries, Clarkson concluded: 'In all my recent travels . . . I have found the need for casework to be overwhelming.'[11] Not only are problems such as juvenile delinquency and divorce increasing rapidly, but 'urbanisation, industrialisation, the breakdown and separation of families, the changing role of women all lead on the one hand to economic development and, on the other, to the confusion of the individual'.[12] With so much confusion in the Third World, she argued, group work and community work cannot cope and the extension of casework services is an urgent requirement.

Although these proposals make an attempt to delineate a role for the profession which is based on an awareness of local social problems, new activities, which are different from the profession's conventional approach, are not envisaged. Manifestations of the maladjustments of modernisation such as crime, family disorganisation and urban destitution are already dealt with by social workers. The claim that these problems will occur with greater frequency does not imply that social workers in developing countries will undertake new tasks to deal with them but instead, that their caseloads and burden of work will increase. Those who propose that social workers can be usefully employed to treat the feelings of bewilderment, confusion, alienation and other psychological maladjustments caused by rapid social change, also propose that therapeutic casework be retained as the primary technique for dealing with these problems of development; indeed, Clarkson and others argued that casework should be given precedence over other methods. How these psychological traumas can be treated in practical terms is not considered. It is difficult to imagine that migrants who feel bewildered will either know that caseworkers can help them or be anxious to seek their advice. As Almazor and others have shown, people in developing countries use social workers usually when they are in dire need of material assistance. Those suffering from acute mental distress are more likely to be referred to psychiatrists than social workers.

In spite of the disruption caused by urbanisation, anthropological research has demonstrated that urban migrants maintain their family ties and turn to their kin in times of trouble. Studies undertaken in Africa have shown that urban migrants are accommodated and supported by relatives, friends or village associations when they come to the cities and that they receive guidance and material aid until they are able to establish themselves. Many retain strong links with their kinsmen who remain in the villages.[13] The image of migrants as confused individuals who are lost materially and spiritually in the urban milieu is not supported by this research. Although sociologists and anthropologists accept that rapid social change causes structural tensions and social disruption, many believe that the psychopathological consequences of modernisation have been exaggerated; today the academic theories of modernisation, which stressed the psychological aspects of social change have been refuted.[14] Nor are the psychopathologies of modernisation the most pressing problems of developing countries; they cannot be compared to the more serious problems of poverty and deprivation in the Third World. The majority of people in developing countries are too poor to be afflicted with the neuroses of modernisation. Social workers who argue that the profession should treat the personal maladjustments of migrants are failing not only to identify relevant forms of practice but to understand the true extent of deprivation in the Third World.

Social Work and Family Planning
Some social workers have argued that if the profession wishes to make a positive contribution to development, it should engage in preventive rather than remedial social welfare. Social workers such as Khinduka have urged that social work should seek to prevent people from becoming poor, for by limiting the incidence of poverty, they would remedy many of the problems they are required to deal with at present: prevention rather than 'individual rehabilitation' should be the profession's main objective.[15]

Although many social workers would support this proposal, preventive programmes are not easy to identify and, with the exception of group work with potentially delinquent youth, social work has not been able to find many areas of professional practice which are clearly preventive in character. One idea, which has been received with some enthusiasm by social workers in the Third World, is the possibility that the profession might become involved in population policy and planning. It has been suggested that if social workers promote family planning and become involved in the delivery of family planning services, they would contribute to the prevention of poverty and deprivation; by encouraging their clients to practise contraception and have fewer children, social workers would help them to meet their material needs and to improve their social and economic circumstances. In addition, other social problems associated with large family size could be averted. For example, Florendo argued that the popular acceptance of family planning in the Third World would have significant preventive implications; not only would the incidence of poverty be reduced but family planning would promote marital harmony and family stability, limit sexual maladjustments, prevent illegitimacy and safeguard maternal and child health.[16]

This idea is not new to social work; in the industrial countries it has been recommended that caseworkers should be aware of the need to advise their clients to seek contraceptive advice if they believe this to be appropriate. In the Third World, the proposal that social work should become involved in population planning has the special attraction of being relevant to development. Today, family planning is regarded by many development economists and sociologists as an essential aspect of development policy. Certainly, social work's involvement in family planning would allow the profession to identify with national development efforts more closely and to demonstrate its concern for development issues. This was the view taken by an expert group of Asian teachers of social work who met in Bangkok in 1974 to consider ways in which social work education in their countries could be made more appropriate to the Third World. They believed that the problems of underdevelopment in the region were a consequence of poverty and population pressure. In Asia, which is exceptionally densely populated, rapid population increases have contributed to 'low standards of living, poor nutrition and housing, poor schooling and poor sanitary and health facilities'.[17] These problems have contributed to the vicious cycle of poverty which, the experts believed, could be broken by population control policies. It was therefore highly desirable that social workers should contribute to this task.

The most comprehensive attempt to examine the question of social work's role in population planning was the International Conference on Social Work Education, Population and Family Planning, which was held in Hawaii in 1970. The participants agreed unanimously that social work should contribute to family planning and most of the conference was taken up with considering ways in which the profession could assume what was described as this 'new responsibility'. Several proposals were made; the obvious recommendation was that a concern for family planning should be instilled into social work students and practitioners. Courses on the subject should be introduced at schools of social work and practising social workers should be encouraged to inform their clients of the importance of family planning and to refer them to specialised agencies for further advice.

Many of the participants made more ambitious proposals; they argued not only that family planning should be a part of conventional practice but a new form of employment for social workers. Some claimed that, because social workers are 'human relations specialists', they are more qualified to deal with those seeking contraceptive advice and to counsel family planning acceptors than medical personnel. It was proposed that schools of social work should 'prepare more graduates who can function in family planning clinics, post partum hospital clinics and other places where the message and services of clinicians can be communicated'.[18] Others suggested that social workers should assume a responsibility for family planning education in the community. In this way, social workers would function not only as counsellors but as motivators and public relations experts who would 'develop the climate of opinion which legitimates and provides acceptance of population policies or a family planning programme'.[19] Some of the delegates proposed that social workers could make a significant contribution to population research; because of their knowledge of the community, they could 'provide feedback and suggested changes to those guiding the programmes and dispensing various kinds of services'.[20] The most ambitious recommendation was made by those participants who believed that social workers would make good family planning directors and managers. Because of their knowledge of human behaviour and special qualifications in human relationships, social workers were most capable of administering and planning population services. In addition, they claimed that their training in community organisation would equip social workers to maintain good levels of service delivery through co-ordinating govern-ment and voluntary family planning agencies effectively.

Although the Hawaii conference was an important event in the profession's search for more appropriate roles in developing countries, the delegates were surprisingly unrealistic and optimistic about social work's ability to assume these responsibilities. The conference's recommendations were based not on a careful assessment of the need for social workers in family planning but on whether the profession's potential for filling or taking over non-medical roles in family planning could be justified. The evidence produced to support this contention was extremely dubious. Many argued that social workers should be made responsible for family planning activities, not because they were technically more competent in the subject or more knowledgeable than others but because they were able to 'convey a sense of human warmth and build up the dignity of those with whom they dealt'.[21] Irwin Sanders, who summarised the findings of the conference, believed that social workers could function effectively as counsellors but he was sceptical about the profession's ability to fill other roles competently. This was, he argued, a dubious claim 'since schools of social work have, for the most part, done little along this line'.[22]

This deficiency could be rectified if schools of social work provided teaching in population and family planning, but Sanders reported that participants from different parts of the world had admitted that their schools did not provide instruction in these subjects, and that social workers in their countries were not involved in the provision of family planning services to any great extent.[23] It would require additional resources and many years before the profession could claim to have adequate expertise in this field. As Florendo pointed out, existing social work training courses would have to be restructured 'in order to make room for family planning in our already overcrowded curricula'.[24] Also, new field work placements and additional staff would be required and schools of social work may lack the resources or be reluctant to make these changes.

Because the field of family planning is already dominated by the medical profession and other specialists such as demographers, motivators, information experts and career administrators, new employment opportunities for social workers in family planning are limited. It is difficult to see how social workers can be incorporated into family planning services except as counsellors. The Hawaii conference's recommendation that social workers should replace specialist demographic research workers, motivators and administrators is most unrealistic; these roles are filled already by experts who are more competent in these fields than social workers. Research into population is a highly technical activity undertaken by sociologists, statisticians and demographers. Training courses for family planning motivators and educators have been established in many developing countries already. The administration of population programmes is rightly or wrongly regarded as the prerogative of medical doctors and civil servants. The profession's desire to be involved in family planning at these levels will certainly be thwarted by the entrenched interests of other professional groups. While there is little doubt that physicians, family planning experts and administrators would be delighted if social workers counselled their clients and referred them to specialised clinics, the profession's chances of taking a controlling interest in the family planning business are limited.

Social Work and Rural Development

The pressing problem of rural poverty is a primary characteristic of underdevelopment and the prospect of social work contributing to its amelioration is attractive. The obvious vehicle for the profession's involvement in this field is community development and some have argued that, because close links between the two exist already, the employment of social workers in community development on a large scale could be facilitated without too much difficulty. As shown previously, links between social work and community development in the Third World do exist but, with the exception of Africa, these are not substantial. With some exceptions, such as Hong Kong, Asian and Latin American schools of social work provide little instruction in community development. Even at anglophone African schools, where more tuition in the subject is provided, community development courses are not given precedence over other social work methods. In most countries where community development services exist, social workers and community development personnel perform very different tasks and are employed by different agencies. Usually, social workers are to be found in the towns and cities while community development personnel work in the rural areas. Only a few countries, such as Ghana, employ professional social workers in community development programmes and integrate these services within one government organisation.

In many countries, community development is regarded as a para-professional field of social welfare. Usually, community development workers are trained at technical institutions which do not have university status. Entrance requirements at these training centres are considerably lower than they are at schools of social work and the courses provided are shorter and less academic. Most community development training institutions place greater emphasis on teaching practical skills than do schools of social work; also, courses in agricultural extension, handicrafts, masonry and carpentry, feeder road construction, domestic livestock husbandry, home economics and other topics are provided. These subjects are not offered at schools of social work.

Historically, community development and social work have different origins. In Africa, community development emerged from the mass education programmes begun by colonial administrators after the Second World War. Community development in India was inspired by the work of Gandhi and Tagore and promoted by the Congress Party and colonial officials such as Brayne. These beginnings owed nothing to social work but there was, as Brokensha and Hodge showed, a gradual infusion of social work ideas into community development.[25] Although community development was based on the principle that local people should participate actively in projects which were designed to promote their welfare, this idea was applied pragmatically. While it is true that Gandhi and Tagore stressed the need for dedicated workers who would be able to encourage village participation, community development was less concerned with concepts than with action; in practical terms this meant that the authorities provided technical expertise, materials and other resources while village people gave their labour.

As the theory of community development evolved, this simple, pragmatic approach acquired ornamentation. In addition to self-help, the principle of self-determination was incorporated into community development. Just as social workers were taught that individuals had fundamental rights to decide on matters affecting their welfare, community development workers were told that the rights of villagers should be respected. In theory, if rural people chose to drink polluted water or live in unhygienic conditions, they had a right to do so. But, while it was believed that community development 'should be carried through on the initiative and hard work of the community itself and should not be organised from outside', this principle was unworkable.[26] It was recognised that villagers did not always know what their 'felt needs' were and community development workers were instructed in the techniques of persuasion to motivate supposedly reluctant villagers to participate in development. These contradictions were seldom recognised by the theorists who wrote at length about the need to encourage traditional communities to be democratic. Also, the concepts of self-determination and democracy were reinforced by

American efforts to establish community development programmes as counter insurgency measures in countries such as the Philippines and Vietnam. In 1962, a British government publication argued that community development should be regarded not only as a means of providing material benefits but as 'a stepping stone to democratic self-government as it is understood in the Western World'.[27] In addition, it was argued that community development workers should be less concerned with providing services and amenities than with promoting attitudinal change. Because superstition and traditionalism were believed to be major reasons for the backwardness of rural communities, workers should function as 'change agents' and seek to awaken rural communities from their traditional slumbers and help them to become dynamic, independent and alive to their own potential.

Through the adoption of these concepts, western liberalism found its way into community development and at schools of social work in the Third World, the theoretical rather than the practical aspects of community development were emphasised. Although theoretical principles were not neglected at vocational community development training centres, they were not venerated as they were at schools of social work. Nor were the relatively unsophisticated trainees subjected to these doctrines to the same extent; in the field, they have been more concerned with practical projects than behavioural change. While they face serious problems of inadequate resources and poor facilities, they have more prospect of contributing to development than do their academically more competent counterparts.

In view of this, it is surprising that those who propose that closer links between social work and community development be fostered, believe that the social worker's superior theoretical knowledge and understanding of human behaviour can promote rural development more effectively. Although social workers such as Cama recognised that community development workers have technical skills in establishing rural development projects, these were not sufficient to bring about rural improvements. Village people, she claimed, do not require services and amenities only; they need to be given insights into their problems and encouraged to be independent and self-reliant. This is required especially in communities which, as she put it: 'are extremely apathetic, lethargic, disorganised, custom bound, isolated and anti-social'.[28] These communities require very skilful handling; because community development workers do not have sufficient expertise to deal with these problems, the skills of social workers and caseworkers especially, are needed.

Dasgupta's attempt to integrate social work theory and community development practice reached similar conclusions.[29] While researching into the effectiveness of community development in West Bengal, Dasgupta realised that the principles of social work were highly compatible with Tagore's ideas on community development. A wealthy but compassionate landowner, Tagore was appalled by the misery of rural life in India, and like Gandhi, believed that rural people could be encouraged to improve their circumstances through self-help. Tagore began to train village development workers informally on his estate at Surul, a village which became known subsequently as Sriniketan, a Bengali word meaning 'home of welfare'. With the help of Leonard Elmhurst, an American agriculturalist, Tagore expanded the work and in 1922, a new training centre was built. Here, recruits were trained, as Dasgupta emphasised, not only to establish village projects and to introduce health, education and sanitary services but to promote local democracy, self-awareness and self-reliance. Tagore believed that it was absolutely essential that his workers encourage rural people to become self-reliant and he was reported to have said that the test of the workers' effectiveness was the ability of the village to dispense with their services. His methodology was formulated in what became known as the principles of *sriniketan*, and these, Dasgupta pointed out, were very similar to those of social work; also, the techniques employed by the rural development workers were almost identical to those used in social work. Because of these similarities, Dasgupta argued that social work could make a useful contribution to rural development. Social workers already possess the knowledge and skills to work in this field; to promote development, the profession should focus its attention on communities instead of individuals and be less concerned with remedial welfare.

Like Cama and others, Dasgupta believed that the provision of services was of secondary importance. To emphasise the need for attitudinal and behavioural change rather than material welfare, he compared two groups of villages in the Birbhum district, near the Visva-Bharati University. The first group had been exposed to the principles of *sriniketan*; using these principles, he claimed that rural development workers had transformed the first group into dynamic, self-aware, democratic and co-operative communities. The second group had not benefited from their intervention and were passive, dependent on outside aid, subject to authoritarian leadership and entirely without ambition and initiative. But they did not lack facilities; local leaders who wielded influence with the authorities had obtained outside help to establish a variety of amenities such as 'schools with big buildings, polished libraries and well decorated classrooms'.[30] While the first group of villages lacked some of these amenities, they were self-reliant, able to identify their needs and solve their problems democratically. Because no attempt had been made to 'touch the rural community at its base and to awaken its dormant potential', the second group had none of these qualities and were infinitely worse off.[31]

A major difficulty with these proposals is the assumption that rural communities require moral upliftment rather than material development. It is claimed frequently that if rural people can be helped to be democratic and self-reliant, they will overcome the poverty which afflicts them. There is little evidence to support this contention; the causes of rural deprivation are not to be found in the hearts and minds of village people. Undoubtedly, they can improve their material circumstances through self-help but they require tangible assistance in the form of expertise, materials and other resources rather than exhortations from social workers. Initiative, democratic procedures, self-awareness and other desirable qualities cannot provide the improved agricultural techniques, infrastructure and other facilities which rural communities need to raise their levels of living. Nor is there much evidence to show that rural people are so lethargic and resistant to change that they require the help of social workers. A recent study, undertaken in Sierra Leone, found that village people were anxious to obtain improved amenities and they were prepared not only to give their labour but to contribute money and materials. Many had undertaken rural development projects on their own initiative without government assistance and the aid of community development workers.[32] If social work is to contribute to rural development, it must do more than provide moral guidance and edification. Unfortunately, at present, there is little evidence that the profession has anything else to offer rural communities.

Social Work and Political Action

The idea that social workers should be committed politically to bring about progressive social change is not a new one, but it has not been popular with most social workers. While the profession has claimed, on numerous occasions, to be concerned with social justice and social reform, it has been reluctant to take concrete action in support of this objective. In the depression years, some social workers urged their colleagues to take a more radical position on the problems of mass unemployment and poverty but this proposal attracted little support. For example, Baldwin's call on American social workers to help the trade unions and to support the establishment of a 'political class party of producers' was too extreme and was dismissed as being subversive. In more recent years, some European and North American social workers have championed radical movements, such as the welfare rights and urban deprivation campaigns, and embraced novel or radical theories ranging from existentialism to classical Marxism.[33] Generally, these have been ephemeral allegiances which have not changed the profession's conventional approach. Although it has been argued that the social worker's role should be one of advocacy and activism, few examples of the practical application of this role exist.[34]

This is true also of the Third World where discussions on the subject have not been extensive. Latin American social workers appear to have debated the issue more than most and while the government of Allende was in power in Chile, some schools adopted a revolutionary position. With this exception, schools of social work in the Third World have not experimented with overtly radical ideas even though proposals for more radical forms of involvement have been made.

Some have argued that social work should promote what has been described by the United Nations and Marxists alike as 'popular participation in development'. Although this concept is poorly defined it has become more fashionable in recent years and is used to denote different things; these include: 'sharing by people in the benefits of development', 'active contribution by people to development', and 'involvement of people in decision making at all levels of society'.[35] These different usages are not only frequently confused but provide vague prescriptions for professional practice. It is difficult to see how social workers can ensure that the benefits of economic growth are distributed equitably or that ordinary people participate in development by helping, for example, to formulate national development plans. While many member states of the United Nations have signed declarations or supported resolutions calling for greater popular participation, many have failed to provide opportunities for their citizens to participate politically, economically or socially in the development process. This is not to deny that social workers can help deprived groups or communities to understand their position in society, to take advantages of whatever legal or constitutional rights they may have and to campaign for progressive social change.

One of the most important sources of inspiration for radical social work, which offers proposals for action of this kind, is the work of the Brazilian pedagogist Paulo Freire. The relevance of Freire's concept of *conscientization* to social work has been examined by authors such as Resnick, Alfero, Kendall and Leonard who agree, albeit with varying degrees of enthusiasm, that it provides an opportunity for social work to promote political change and reform.[36] Previously a professor of education at the University of Recife, Freire took a special interest in adult education and was involved in literacy training among rural communities in North East Brazil in the late 1940s and early 1950s. He realised that conventional methods of adult education were inappropriate to the needs of the rural poor. These methods were authoritarian, based on rote learning and had little relevance to the social and political circumstances of peasant communities. The alternative method, which Freire developed, attempted to stimulate an awareness of broader political and social issues; it replaced paternalistic approaches to education with a dynamic interpersonal dialogue between students and instructor through which the poor would arrive at a proper understanding of their position in society and of the factors which had caused their deprivation.[37] The term, *conscientization* was used to denote the 'awakening of consciousness' which followed. Although Freire did not specify what subsequent changes this awakening might bring about, he believed that if social dissatisfaction followed, it was inherent in the broader political situation. As Resnick suggested: 'an almost inevitable consequence is political participation and the formation of interest groups such as community organisations and labour unions'.[38] The potential of Freire's approach was recognised by the Movement for Basic Education, an educational radio service sponsored by the Church which began to use it on a large scale, and by the Brazilian government. Fearing its revolutionary implications, the military authorities imprisoned and subsequently exiled Freire in 1964 and censored his writings.

The techniques which are inherent in the process of *conscientization* are not dissimilar to those of social work or community development but, unlike social work, the focus is not introspective and the purpose of encouraging people to gain insights into their circumstances is very different. Instead of helping people make a better adjustment to their circumstances, *conscientization* gives insights so that people can change their circumstances. Because man is capable, as Alfero put it: 'of influencing and transforming his reality', social work should contribute to this through 'an educational function which is enabling and conscientizing'.[39]

Freire's approach was adopted explicitly by the Catholic University of Chile as a technique of social work intervention and it was taught within a broader revolutionary framework of academic instruction. In addition to conventional academic subjects, courses in radical theory were provided. A unit entitled 'Introduction to the Analysis of National Reality' dealt with the ideas of Marx, Lenin, Mao and Latin American socialists such as Guevara. Students were instructed in the technique of *conscientization* at 'theoretical practical workshops' where, together with their teachers, they engaged in the process themselves and shared their experiences of applying it to social work practice. Field work was given much emphasis and students were sent to work chiefly with peasant communities and agricultural workers. In addition to these settings, placements were arranged in neighbourhood councils, trade unions, day care centres, co-operatives and land reform agencies. The school's prospectus revealed that the training provided had 'the broad aim of raising the consciousness of the working class, of co-operating in the strengthening of popular organisations and of offering special programmes to meet the needs of the popular class'.

Whether they are phrased explicitly in ideological terms or not, techniques such as these can be used by social workers in group and community work. Groups of women or squatters or unemployed youth can be established and organised. Although the extent to which poor people can become active politically depends on the prevailing political situation, social workers can make a contribution in practical ways through establishing co-operatives or other self-help groups. Urban community development has come closest to realising this potential in the Third World; indeed, the proponents of urban community action are in agreement with the broad principles of community development, arguing essentially that a more radical attitude among workers is required. Social workers have been involved in urban community development projects in some countries where squatter communities have been organised to utilise available urban amenities or to make demands on the authorities for improved facilities. As Turner has shown, marginal urban groups in Latin American cities can be mobilised effectively in this way.[40] The Klong Toey project in Bangkok was not explicitly radical or committed to a specific ideology but social work students from Thammasat University have encouraged local residents, who live in the most appalling conditions of urban squalor, to improve their circumstances through co-operative effort. This has resulted in greater political awareness in the community and a willingness to take action and resist arbitrary bureaucratic decisions.[41]

Examples of this kind are isolated. Opportunities for political activism in the Third World are limited and, as Resnick showed, exist chiefly in countries with liberal or progressive governments. In repressive societies, where it is needed, radical social work will be resisted. The best example of radical social work in action flowered under a socialist government and came to an abrupt end after 1973 when the military seized power in Chile; the junta closed the country's schools of social work and after a thorough purge of 'subversive elements' allowed some to re-open and they are run now under close state surveillance.

Opposition from repressive governments is one problem; as social workers such as Monica Yu Hung showed, the attitudes of most social workers towards activism are negative. Describing how a group of social workers in Hong Kong assisted a slum community to protest vigorously at the government's lack of concern about their circumstances, she claimed that their efforts were frowned on by most social workers in the colony. The Li Yan villagers had been moved to a temporary 'resite area' by the Department of Resettlement in 1968 and were promised new housing within eighteen months. By 1972, they had not been rehoused and understandably, they were angry and frustrated. Aided by social workers they petitioned the authorities unsuccessfully and then staged a 'sit-in' which led to conflict with the police. Although some community leaders and social workers were arrested, the publicity attending the demonstration was such that the villagers were rehoused soon afterwards. Instead of applauding their efforts, social workers in Hong Kong were unimpressed by their radical colleagues. Many felt, as Hung reported, 'that this sort of activity is a piece of unrefined or even immature behaviour', which would discredit the profession.[42] This was a blow to those who had made sacrifices to secure justice for a deprived community. Political action by social workers, Hung argued, is likely to be resisted by most of their colleagues who, rejecting the radicalisation of social work, reveal their true allegiance to established power groups in society.

Social Work and Social Planning
Today it is recognised that development planning is an essential

instrument of economic policy in developing countries, and many governments have established central planning agencies which are responsible for the formulation and implementation of national development plans. Although these government bodies are concerned chiefly with economic matters they are responsible also for social expenditure and provide allocations to sectoral ministries such as education, health, housing and social welfare. Originally, these social services were neglected and, as was shown previously, social welfare was thought to be of secondary importance to economic growth. In time, the social aspects of development were given more attention and today, there is a greater awareness of the need for social planning in the Third World.

This has been fostered by the United Nations which has urged the governments of developing countries to undertake research into social need and to formulate social policies and plans to deal with it. The United Nations has sponsored expert meetings and conferences on the subject and has recommended that specialist training courses for social planners be established. Although few countries have taken adequate steps to promote effective social planning, some progress has been made. Opportunities for training in social planning have been created and some governments now employ social planners to work in their planning ministries.

Social workers have shown much interest in these developments and some have argued that the profession should involve itself in development by assuming a responsibility for social policy and planning. Addressing the Sixteenth International Congress of Schools of Social Work, Gerima proposed that social workers should participate in the preparation of national development plans and take a special responsibility for the sectoral planning of social welfare services.[43] Similarly, Hokenstadt argued that social workers should be trained in social planning so that they would be able to 'influence technological and social change rather than merely reacting to its consequences'.[44] To achieve this, schools of social work should introduce a variety of courses related to social planning; as Khinduka put it: 'curricula of schools of social work in the Third World should lay considerably greater stress on subjects such as social change, planning, economic growth, public administration ...'[45]

However, there are several reasons why it is unlikely that the profession will become involved in social development planning on a substantial scale in the future. One reason concerns the considerable change in direction which social work will have to take if it is to commit itself to this activity; it would negate the principle of direct intervention which is fundamental to social work. While other proposals for the profession's involvement in development, whether these be family planning or advocacy, maintain social workers in face to face relationships with their clients, planners do not work with people in the community directly. Such a shift in the profession's emphasis towards social policy, as Butrym pointed out: 'puts in question the very core of its identity, namely its concern with actual persons rather than abstract ideals'.[46] Similarly, there is a historical suspicion of substantial state intervention among social workers which has maintained the profession's commitment to direct service and the ideals of individualism and self-reliance. As Younghusband showed, the animosities between the founders of social work and the Fabians in Britain arose from differences of opinion on this issue.[47] Although opinions have changed since then, social work is still concerned primarily, as Khinduka put it eloquently, 'with the biography of the person rather than the drama of society'.[48]

As shown previously, studies of the curricula of schools of social work in the Third World have found that teaching in social policy is neglected and that few courses in social planning have been established. Obviously, social work's lack of expertise in social planning can be remedied; some social workers such as Nakamura have argued that it is of the utmost urgency that the profession prepare itself for this task. In Japan, he reported, younger social workers were being drawn to Marxism because of their disillusionment with conventional social work. To maintain their allegiance, social work must take an active interest in social policy and planning and develop 'a broader perspective to see the living environment of people totally'.[49]

It has been pointed out that schools of social work in the United States provide courses in social planning which could be replicated in developing countries. But this teaching and the growing literature on the subject in the industrial countries is not concerned with development planning and has little relevance to the Third World. The concept of social planning in American social work is related to community organisation; community organisers are trained in planning so that they may be better able to co-ordinate local voluntary and public welfare organisations. In developing countries, community organisation is hardly practised; the skills of community welfare planners would be of no use to centralised planning authorities which are concerned with national development and not with the co-ordination of local welfare agencies. Even if this expertise could be applied at the local level, it is unlikely to make much impact on the social problems of underdevelopment; these require, as Jagannadham put it: 'massive state action rather than sporadic work by voluntary and statutory agencies'.[50]

If social workers are to be trained to participate in development planning, they will require technical skills which bear little resemblance to community welfare planning, let alone conventional social work. Additional staff will have to be recruited to teach a wide range of new subjects such as development economics, demography, social development, statistics and the skills of computer programming, data processing, cost-benefit analysis, budgetary planning, operations research and other techniques. This has not been appreciated adequately by those who have urged the profession to involve itself in social planning. Instead it has been argued that the social worker's skills in dealing with people is a sufficient qualification for this task. Some have claimed that because social planners and administrators should be 'warm, communicable, flexible in disposition' and have, what one writer described as 'human touch', it is desirable that social workers, who possess these qualities, be appointed to these positions.[51] But governments have not been persuaded by these arguments and, in spite of their human relations skills, social workers have not been involved in policy making and social planning at senior levels of administration in many countries. Even in India, where social work is well established, social policies are formulated by politicians, professional planners and career civil servants and not by social workers.[52] Although Indian social workers have lamented this fact, claiming that their concern for human welfare is sufficient justification for their involvement in these activities, they have no knowledge of management, policy analysis or planning. It is unlikely that governments will replace experienced administrators and planners with social workers who are not competent to undertake complex planning tasks.

8 Social Work in the Third World – The Need for a Pragmatic Approach

The world-wide expansion of social work in the 1950s and 1960s was characterised by a general sense of optimism and satisfaction. Social workers throughout the world believed that they were dealing effectively with social problems and, because of this, regarded the internationalisation of social work as an achievement of considerable importance. The literature of social work gave many examples which purported to show how social workers were applying the profession's principles to treat social problems in developing countries. Also, as examples of social work's relevance to the traditions, customs and religious beliefs of different societies were provided, it was believed that social work was compatible with the highest humanitarian ideals of all cultures.

By the 1970s, this spirit of optimism had waned. Social workers in developing countries were criticised, both by members of the profession and by outsiders, for their limited concern with the problems of individual maladjustment and their neglect of broader social issues. Teachers of social work were accused of adopting American concepts and theories uncritically and of aiding the diffusion of inappropriate approaches to developing countries; this, it was argued, was just another manifestation of the perpetuation of colonial influences which maintained the Third World's dependence on the industrial countries.

This book has attempted to review these criticisms and to discuss different aspects of social work education and practice in the Third World. Generally, its findings are pessimistic. It has argued that, because of its dependence on western ideas, social work education in developing countries is unsuited not only to the demands of practice but to the amelioration of the pressing social problems of these countries. It has attempted to demonstrate that social work practice in the Third World is based on a narrow, colonial conception of social need and social welfare and that social work practitioners face serious problems of inadequate resources and poor conditions of service which impede their effectiveness to deal even with the conventional problems of urban poverty and maladjustment which are presented to them. It has examined the profession's response to these criticisms by discussing some proposals which have been made for social work's involvement in development. But, because many of these are unrealistic and ambitious, they have not offered feasible solutions to the problems of social work in the Third World.

Of course, these are generalisations and in some countries, schools of social work and social work practitioners have made commendable efforts to rectify the inappropriate curricula and professional roles bequeathed to them by colonialism and the stewards of modernisation. Moreover, there are enormous differences between developing countries and, for this reason, it is impossible to provide universal answers to the questions which this book and similar publications have raised. But it is possible and necessary to attempt to summarise, in general terms, the obstacles which prevent social work from making a more appropriate contribution in the Third World. At the risk of repetition, these are considered briefly with reference to social work education and social work practice in developing countries for it is only when the failures and inadequacies of social work are understood properly that solutions can be found.

The Problems of Social Work in the Third World

The inappropriateness of social work education in the Third World has been a major issue in this book. Although many schools of social work have introduced background courses and, in some cases, short courses on social work intervention which take local cultural conditions into account, the status accorded to American theories of social casework and the principles of generic social work has seriously inhibited the development of relevant forms of instruction. In spite of claims to the contrary, psycho-dynamic theories of casework and the abstract principles of social work intervention dominate the training approach adopted at most schools. The cultural irrelevance of this instruction requires little further comment; as Almazor and others have shown, the liberal values governing social work theory have no meaning in traditional culture. Social work professors argue that this teaching is necessary because of the skills it imparts and because of the insights it gives students into human behaviour. While it may well be desirable that they should be trained to understand the dynamics of human personality, there is little point in teaching students in developing countries to understand the workings of the American mind. If instruction in human relationships is required, it must be based on a culturally appropriate psychology. However, it is questionable whether schools of social work should place as much emphasis as they do on 'human relations' skills. Social workers have made much of these skills, claiming that because they have a superior understanding of human nature they are capable of undertaking a variety of tasks and of assuming new, developmental responsibilities. But these claims have not impressed employers and social workers have not been invited to become social planners or population programme directors because they have a knowledge of human behaviour. These activities, like the problems of underdevelopment, require practical responses and technical, rather than theoretical, skills.

Because of an excessive reliance on theory, social work education in many developing countries fails to prepare students adequately to undertake the practical tasks required of them by ministries of social welfare and other employers. Social work education in many countries amounts to a general academic education; the greater part of the instruction students receive is devoted to background courses in psychology, sociology and other social science and arts subjects, and much of their training in social work is devoted to learning the theories and principles of social work intervention. Often, field placements in relevant agencies provide the only opportunity for inculcating practical skills. Since the government is the chief employer of social workers in many developing countries, there is an urgent need for schools of social work to prepare students to work competently in statutory settings, instead of leaving them to learn the procedures of statutory intervention and the intricacies of implementing the social legislation of their countries after graduation.

The question of the relative emphasis which should be given to theoretical and practical instruction at schools of social work has been debated since social work training courses were first established in Britain and the United States at the end of the nineteenth century. Although it may be necessary that social workers should have general academic abilities and a theoretical appreciation of human behaviour and the society in which they work, it is more important that they have the technical abilities to perform their duties effectively. This is most important in the Third World; if the profession is to involve itself in development, schools of social work must provide instruction in subjects which will contribute to the amelioration of poverty and deprivation in practical ways.

The adoption of western approaches to social work education has resulted in courses which are unrelated, in many cases, to the levels at which social workers find employment and also, to the levels at which social work intervention is required by the community. This issue has not been discussed adequately and it is another cause of the inappropriateness of social work education. Because schools of social work in the United States and Britain were established at universities, it was recommended that social work training in the Third World should be introduced at the same level. In some countries, where there is a surplus of graduates, university trained social workers are employed as field workers but in many others, where a university education holds the prospect of rapid promotion, graduates are not eager to begin their careers at field level positions and are especially anxious to avoid a posting in the rural areas. Frequently, graduates are given responsibilities for administration for which they have not been trained properly and, at the same time, inadequate training facilities for field level workers are provided. The problem has been recognised in some countries and efforts have been made to solve it. For example, in Ghana, basic grade social workers are trained at the government's School of Social Welfare and after a suitable period in the field, those with ability are nominated for further training at the university. In the past, promotion within the country's social welfare service has been related to further professional training and most social work students at the University of Ghana are on release from the Department of Social Welfare and Community Development for the duration of their training. There has been some discussion of the need to develop paraprofessional courses in the Asian and Pacific region and an attempt has been made to deal with this problem in Indonesia, where the government has established social work training facilities at the secondary school level.

One difficulty is that these workers may not be given adequate salaries or promotion prospects and they may not be regarded as professional social workers. Attempts to differentiate between professional social work education and non-professional social welfare training have not been entirely successful, but there is some agreement among social workers about the standards required for professional recognition; as was shown previously, an important criterion is whether or not social workers are trained at universities. This is paradoxical, for the élitist character of social work education in many developing countries has hampered the profession's efforts to become involved in development. Non-professional personnel, such as community development workers, have made a greater contribution to development than university trained caseworkers.

The inappropriateness of social work education in developing countries is revealed even more dramatically when the roles of social work practitioners in the Third World are examined. Although many case histories of social work practice in developing countries claim that social workers help individuals to gain insights into their behaviour, strengthen their personalities and so cope more effectively with their problems, most practising social workers do not apply the theories of western casework or the principles of social work intervention which they have been taught. In addition to their cultural inappropriateness these principles cannot be applied usefully because of the nature and urgency of the problems social workers deal with; the idealised case histories of social work intervention in the Third World belie the fact that social workers in developing countries deal with people who are in dire need of material assistance, or who require other tangible and immediate solutions to their problems. Their clients are the destitute, homeless and handicapped of Third World cities; many are neglected, abused or abandoned children or women who have been deserted by their husbands and left without means of support. Many social workers deal with beggars and vagrants apprehended by the police and with young offenders placed under their jurisdiction by the courts. Social workers in the Third World admit that they are too overworked to be able to function as para-psychologists concerned with the personality development of their clients. Instead they deal, as best they can, with the crises of urban destitution and maladjustment and devote their time to responding to requests for urgent material assistance, securing residential places and dealing with judicial child committal, probation and maintenance cases. The demands made upon them are such that their potential for playing psycho-therapeutic roles is severely limited.

Studies of social work practice in developing countries have shown that social workers are unable to undertake these remedial welfare activities effectively because of inadequate resources and facilities. Many governments in the Third World have not only retained the residual social policies of colonialism, but have also relegated social welfare services to a level where they enjoy less priority than tourism and sport. Social workers are not provided with resources which are sufficient to help the destitute, or house the homeless, or even to place neglected children, or the handicapped and abandoned old people in suitable residential institutions. Although social work cannot be held responsible for this, the profession has been remarkably uncritical of the problem of inadequate resources and it has not campaigned vociferously for the provision of more extensive, basic welfare services. Indeed, this pressing issue is hardly mentioned in the profession's literature.

Social work's excessive concern with remedial social welfare in developing countries has attracted as much criticism as has inappropriate social work education and this has been a second major theme of this book. Some writers have urged the profession to abandon its curative conception of social welfare in favour of a developmental approach through which social workers will contribute to the amelioration of the social problems of underdevelopment and help to meet basic needs. Although few social workers accept that the profession should not be responsible for remedial activities, more are beginning to support this idea. Early publications which raised this issue were followed by a succession of articles which endorsed the view that social work should be involved actively in development but, apart from condemning social workers for failing to promote the development of their countries and exhorting them to indigenise, few made tangible or practical proposals. There is little indication that anything much has been achieved; with some exceptions, such as community development courses, few schools of social work in developing countries provide extensive instruction in subjects which are concerned with development, or which prepare students to undertake developmental tasks. As was shown previously, where teaching of this kind is provided, it has not displaced western theories of social work. In addition, few opportunities for the employment of social workers in occupations which are concerned with development have been created.

There are many reasons for social work's failure to adapt itself to the circumstances of developing countries and to involve itself in new, developmental activities. For example, there has been insufficient discussion of the constraints which inhibit the profession's involvement in new fields of practice. Instead, proposals that social work become responsible for family planning, rural development or social policy have been met with such apparent enthusiasm at international conferences that the practical difficulties have been ignored. If social workers had examined them more carefully, they would have realised that some of these proposals are unrealistic; some require that the basic features of social work, which give the profession a unique identity, be discarded in favour of activities which have nothing in common with social work at all. This is true especially of suggestions that social work should become responsible for social policy and planning in developing countries.[1] Understandably, there are many who are reluctant to support changes which will lead the profession away from direct intervention. The expertise of social workers and their potential for employment in new fields has not been properly assessed. While it has been claimed that a variety of new courses could be introduced at schools of social work in the Third World, the threat which some of these proposals pose to social work educators has not been considered. It is unlikely that those who teach social work will support changes in social work training which are so drastic that they will become redundant.

Those who propose that social work assume new, developmental responsibilities have neither considered these practical difficulties nor have they debated some of the more fundamental issues concerning social work in the Third World. As a profession, social work cannot provide solutions, as many have claimed, to the social problems of developing countries by involving itself in developmental activities. The problems of Third World poverty must be dealt with at the highest political level; concerted international action and political determination are required to bring about significant improvements in living standards in developing countries. Indeed, when the enormity of the problem and the extent of poverty and deprivation in the Third World is recognised, the question of social work's involvement in development pales into insignificance and it is understandable that those who are more familiar with these issues than social workers will see no point in the perpetuation of social work in the Third World and call for its abolition. But social work is not likely to be disbanded; governments and the international agencies have supported the establishment of social work in developing countries and today it is entrenched. Here is a contradiction which few have recognised; while many Third World governments have encouraged the professional growth of social work, they have not provided the resources which social workers require to carry out their duties properly. Whether this is so because of scarce resources or international pressure on governments to recognise social work in principle, if not in fact, is debatable; it may be argued also that because the political élites of developing countries have no intention of redistributing income and wealth to eradicate poverty, they use social work as a palliative and as a means of camouflaging the real causes of deprivation in the Third World. Social workers may not like this interpretation but they must be prepared to respond to it and realise that their role in developing countries has deeper political implications.

The problems of social work in the Third World make for depressing reading and explain the demoralisation of many social workers in developing countries today. Although there are no simple solutions, the profession will not resolve the dilemmas it faces by embracing some of the grandiose proposals for its involvement in development, which were discussed previously. Nor is it a solution to claim that because social workers have neither the resources nor the expertise to solve the problems of underdevelopment, they should confine themselves to conventional remedial activities. While there is a commendable note of common sense in this suggestion, it is a conservative recipe which legitimates the transfer of an inappropriate western approach to the Third World and confirms the belief that social work is no more than a technique for dealing with the most conspicuous manifestations of urban need.

Solutions to these problems can be found only if social workers attempt to identify and rectify inappropriate forms of social work education and practice in their own countries. They may not solve the problems of underdevelopment by modifying unsuitable educational practices and professional roles, but they will increase their relevance to the needs and circumstances of their societies and make a more useful contribution to the amelioration of basic social problems in the Third World. Among the new attempts which have been made to formulate appropriate approaches to social work education and social work practice in developing countries, those which have proceeded pragmatically have been the most successful. Two examples have been selected to illustrate how a pragmatic approach can be developed and implemented. The first deals with an attempt to identify appropriate fields of practice in the Philippines, and the second describes an attempt to introduce appropriate social work education in Sierra Leone in West Africa.

Developing Appropriate Roles for Practice – The Case of the Philippines

Social work is well established in the Philippines; there are eleven university schools of social work which are affiliated to a national professional association and all offer a four-year Bachelor's degree in the subject. In addition, post-graduate Master's and doctoral degrees are awarded. American ideas have influenced social work education in the Philippines profoundly. Many Filipino social workers have been trained in the United States and close links exist with American social work schools. American influences are revealed not only in social work education but in the provision of social welfare services in the Philippines. In 1915, during the period of American colonial rule, a national public welfare board was created to deal with social welfare matters on a limited scale and in 1919, a Bureau of Dependent Children, similar to the American Children's Bureau, was established. Apart from minor administrative changes, no substantial reorganisation took place until 1939, when legislation was enacted to create the Department of Health and Social Welfare. The Bureau of Dependent Children and other public welfare bodies were placed under its jurisdiction. In 1947, when the Social Welfare Commission was created, welfare services were placed under direct presidential supervision. Known subsequently as the Social Welfare Administration, it remained in the Office of the President until 1968 when an autonomous, cabinet-level Department of Social Welfare was established.

As in many other developing countries, the Department was concerned chiefly, as one Filipino newspaper put it: 'with the welfare of the handicapped, the unwanted and the unloved, like the orphans and waifs who either ran away from home or were turned out by their parents'.[2] Indeed, child care was among the first responsibilities assumed by public welfare services in the Philippines. The first government orphanage was established in 1917, two years before the creation of the Bureau of Dependent Children and since then, the burden of caring for orphaned, neglected, abandoned and illegitimate children has been considerable. The Department was also made responsible for poor relief; the first public assistance measures were introduced in 1941 and during the war, the Department co-ordinated emergency relief services. It has retained this function providing food, clothing, medicines and other forms of aid to fire victims and those displaced by natural disasters, especially typhoons which occur perenially.

As a major employer of social workers, the Department's limited remedial welfare activities were compatible with social work education in the country. Social work training courses laid great stress on casework methods and although the Philippines is one of the few developing countries which has locally produced teaching materials, most of these are so dependent on American ideas that their authors could have spared themselves the effort. For example, a textbook published in 1972 described eighteen cases dealt with by social workers in the Philippines, including those employed by the

Department of Social Welfare. Most were concerned with psychiatric, adolescent, marital and other personal problems and all were designed to illustrate how caseworkers help their clients in emotional distress to gain insights into their problems and improve their capacity for personality growth.[3]

Social work's lack of relevance to the needs of the Philippines was recognised gradually. Filipino social workers such as Almazor began to question the usefulness of American theories, and others were critical of the profession's concern with the psychological maladjustments of individuals. The Department of Social Welfare's role as an agency which provided help only in times of crisis was also criticised and many were aware that its poor public relations image had exacerbated the problem. The Department was concerned that the 'traditional meaning of social welfare as "doleout" had persisted not only among the poor but among the more informed sectors of society as well'.[4] The attitudes of the rich and influential in Filipino society towards social welfare was summarised by the President's wife who said: 'Social welfare must lead the poor to a life of self-reliance and not to a lifetime of begging.'[5] Addressing the First Asian Conference of Ministers Responsible for Social Welfare, which was held in Manila in 1970, President Marcos pointed out that it was his government's policy to discourage handouts to those in need. 'We believe in helping the poor', he said, 'but we believe in making the poor self-reliant, dignified and self-respecting'.[6] The Asian conference of welfare ministers was less concerned about the problem of scroungers than with the need to broaden the scope of social welfare services in developing countries. It recommended, for example, that social welfare ministries should undertake social planning, take steps to deal with the problem of unemployment, encourage non-formal education, promote an awareness of population issues and take a special interest in the needs of pre-school children.[7]

The criticisms which had been levelled at social work and social welfare services in the Philippines, and the impact of the Asian ministers' conference, in which the Department's officials participated actively, were instrumental in re-structuring its activities. Certainly, political pressure, which had been exerted on the Department to end its public assistance activities, compelled it to find alternative ways of distributing poor relief. In 1976, following the promulgation of Presidential Decree 994, the Department became known as the Department of Social Services and Development and it adopted a six point programme which would foster its new 'productivity and

developmental thrust'.[8] Known by the acronym SPDEFS, the
Department's services were reorganised as Self Employment
Assistance, Practical Skills Development and Job Placement, Day
Care Services and Supplemental Feeding, Emergency Assistance,
Family Planning Motivation and Special Social Services.

As in most developing countries, social welfare services in the
Philippines were concentrated in urban areas and there was a serious
lack of data about social need in the country. To implement its new
approach, the Department's administrative structure was reorganised
and it established a network of service delivery units organised under a
regional system of administration. Today a substantial degree of
coverage has been achieved; there are 13 regional authorities which
are responsible for 78 provincial offices, 57 offices in towns and cities
throughout the country and 450 unit offices. Some indication of the
extent of its coverage is shown by the fact that roughly 90 per cent of
the Department's staff work in the regions.[9] The Department has
implemented research, monitoring and planning procedures and
unlike most developing countries, it has collected detailed statistics on
its work and on the community it serves. Each regional office has a
research and planning section which is also responsible for identifying
targets in its locality. Broadly, the Department hopes to concentrate its
resources on the poorest 30 per cent of the population; to reach this
goal, regional welfare planners have identified the poorest 'barangays'
in their areas. The barangay, which is the smallest unit of local
government in the Philippines, will serve as a focal point for the
delivery of services. By adopting a 'barganic' approach, the
Department hopes to direct its efforts towards needy communities
rather than individuals and to involve local people in activities which
will promote their own welfare.

The Self-Employment Assistance Programme is a modified social
assistance scheme which provides small capital loans instead of poor
relief to needy families; under the scheme they are helped to establish
'income generating' projects which will lead, hopefully, to financial
self-sufficiency. In one region in Luzon in 1977, approximately 14,000
needy families, disabled people, unemployed youth and victims of
natural disasters were advanced loans to establish projects of this kind.
These included agricultural production ventures such as duck raising,
mushroom cultivation and poultry farming; handicraft projects such
as pottery, matweaving and basketry and vending or selling cooked
food, fruit, vegetables or refreshments. During 1977, this regional
office spent more than one million pesos on these projects.[10]

The Practical Skills and Job Placement service provides vocational training to help needy people to become self-employed or find work as wage earners. Vocational instructors have been recruited to teach skills such as woodwork, crafts, sewing, carpentry, motor mechanics and electrical repairs. While some are found employment through the job placement service, many are helped through the Self-Employment Assistance scheme to establish their own businesses. The Department believes that it is profitable to train groups of people in their homes or communities; for example, barangay co-operatives of out of school youth or women have been established and under the guidance of vocational instructors, they have produced a variety of craft and other products for sale. More than 140,000 people throughout the Philippines benefited from this service in the 1977 fiscal year.[11]

The Day Care and Supplemental Feeding scheme utilises the baranganic approach fully; local communities are encouraged to build their own nursery schools which are staffed by the Department's workers with assistance from local volunteers. In an attempt to ameliorate the serious problem of malnutrition among pre-school children, the Department provides the ingredients for meals; balanced diets are prepared and the children's food is cooked by local helpers. In one region in the Visayas, no less than 412 day care centres, serving about 67,000 children, had been established by 1978. In that year, eight more communities built nursery schools which are run now by the Department's day care workers and local women.[12]

The Emergency Assistance programme has been in existence for many years and owing to the country's susceptibility to natural disasters, large numbers of families require help each year. In 1977, the Philippines was struck by two typhoons, serious floods in Mindanao and the Visayas, and two earthquakes. More than half a million people were affected. Because they require urgent help, much emergency relief is in the form of immediate grants of food, clothing or money but the Department has introduced 'food for work' schemes to support communities seeking to repair the damage caused by natural disasters, and those who have lost their source of livelihood are eligible for Self-Employment Assistance. Also, the Department has convened 'disaster preparedness' workshops in areas at risk to formulate contingency plans with the help of local community leaders and officials.

The Family Planning Motivation, Population Awareness and Sex Education service is designed to involve the Department's workers in the promotion of family planning. Although the Department does not supply contraceptives and clinical services, it believes that its workers should foster the ideals of family planning among their clients and others in the community. Social workers have been trained to give lectures on the subject and emphasis is given to family planning motivation and sex education among young people. Region III in Pampanga reported that in 1977, it had trained forty-five of its workers in family planning motivation; they had given talks to more than 20,000 young people and counselled 11,000 of their clients.[13]

The Department's Special Social Services comprise its conventional welfare activities such as adoption and foster care, probation, residential services, rehabilitation of the disabled and casework with the psychologically disturbed, drug addicts and others with personal problems. Although the Department has retained its responsibility for providing these services, they are not its most important activities, as they are in many other countries, nor do they consume most of its resources. Some indication of the extent to which the Department has redirected its efforts towards developmental services is shown in its budget; for example, in region VI in the Visayas, only 8.5 per cent of the budget of 2.7 million pesos was spent on Special Social Services in 1978.[14]

Obviously, these activities are not solutions to the country's social problems and the Department has been honest about its shortcomings. It recognises that many unemployed young people who have been trained in practical skills have not found work; many self-employment assistance loans have not been repaid and not all of these projects are viable or profitable. Nevertheless, there have been successes and many poor families have benefited from its new approach. Certainly, these developments have significant implications for social work in the Philippines; social workers are now involved in a range of activities which have little in common with western, therapeutic casework even though their training has not equipped them to undertake these developmental tasks. That they have implemented these services is to their credit but it remains to be seen whether social work education in the Philippines will modify existing training approaches to produce graduates who have the skills required by the Department.

Developing Appropriate Social Work Education – The Case of Sierra Leone

Unlike the Philippines, there is no university school of social work in

Sierra Leone even though the country's university is among the oldest in Africa. On the other hand, social welfare services have been provided for many years. A division was created within the Department of Education in 1941 to deal with the problems of child neglect, vagrancy and juvenile delinquency in Freetown, the capital. In 1951, a separate Department of Social Welfare was established; by the mid 1950s, the Department had opened offices in provincial towns such as Kenema and Moyamba and several residential institutions had been built. Inspired by the successes of community development programmes in other British territories in West Africa, the Department introduced adult literacy classes, youth work, rural works projects and other community development activities during this period. When Sierra Leone became independent in 1961, the Department was renamed the Ministry of Social Welfare and in addition to its remedial services, it was made responsible for rural community development. In spite of this, many community development projects in the rural areas were organised locally by the District Councils or Chiefdom authorities and international agencies such as the Peace Corps and the American organisation CARE supported these activities. When the District Councils were abolished in 1972, the Ministry assumed responsibility for their community development functions and absorbed many of their staff. The Ministry was reorganised and renamed in 1974 when it became known as the Ministry of Social Welfare and Rural Development; it amalgamated briefly with the Ministry of Education in 1976 but now is autonomous again.

Today, the Ministry has an office in each of the country's twelve administrative districts; a study undertaken in 1977 found that 87.5% of its personnel work in these rural districts while the remainder are employed in the capital at the Ministry's headquarters, the city social welfare office and residential institutions.[15] The Ministry's rural development and social welfare functions are integrated fully; a district office is responsible not only for rural development projects but for youth work, adult education, women's work, probation, child care and family casework services. Although most field workers are assigned to one task at a time, their functions are interchangeable and senior personnel undertake a variety of different activities; for example, they may be responsible for supervising community development projects, settling marital disputes and preparing reports for the juvenile court. Because of this, the Ministry's approach may be described as generic; its workers are employed in different fields simultaneously and it uses casework, group work and community work methods comprehensively.

Social welfare training in Sierra Leone began in 1962 when a training centre for the Ministry's staff was established in the provincial town of Bo, the country's second largest town. However, the training centre functioned sporadically and eventually it was closed. Apart from the courses offered at the centre, many of the Ministry's personnel have had no special training in social work or community development. Only a quarter hold post-secondary school qualifications and, of these, most were trained abroad in countries such as Britain, the United States, Canada and Israel. These qualifications are concentrated among the Ministry's senior staff.[16]

Recognising the need for proper training facilities, the government of Sierra Leone obtained credit from the International Development Association to establish a new centre. The credit agreement required that prior to the release of funds for construction, the training needs of the Ministry's personnel be assessed carefully and that foreign consultants be recruited to advise on a suitable curriculum. Initially, it was hoped that the services of social work experts would be obtained and one or two foreign social workers made preliminary visits to the country. But there was some uncertainty about the type of training required; a conventional school of social work affiliated to the university would produce graduates who would be overqualified and unlikely to work in the rural areas. Also, the Ministry's activities demanded that proper emphasis be given to rural community development. On the other hand, the Ministry's family casework, residential care and probation services could not be neglected for these activities also required trained personnel.

Their solution to this problem lay not in transplanting social work or community development training approaches from other countries to Sierra Leone but in establishing courses which would be appropriate irrespective of whether or not they conformed to ideas accepted internationally. For this purpose, a project team of Sierra Leoneans, assisted by short-term foreign consultants, was appointed.[17] Its first task was to undertake a thorough review of the work of the Ministry; budgets, annual reports and field activities were studied. This was supplemented by a comprehensive survey of the staff; information about their duties, conditions of work, resources and previous training as well as their frustrations and problems was obtained. Secondly, a sample survey of families in villages in the rural areas and in one provincial urban centre was undertaken; families were questioned not only about their welfare problems but about health, education, housing, sanitary facilities, nutrition, child care and other matters. Specifically, information about their knowledge, utilisation and attitudes towards government social services was obtained. In addition, headmen and other community leaders were interviewed to determine the extent to which their villages had been involved in rural development activities and whether or not they had received assistance from the Ministry or other agencies for this purpose. The project team's third task was to use this information to formulate detailed policy proposals for the training of the Ministry's staff. Its specific objective was to balance the requirements of the Ministry on the one hand with the needs of ordinary people on the other; in this way, it was hoped that realistic and useful proposals could be made.

In the absence of alternative sources of data, the surveys were of crucial importance. In some respects, their findings were depressing. The community needs survey revealed the discrepancies of access to social services between urban and rural areas, and showed also that substantially more public resources are required to improve village welfare.[18] The personnel study showed that there was a high degree of frustration among the Ministry's staff because of inadequate resources; many reported that they could not carry out their duties effectively because of shortages of funds, equipment, transport and other facilities. Although these problems could not be solved through improved training but only through determined government action, the project team believed that the need for appropriate courses in social welfare and community development was revealed clearly.

The surveys also showed that the perceptions of the Ministry's staff of their training requirements were not congruent with the needs of ordinary people. The personnel were invited to make recommendations about the courses they wished to be included in the centre's curriculum. Although a very large number of suggestions were made, including that esoteric academic subjects such as Philosophy and English Literature be taught, the largest concerned social work subjects. Many of the Ministry's staff were anxious that professional social work courses be provided and many expressed the view that priority should be given to casework, probation and child care; relatively little emphasis was placed on the teaching of developmental skills.[19] On the other hand, the community needs study showed that priority should be given to rural development; need was greatest in the rural areas and demand for improved facilities was considerable.

Villagers not only expressed the desire to have clean drinking water, roads and bridges to have access to markets, schools and clinics, better methods of house construction and improved health and educational services, but demonstrated their willingness to give their labour and contribute financial resources to secure these amenities. Many had organised self-help projects on their own initiative but it was clear that they required additional expertise and material aid.[20] The surveys showed that it was necessary that the Ministry's staff possess the practical skills, for example, 'to be able to show villagers how to mix concrete, carry out simple joinery, dig wells and install pumps, construct feeder roads, culverts and bridges'.[21]

These findings were incorporated into the project team's proposals which recommended that social work and community development training be given simultaneously and that emphasis be placed on teaching practical skills which would benefit rural communities. The team proposed that students should be taught the broad principles of social work and community development within a generic approach but urged that this should be related specifically to the demands of practice in Sierra Leone and that technical rather than theoretical skills in both subjects should be stressed; these included report writing, case recording, statutory welfare procedures, administrative routines, handicrafts, construction techniques, horticulture and small livestock husbandry. In addition, they recommended that background courses in public health and especially maternal and child health, adult education, nutrition, agriculture and public administration in Sierra Leone be provided. After these proposals were approved by the government in 1978, a detailed curriculum was prepared by the project team together with the centre's newly appointed teachers. The curriculum was tested on a small group of students selected from among the Ministry's staff so that those with field experience could contribute to the evaluation of the courses. The pilot training course was held in 1979 and after the evaluation was completed, the centre became fully operational in 1980.

Although students are introduced to the broad principles of social work and community development, the centre's courses have little in common with the curricula of schools of social work in other countries. Training in the techniques of casework, group work and community work have been linked to specific practical tasks; casework skills are taught within the framework of statutory social welfare procedures, group work techniques are inculcated within the teaching of youth work, adult education and women's work while community work methods are incorporated within practical instruction in rural community development. In each, theory has been minimised and limited use has been made of western concepts; the terms casework, group work and community work have been avoided and the centre's graduates will be known neither as social workers nor as community development workers but as 'social development workers'.

The avoidance of western theory created a demand for relevant teaching materials; obviously, western publications were unsuitable and would have defeated the project team's efforts to develop courses which were appropriate to Sierra Leone. Together with the centre's staff, the team have prepared suitably illustrated and relatively simple textbooks in each subject. These have been produced at surprisingly little cost and yet, they are wholly suited to the needs of students. In addition, case study materials and a variety of audio visual aids have been prepared.

Those who are trained at the centre will not be familiar with western social work theories or with the names and publications of leading academic social workers in Europe and North America. They will not be university graduates and others will be sceptical of their intellectual abilities. But they will have the skills to work with needy individuals, groups and communities and to contribute to the development of their country. Whether they will be recognised internationally as social workers and accorded recognition for their efforts to promote development is debatable.

Elements of a Pragmatic Approach

These two case studies have been selected to illustrate how appropriate social work roles and training practices can be identified; they are not intended to serve as models which should be replicated in other countries. Professional roles which are suited to the Philippines may not be relevant to other societies; similarly, training practices devised in Sierra Leone may not apply to other nations. The enormous cultural, economic, social and political differences between those nations which are referred to collectively as the Third World, preclude any attempt to prescribe alternative forms of social work which have universal relevance. These differences demand that solutions to the problems of professional imperialism in social work be found locally by local social workers with reference to the needs and circumstances of their own countries. Because of this, no attempt will be made in this book to identify new forms of social work which may be more relevant to developing countries. To do so would contradict its central argument and invalidate its critique of professional imperialism; instead, the requirements of appropriate social work and the characteristics of appropriate professional roles and training practices will be described in general terms.

The criticisms which were made in the previous chapter of attempts to identify alternative forms of social work practice were designed to introduce an element of healthy scepticism into the debate. Although some of these proposals were severely criticised, all are to be commended for urging the profession to involve itself in activities which are related more closely to development. Also, some are viable in principle; certainly, there can be no quarrel with the idea that social workers should become involved in rural development, or in community work with urban slum dwellers, or that they should become advocates of the poor and deprived, or that they should take a greater interest in family planning, adult education or nutrition. But if social workers are to adopt these roles, they must do so pragmatically; their implications for social work education must be examined realistically and the profession's potential for becoming involved in these activities must be assessed properly. Also, social workers must recognise that they are not qualified to assume a variety of new responsibilities simply because they have a theoretical knowledge of human behaviour.

The two case studies demonstrate the need for pragmatic responses to the problems of social work in the Third World and although they dealt with different aspects of the profession's role in developing countries, they shared common features which were compatible with pragmatic social work. Firstly, they attempted to formulate appropriate training practices and professional roles within the framework of social work's existing approach instead of abandoning it. The essential features of this approach are professionalisation, direct intervention through face to face contact with people, a commitment to the amelioration of social problems and a focus on the needs of individuals and their families, groups and communities. This is the first requirement of a pragmatic and appropriate approach; social work must deal with social problems in developing countries through direct service and it can do this in ways which differ significantly from conventional therapeutic casework. Although the content of social work training in Sierra Leone and the nature of social work practice in the Philippines had little in common with western social work, neither discarded the profession's commitment to direct service and the other basic characteristics of social work intervention. As was argued previously, proposals for the profession's involvement in development, which discard these basic features, are the least likely to be implemented. This is not to suggest that social workers should not be given responsibilities for administration, research, planning and policy making; as was shown previously, social workers, and graduates especially, are responsible for these activities in some countries. Where a demand for this type of involvement exists, schools of social work must give appropriate emphasis to these subjects and specialist post-basic courses should be offered. But these must be related specifically to the administration of social work services; training courses of this kind must be compatible with the profession's commitment to direct service and must prepare specialists who will facilitate the effective deployment of social workers in the field.

A second requirement of a pragmatic approach is that more emphasis be given to practical than theoretical skills. In Sierra Leone and the Philippines, it was recognised that the theoretical knowledge of human behaviour and the skills in dealing with human relationships, which social workers claim to possess, were of little relevance to the problems of underdevelopment in these countries. In Sierra Leone, considerably more teaching in practical tasks, ranging from implementing statutory procedures to building bridges, was provided than was instruction in the theoretical principles of social work and community development. Similarly, in the Philippines, social workers were expected to undertake practical tasks of tangible benefit to people and communities rather than limiting themselves to promoting behavioural and attitudinal change.

Thirdly, pragmatic social work in the Third World must be concerned with the most pressing social problems of developing countries. Although these must be identified locally, the nature and extent of poverty and its various manifestations must be recognised and given priority; social workers must seek to involve themselves in activities which will contribute to the amelioration of these problems. Social workers will still be needed to deal with the personal problems of individuals and their families and maintain their commitment to needy children, the disabled, the elderly and others with problems which require remedial intervention, although these activities should not be the profession's only or even primary concern. In both case studies, social work's responsibilities for existing welfare problems was retained, but in Sierra Leone more emphasis was given to training in community development than casework and in the Philippines, social workers devoted more of their efforts to developmental than to remedial social welfare.

A concern with the social problems of underdevelopment will lead the profession into new fields such as those illustrated in the case studies. In some countries, social workers may participate in rural development on a large scale and in view of the pressing needs of rural areas in the Third World, this should be encouraged. In others, they may focus their attention on marginal urban groups. Certainly, social work has considerable potential for becoming much more actively involved in development by working with deprived communities both in rural and urban areas. In some countries, an effective advocacy role may be feasible while in others, community work may be concerned with the provision of basic amenities and services or with the creation of co-operatives and other self-help groups. Social workers may participate more widely in the promotion of non-formal education, family planning, primary health care and nutrition, and in projects designed to generate income and employment. It is hoped that unique fields of service may be identified; also social workers in different societies may become involved in several developmental tasks simultaneously but in all cases, appropriate social work must be concerned with meeting basic social needs.

Finally, pragmatic social work in developing countries must be based on the principle of indigenisation. Defined properly, indigenisation means appropriateness; professional social work roles must be appropriate to the needs of different countries and social work education must be appropriate to the demands of social work practice. As this book has shown, social work practice in the Third World has been based on professional roles which were developed in the West and transmitted to developing countries through colonialism. Similarly, social work education has been based on western theories which have little relevance to the needs of developing countries and the requirements of practising social workers. Indigenisation demands that these absurdities be corrected.

Indigenisation requires also that new professional roles be identified not only with reference to the circumstances of different countries but to the opportunities available for new forms of involvement. Proposals made at international conferences should not be adopted simply because they offer an alternative to western casework; their potential application must be realistically assessed on the basis of unmet needs and within the limits of available opportunities. Obviously, there is little point in social workers aspiring to become population experts, social administrators or rural development workers if there are no openings in these fields; in some countries, these tasks are undertaken competently by others and in other countries, there may be no need for some of these activities. For example, the integration of social work with community development in Sierra Leone was possible because these functions were integrated administratively. In the Philippines, on the other hand, community development services are provided by the Department of Local Government and Community Development which recruits its own professional personnel from university graduates who have specialist qualifications in this subject. Instead of aspiring to become responsible for community development, the Department of Social Services and Development identified new fields of practice, realistically taking into account needs which existing services were not attempting to meet.

The indigenisation of social work practice must be accompanied by the indigenisation of social work education; schools of social work must devise curricula which will prepare students adequately for professional practice, however this is defined in their own countries. Also, social work education must be offered at a level which is appropriate to the requirements of different societies; students may have to be trained to different standards and exposed to different curricula to undertake different tasks. The pervasive and powerful influence of American social work theory remains one of the greatest obstacles to the development of indigenous social work education in the Third World. Although many social work educators are reluctant to dispense with these theories entirely, often because they are fearful of the academic void which they believe would result from the renunciation of western theory, it is possible as the Sierra Leonean case study demonstrated, to provide alternative curricula and appropriate teaching materials. It is vitally important that priority be given to the production of appropriate textbooks, journals and other teaching aids. Facilities for their publication exist in the majority of developing countries today and it has been shown, in fields such as adult education and community development, that teaching materials which are suited to local conditions can be prepared at little cost.

These four characteristics of pragmatic social work may serve as guidelines to social workers who are seeking to increase their profession's relevance to the needs and circumstances of their countries. This raises the issue of whether it is likely that appropriate social work roles and training practices will be formulated in the Third World. Although the prospects are bleak, it is true that social workers in developing countries today are much more aware of the inadequacies of their profession than they were previously and that they now may be more prepared to take action. Certainly, a pragmatic re-orientation of social work in the Third World must begin with an assessment of the profession's failures. Although criticisms of social work in developing countries have been aired in the literature and at international conferences, there have been very few national gatherings of social workers which have debated these issues vigorously with specific reference to their own countries. Unfortunately, social workers in developing countries seldom meet each other in this way and often, where professional associations exist, they are weak or poorly organised. It is a serious indictment of social work in most developing countries that national gatherings are seldom held, local journals and magazines do not exist and research into social work issues is not undertaken. Schools of social work could take the lead if their teachers dedicated themselves to this task; regular meetings and conferences could be held and local magazines could be published to provide a forum for discussion. In this way, social workers could stop talking about the need to indigenise and begin to put its ideals into practice. The strengthening of national professional groups, which will involve themselves in a collective debate on the profession's shortcomings in their societies must be given priority, as this is the first step in the formulation of an appropriate, pragmatic approach.

Although the emergence of strong professional bodies can lead to greater conservatism and self-interest, professional associations can function also as political pressure groups which campaign for reforms and more resources which will benefit others. Social workers in developing countries can exert pressure on governments if they do so collectively and adopt a more radical stance. They cannot maintain a vague allegiance to ethical neutrality in the face of entrenched inequality and injustice; a decisive commitment to progressive social change must be an integral part of the profession's role in the Third World. However, it is unlikely that social workers will adopt this role readily. Social work has not proved to be a vehicle for protest in the past even though its potential for pressure group politics is considerable. Nor may social workers in developing countries be able to mobilise themselves collectively to remedy inappropriate forms of social work. Consensus on these issues may not be possible and some may fail to appreciate the need for change.

Attempts to implement a pragmatic approach in developing countries require the support of the international social work community; if social work education in the Third World is to be freed from inappropriate ideas, the responsibility for ending this dependence must be shared equally between schools in the industrial and developing countries. It is unforgivable that western schools of social work still accept students from the Third World without providing courses which are suited to their needs. The use of aid revenues to train social work students who come from countries where schools of social work exist, should also be condemned. Western governments should cease to provide scholarships for social work education in Europe and North America, but should divert their aid revenues to establishing or strengthening local training facilities. Instead of sponsoring their education in the West, it is preferable that aid be provided for the third country training of social work students who come from nations where no schools of social work exist.

Similarly, foreign assistance to schools of social work in the Third World should be re-examined. Western teachers, who take their sabbaticals abroad to lecture in developing countries on the latest theories or techniques of social work intervention, should be made aware of their responsibility for transmitting alien ideas. While it is unlikely that these exchanges will cease, these visitors should seek to learn during their travels rather than teach. Social work experts who are sent abroad to help develop curricula at schools of social work in the Third World should be selected more carefully and an essential criterion for their employment should be their ability to promote an indigenous and pragmatic approach. The resources which are now spent on financing expert missions, international conferences and study tours could be used more profitably to foster the development of appropriate social work education in tangible ways. For example, resources are needed urgently to meet the critical problem of inadequate teaching materials which is a major impediment to indigenisation. The allocation of aid resources for this purpose should be encouraged.

A serious assessment of the problems of social work in different developing countries undertaken by social workers locally and supported internationally may point the way towards solutions; by adopting a pragmatic approach, appropriate forms of social work can be identified. Although social work will retain its basic characteristics and commitments, professional imperialism can be ended only if unique forms of social work practice and training are adopted in different developing countries; indeed, the term 'social work' may not be used universally in future. It remains to be seen whether social workers in developing countries will respond to the challenge, or whether the international social work profession will tolerate these changes and permit such a flexible interpretation of social work in the Third World.

Notes and References

Chapter 1

1. G. Konopka: The Methods of Social Group Work. In W. Friedlander (Ed.): *Concepts and Methods of Social Work*, Englewood Cliffs: Prentice Hall, 1958, p. 116.
2. M. S. Gore: The Cultural Perspective of Social Work in India. In Council on Social Work Education: *An Intercultural Exploration*, New York: 1967, p. 97.
3. Ibid. p. 87.
4. M. Roof: *Voluntary Societies and Social Policy*, London: Routledge and Kegan Paul, 1957, p. 7.
5. R. Chambliss: *Social Thought*, New York: Holt, Rinehart and Winston, 1954, pp. 25–6.
6. See for example, F. A. Hayek: The Roads to Serfdom and A. Seldon: Welfare by Choice. In A. V. S. Lochhead (Ed.): *A Reader in Social Administration*, London: Constable, 1968.
7. M. Bruce: *The Coming of the Welfare State*, London: Batsford, 1961, p. 138.
8. Especially through the work of R. M. Titmuss, first professor of this subject at the University of London. See for example, his *Social Policy: An Introduction*, London: Allen and Unwin, 1974.
9. H. Maas: Social Casework. In Friedlander, op. cit. p. 19.
10. H. H. Perlman: *Social Casework: A Problem Solving Process*, Chicago: University of Chicago Press, 1957, p. 27.
11. M. Richmond: *Social Diagnosis*, New York: Russell Sage, 1917, p. 25.
12. F. Biestek: *The Casework Relationship*, London: Allen and Unwin, 1961, p. 25.
13. Ibid. p. 19.
14. Maas: op. cit. p. 21.
15. H. H. Stroup: *Social Work: An Introduction*, New York: American Book Co., 1960, pp. 1–2.
16. Konopka: op. cit. p. 126.
17. Ibid. p. 153.
18. Stroup: op. cit. p. 356.
19. A. Dunham: Community Organisation. In *Social Work Yearbook*, National Association of Social Workers, 1943, p. 286.
20. G. Carter: Community Organisation Methods. In Friedlander: op. cit. p. 239.
21. One notable exception is S. Brair and H. Miller: *Problems and Issues in Social Casework*, New York: Columbia University Press, 1971.
22. Friedlander: op. cit. p. 2.
23. This definition was proposed in W. I. Newstetter's paper What is Social Group Work? read at the 62nd National Conference of Social Work in 1935.

24. V. M. Sieder: What is Community Organisation Practice in Social Work? *Proceedings of the 83rd National Conference of Social Work*, 1951.
25. Friedlander: op. cit. p. 3.
26. Ibid. p. 10.

Chapter 2

1. M. Bruce: *The Coming of the Welfare State*, London: Batsworth, 1961, p. 24.
2. Ibid. p. 33.
3. Hawksley's address was entitled: *The Charities of London and Some Errors in their Administration with Suggestions for an Improved System of Private and Official Relief.*
4. See: H. Bosanquet: *The History and Mode of Operation of the Charity Organization Society*, London: Longmans, 1874. C. S. Mowat: *The Charity Organisation Society 1869–1913*, London: Methuen, 1961. A. F. Young and E. T. Ashton: *British Social Work in the Nineteenth Century*, London: Routledge and Kegan Paul, 1956.
5. C. S. Loch: *How to Help Cases in Distress*, London: Family Welfare Association, 1883. A Clay (Ed.): *A Great Ideal and its Champion: Papers and Addresses by the Late Sir Charles Stewart Loch*, London: Allen and Unwin, 1923.
6. S. A. Queen: *Social Work in the Light of History*, Philadelphia: Lippincott, 1922, p. 134.
7. See H. O. Barnett: *Canon Barnett: His Life, Work and Friends*, London: Murray, 1922. J. A. R. Pimlott: *Toynbee Hall: Fifty Years of Social Progress*, London: Dent, 1935.
8. M. J. Smith: *Professional Training for Social Work in Britain*, London: Allen and Unwin, 1965.
9. E. G. Meier: *A History of the New York School of Social Work*, New York: Columbia University Press, 1954.
10. Her views on the subject were published in *Social Welfare and Professional Education*, Chicago: University of Chicago Press, 1931. See also, R. Lubove: *The Professional Altruist: The Emergence of Social Work as a Career*, Cambridge: Harvard University Press, 1965.
11. F. J. Bruno: *Trends in Social Work 1874–1956*, New York: Columbia University Press, 1957.
12. E. E. Southard: *The Kingdom of Evils*, New York: MacMillan, 1922. Previously, in 1919, Jarrett urged the National Conference of Charities and Corrections to take greater cognisance of psychiatric ideas. Healy's paper was entitled: *The Bearings of Psychology on Social Casework*.
13. M. Richmond: *Social Diagnosis*, New York: Russell Sage, 1917. See also, *What is Social Casework?* New York: Russell Sage, 1922.
14. Quoted in Bruno: op. cit. p. 187.
15. Ibid.
16. Op. cit. p. 125.
17. K. Woodroofe: *From Charity to Social Work*, London: Routledge and Kegan Paul, 1962, p. 129.
18. See C. B. Stendler: New Ideas for Old: How Freudianism was Received in the United States. *Journal of Educational Psychology* Vol. 38 (1947) pp. 57–68. A. A. Brill: The Introduction and Development of Freud's Work in

the United States. *American Journal of Sociology* Vol. LXV (1939) pp. 318–25.

19. Z. Butrym: *The Nature of Social Work*, London: MacMillan, 1976, p. 23.
20. J. Addams: *The Spirit of Youth and the City Streets*, New York: MacMillan, 1912.
21. G. Coyle: *Social Progress in Organized Groups*, New Hampshire: Topside, 1930. See also, *Studies in Group Behaviour*, New York: Harper, 1937 and *Group Experience and Democratic Values*, New York: Women's Press, 1948.
22. The findings of this and subsequent study groups were edited by R. P. Lane: Reports of Groups Studying Community Organization Process. In *Proceedings of the 67th National Conference of Social Work*, 1940
23. P. J. Stickney and R. P. Resnick: *World Guide to Social Work Education*, New York: International Association of Schools of Social Work, 1974, p. 181.

Chapter 3

1. Terms such as 'colonialism', 'imperialism', 'developing country' and 'Third World' are used widely in development studies but controversy about their proper meaning and precise definition remains unresolved. See, for example, J. E. Goldthorpe: *The Sociology of the Third World*, Cambridge: Cambridge University Press, 1975, p. 40. L. Wolf-Phillips: Why Third World? *Third World Quarterly* Vol. 1, no. 1 (1979) pp. 105–14. P. Worsley: How Many Worlds? *Third World Quarterly* Vol. 1, no. 2 (1979) pp. 100–107.
2. See, for example: J. Bowle: *The Imperial Achievement: The Rise and Transformation of the British Empire*, London: Secker and Warburg, 1974.
3. Ibid. p. 125.
4. United Nations: *Measures for the Economic Development of the Underdeveloped Countries*, New York: 1951.
5. P. N. Rosenstein-Rodan: Problems of Industralization of Eastern and South Eastern Europe. *Economic Journal* Vol. 53 (1943) pp. 205–11.
6. R. Nurske: The Case for Balanced Growth. In G. M. Meier (Ed.): *Leading Issues in Economic Development*, New York: Oxford University Press, 1976, pp. 640–43.
7. R. F. Harrod: *Toward a Dynamic Economics*, New York: St Martins, 1948 and E. D. Domar: Capital Expansion, Rate of Growth and Employment. *Econometrica* (1946) pp. 137–47.
8. W. W. Rostow: *The Stages of Economic Growth: A Non-Communist Manifesto*, Cambridge: Cambridge University Press, 1960 and *The Economics of Take-Off Into Sustained Growth*, London: MacMillan, 1963.
9. W. J. Goode: *World Revolution and Family Patterns*, Glencoe: Free Press, 1963.
10. B. F. Hoselitz: Social Stratification and Economic Development. *International Social Science Journal* Vol. 16 (1964) pp. 237–51.
11. B. F. Hoselitz: *Sociological Factors in Economic Development*, Glencoe: Free Press, 1960.
12. E. E. Hagen: *On the Theory of Social Change*, Homewood: Dorsey, 1962. D. C. McClelland: *The Achieving Society*, Princeton: Van Nostrand, 1961 and A Psychological Approach to Economic Development. *Economic Development and Cultural Change* Vol. 12 (1964) pp. 320–24.

13. A. Inkeles and D. H. Smith: *Becoming Modern*, London: Heinemann, 1974.
14. See D. M. Heer: *Society and Population*, Englewood Cliffs: Prentice Hall, 1968, pp. 10–12.
15. See D. Lerner: *The Passing of Traditional Society*, Glencoe: Free Press, 1958, p. 58.
16. W. E. Moore: *Social Change*, Englewood Cliffs: Prentice Hall, 1963, p. 89.
17. See, for example, P. Baran: *The Political Economy of Growth*, Harmondsworth: Penguin, 1973. C. Furtado: *Development and Underdevelopment*, Berkeley: University of California Press, 1964. A. Gunder-Frank: *Capitalism and Underdevelopment in Latin America*, Harmondsworth: Penguin, 1971. T. Dos Santos: The Crisis of Development Theory and the Problem of Dependence in Latin America. In H. Bernstein (Ed.): *Underdevelopment and Development*, Harmondsworth: Penguin, 1973. W. Rodney: *How Europe Underdeveloped Africa*, Dar Es Salaam: Tanzania Publishing House, 1972. S. Amin: *Neo-Colonialism in West Africa*, Harmondsworth: Penguin, 1973.
18. Frank's analysis of the inadequacies of sociological modernization is one of the best known critiques; see his *Sociology of Development and Underdevelopment of Sociology*, London: Pluto, 1971.
19. M. Brown: Where do we go from Here? *Social Service Quarterly* Vol. 31 (1957) pp. 112–16.
20. United Nations: *Training for Social Work: An International Survey*, New York: 1950. See also the second survey, published in 1955 and the third survey, published in 1959.
21. United Nations: *Training for Social Work: Fourth International Survey*, New York: 1964.
22. R. Rashid: Social Work Practice in Pakistan. In Council on Social Work Education: *An Intercultural Exploration*, New York: 1967, p. 107.
23. P. J. Stickney and R. P. Resnick: *World Guide to Social Work Education*, New York: International Association of Schools of Social Work, 1974, p. 95.
24. Ibid. p. 141.
25. Ibid. p. 112.
26. Ibid. p. 226.
27. Ibid. p. 116.
28. H. Nagpaul: Social Work Education in India. In S. K. Khinduka (Ed.): *Social Work in India*, Allahabad: Kitab Mahal, 1965, p. 224. See also, India, Ministry of Education and Social Welfare: *Handbook on Social Work Education Facilities in India*, New Delhi: 1976, p. 9.
29. S. Weisner: *Professional Social Work in Kenya*, Lower Kabete: Kenya Institute of Administration, 1972, pp. 3–5.

Chapter 4
1. P. J. Stickney and R. P. Resnick: *World Guide to Social Work Education*, New York: International Association of Schools of Social Work, 1974, p. v.
2. Ibid. p. 293.
3. L. She: The Early Development of Social Work Education in Hong Kong. *International Social Work* Vol. 21, no. 4. (1978) pp. 31–43.
4. E. L. Younghusband: *Training for Social Work in Hong Kong*, Hong Kong: Government Printer, 1960.

5. J. D. Chaisson *et al.*: *Training for Social Work in Hong Kong*, Hong Kong: Government Printer, 1963.
6. For further information see P. Hodge: Social Welfare Training in Ghana. *Social Service Quarterly* Vol. 31 (1957) pp. 117–21.
7. M. O'Collins: Introducing Social Work Education at the University of Papua and New Guinea. *International Social Work* Vol. 21, no. 4 (1973) pp. 20–25.
8. United Nations: *Training for Social Welfare: Fifth International Survey*, New York: 1971. See also, United Nations: *Training for Social Work: Fourth International Survey*, New York: 1964.
9. P. J. Stickney and R. P. Resnick: op. cit. p. v.
10. Ibid. p. ix.
11. United Nations: op. cit. p. 53.
12. Ibid. p. 27.
13. A. Yiman: *Curricula of Schools of Social Work and Community Development Training Centres in Africa*, Addis Ababa: Association for Social Work Education in Africa, 1974.
14. See also, R. F. Sedler: Social Welfare in a Developing Country: The Ethiopian Experience. *International Social Work* Vol. 11, no. 2 (1968) pp. 36–44.
15. See also, P. T. Brown: Social Work Education in Zambia. *International Social Work* Vol. 14, no. 1 (1971) pp. 42–7.
16. United Nations: op. cit. p. 52.
17. India, Ministry of Education and Social Welfare: *Handbook on Social Work Education Facilities in India*, New Delhi: 1976.
18. A. C. Almazor: The Profession of Social Work in the Philippines. In Council on Social Work Education: *An Intercultural Exploration*, New York: 1967, p. 125.
19. H. Nagpaul: Social Work Education in India. In S. K. Khinduka (Ed.): *Social Work in India*, Allahabad: Kitab Mahal, 1965, p. 244.
20. Two early reviews of social work education in developing countries, which drew attention to these similarities, are M. Branscombe: Curriculum Planning for Social Work in Newly Developing Countries. *International Social Work* Vol. 4, no. 3 (1961) pp. 1–3 and J. M. Robertson: Observations on Some Aspects of Social Work Education in Developing Countries. *International Social Work* Vol. 6, no. 2 (1963) pp. 19–21.
21. A. Yiman: op. cit. p. 51.
22. A. Shawkey: Social Work Education in Africa. *International Social Work* Vol. 15, no. 3 (1972) pp. 3–16.
23. P. T. Brown: op. cit.
24. D. W. Dunning: Limits to the Amount of Noise, *International Social Work* Vol. 15, no. 2 (1972) pp. 4–7.
25. United Nations: op. cit. p. 74.
26. R. C. Jones: Training for Social Work in Latin America. *Social Service Quarterly* Vol. 23 (1949) p. 24.
27. V. Paraiso: Education for Social Work in Latin America. *International Social Work* Vol. 9, no. 2 (1966) p. 19.
28. Ibid. p. 20.
29. United Nations: op. cit. p. 27.

30. H. Nagpaul: The Diffusion of American Social Work Education to India. *International Social Work* Vol. 15, no. 1 (1972) pp. 3–17.
31. D. Drucker: *An Exploration of Social Work in Some Countries of Asia with Special Reference to the Relevance of Social Work Education to Social Development Goals*, Bangkok: ECAFE and UNICEF, 1972.
32. P. T. Thomas: Social Work Education and Training in India. In India, Planning Commission: *Social Welfare in a Developing Economy*, Faridabad: 1963, p. 67.
33. Ibid. p. 68.
34. H. Aptekar: Social Work in Cross-Cultural Perspective. In S. K. Khinduka op. cit. p. 123.
35. J. D. Chaisson *et al.*: op. cit. p. 1 and 23.
36. P. J. Stickney and R. P. Resnick: op. cit. p. 144.
37. H. Nagpaul: Social Work Education in India: op. cit. p. 247.
38. S. Farman-Farmaian: Social Work Education and Training. In India, Planning Commission: op. cit. p. 60.
39. H. Nagpaul: The Diffusion of American Social Work Education to India: op. cit. p. 11.
40. J. M. Hoey: Professional Implications of International Social Work Development. In C. Kasius (Ed.): *New Directions in Social Work*, New York: Harper, 1954, p. 87.
41. H. Aptekar: American Social Work Literature. In India, Planning Commission: op. cit. p. 78.
42. Editorial in *International Social Work* Vol. 15, no. 4 (1972).
43. P. J. Stickney and R. P. Resnick: op. cit. p. v.
44. Editorial in *International Social Work* Vol. 18, no. 1 (1975).
45. For a more detailed discussion of community work training at schools of social work in the Third World see J. Midgley and Z. Adler: Community Work Teaching at Schools of Social Work in Developing Countries. *Community Development Journal* Vol. 13 (1978) pp. 131–139.
46. Information about these placements are provided by E. Brooks: Village Productivity Committees and Social Development in Zambia. *International Social Work* Vol. 17, no. 1 (1974) pp. 35–42.
47. E. M. Clarkson: The Contribution of British Social Work to Developing Countries. *International Social Work* Vol. 19, no. 1 (1976) p. 4.

Chapter 5

1. For a fuller discussion of these issues see P. Hazard: *European Social Thought in the Eighteenth Century*, London: Hollis and Carter, 1954. L. T. Hobhouse: *Liberalism*, London: Thornton Butterworth, 1934. S. Lukes: *Individualism*, Oxford: Blackwell, 1973.
2. M. Bruce: *The Coming of the Welfare State*, London: Batsford, 1961, p. 78.
3. W. Friedlander (Ed.): *Concepts and Methods of Social Work*, Englewood Cliffs: Prentice Hall, 1958, p. 2.
4. See R. Williams: Value Orientations in American Society. In H. Stein and R. Cloward (Eds): *Social Perspectives on Behaviour*, Glencoe: Free Press, 1958, pp. 288–314 and R. Williams: *American Society: A Sociological Interpretation*, New York: MacMillan, 1968.

5. M. Pumphreys: *Teaching of Values and Ethics in Social Work Education*, New York: Council on Social Work Education, 1959. See also, H. Bisno: *The Philosophy of Social Work*, Washington: Public Affairs Press, 1952.
6. G. Konopka: Methods of Social Group Work. In W. Friedlander: op. cit. p. 118.
7. E. L. Younghusband: *Social Work and Social Change*, London: Allen and Unwin, 1964, p. 104.
8. F. Biestek: *The Casework Relationship*, London: Allen and Unwin, 1961, p. 137.
9. S. Briar and H. Miller: *Problems and Issues in Social Casework*, New York: Columbia University Press, 1971, p. 35.
10. W. Friedlander: op. cit. p. 3.
11. S. Briar and H. Miller: op. cit. p. 37.
12. H. Stein: Observations on Determinants of Social Work Education in the United States. In Council on Social Work Education: *An Intercultural Exploration*, New York: 1967.
13. W. Friedlander: op. cit. p. 3. See also, A. Keith-Lucas: A Critique of the Principle of Self-Determination. *Social Work* Vol. 8 (1963) pp. 61–71 and S. Bernstein: Self-Determination: King or Citizen in the Realm of Values. *Social Work* Vol. 5 (1960) pp. 3–8.
14. S. K. Khinduka (Ed.): *Social Work in India*, Allahabad: Kitab Mahal, 1965, p. 27.
15. K. Huang: Matching Needs with Services: Shoes for Chinese Feet. *International Social Work* Vol. 21, no. 4 (1978) pp. 44–54. The problems of applying western social work principles to immigrant cultural minorities in the industrial countries is discussed also in this article but see, for example: J. Ellis (Ed.): *West African Families in Britain*, London: Routledge and Kegan Paul, 1978.
16. For a discussion of the relevance of these values to western religions other than Christianity see A. Kutzik: *Social Work and Jewish Values*, Washington: Public Affairs Press, 1959.
17. H. Aptekar: Social Work in Cross-Cultural Perspective. In S. K. Khinduka: op. cit. p. 120.
18. S. F. Desai: Zoroastrianism – Its Ideology and Social Work Values. *Social Work and Development Newsletter* (ESCAP) no. 11 (1974) p. 14.
19. R. Rashid: Social Work Practice in Pakistan. In Council on Social Work Education: op. cit. p. 139.
20. M. Hasegawa: Zen and Social Work. *Social Work and Development Newsletter* (ESCAP) no. 31 (1974) p.13.
21. F. M. Yasas: Gandhian Values and Professional Social Work Values. In S. K. Khinduka: op. cit. p. 81.
22. A. M. Muzumdar: Mahatma Gandhi's Contribution to Social Welfare. In S. K. Khinduka: op. cit. p. 81. See also, A. M. Muzumdar: *Social Welfare in India: Mahatma Gandhi's Contribution*, London: Asia Publishing House, 1964.
23. India Planning Commission: *Social Welfare in a Developing Economy*, Faridabad, 1964, p. 18.
24. See for example, a discussion of these issues in R. M. Titmuss: *The Gift Relationship*, Harmondsworth: Penguin, 1971.

25. G. Wijewardena: Humanism and the Values of Social Work in Asia. In Council on Social Work Education: op. cit. p. 115.
26. *Ibid*, p. 416.
27. M. H. Liyanage: Buddhism and Social Work Education. *Social Work and Development Newsletter* (ESCAP) no. 11 (1974) p. 11.
28. S. F. Desai: op. cit. p. 15.
29. H. Aptekar: op. cit. p. 122.
30. Council on Social Work Education: op. cit. p. 76.
31. G. Wijewardena: op. cit. p. 110.
32. E. M. Clarkson and A. Halim: A Bangladesh Case History *International Social Work* Vol. 17, no. 2 (1974) pp. 18–20.
33. W. Clifford: *A Primer of Social Casework in Africa*, Nairobi: Oxford University Press, 1966.
34. Ibid. p. 14.
35. Ibid. p. 82.
36. A. C. Almazor: The Profession of Social Work in the Philippines. In Council on Social Work Education: op. cit.
37. Ibid. p. 134.

Chapter 6

1. W. Clifford: *A Primer of Social Casework in Africa*, Nairobi: Oxford University Press, 1966, p. 14.
2. E. M. Clarkson and A. Halim: A Bangladesh Case History. *International Social Work* Vol. 17. no. 2 (1974) pp. 18–20.
3. These data are taken from World Bank: *1978 World Bank Atlas*, Washington: 1978 and World Bank: *World Development Report, 1978*, Washington: 1978.
4. *1978 World Bank Atlas:* op. cit.
5. World Bank: *World Development Report, 1978*, op. cit. pp. 1–3.
6. United Nations: *1974 Report on the World Social Situation*, New York: 1975, p. 6.
7. Ibid.
8. United Nations: *1978 Report on the World Social Situation*, New York: 1979, p.18.
9. P. Donaldson: *Worlds Apart*, Harmondsworth: Penguin, 1971, p. 14. For a different view on this question see P. T. Bauer: *Dissent on Development*, London: Weidenfeld and Nicolson, 1971, pp. 49–67.
10. United Nations: *1974 Report on the World Social Situation*, op. cit. p. 6.
11. World Bank: op. cit. p. 33.
12. G. Myrdal: *The Challenge of World Poverty*, Harmondsworth: Penguin, 1970, pp. 322–3.
13. F. Paukert: Income Distribution at Different Levels of Development. *International Labour Review* Vol. 108 (1973) p. 108. See also, H. Chenery et al.: *Redistribution with Growth*, London: Oxford University Press, 1974.
14. P. Donaldson: op. cit. p. 45.
15. United Nations: *Report on the World's Children*, New York: 1970.
16. Quoted in J. McHale: *World Facts and Trends*, New York: Collier, 1972, p. 8.

17. Ibid. p. 41.
18. S. K. Khinduka: Social Work in the Third World. *Social Service Review* Vol. 45 (1971) p. 63. See also, World Bank: op. cit. p. 108.
19. J. McHale: op. cit. p. 82.
20. Ibid.
21. Quoted Ibid. p. 83.
22. United Nations: *1974 Report on the World Social Situation*, op. cit. p. 16.
23. Ibid.
24. Population Council: *Population and Family Planning Programs: A Factbook*, New York: 1976, p. 5.
25. World Bank: *Rural Development Sector Policy Paper*, Washington: 1975.
26. Quoted ibid. p. 81.
27. P. Donaldson: op. cit. p. 115.
28. World Bank: *Rural Development Sector Policy Paper*, op. cit. pp. 83-4.
29. A. V. S. Lochhead: Training for Social Work. In India, Planning Commission: *Social Welfare in a Developing Economy*, Faridabad: 1964, p. 44.
30. P. T. Thomas: Reflections on the Philosophy of Social Work. In S. K. Khinduka (Ed.): *Social Work in India*, Allahabad: Kitab Mahal, 1965, p. 69.
31. M. S. Gore: The Cultural Perspective in Social Work in India. In Council on Social Work Education: *An Intercultural Exploration*, New York: 1967, p. 101.
32. Ibid. pp. 101-2.
33. R. Rashid: Social Work Practice in Pakistan. In Council on Social Work Education: op. cit. p. 146.
34. S. Farman-Farmaian: Social Work Education and Training. In India, Planning Commission: op. cit. pp. 56-7.
35. Teheran School of Social Work: *Analysis of Training Experiences Since 1958*, Teheran, 1974.
36. S. Weisner: *Professional Social Work in Kenya*, Lower Kabete: Kenya Institute of Administration, 1972, p. 18.
37. V. Jagannadham: Social Policy and Social Work. In S. K. Khinduka (Ed.): *Social Work in India*, op. cit. p. 155.
38. S. Weisner: op. cit. p. 40.
39. India, Ministry of Education and Social Welfare: *Report, 1974-5*, New Delhi: 1975, paras. 1.06 and 10.08.
40. Ghana: *Annual Report of the Department of Social Welfare and Community Development*, Accra: 1966, p. 30.
41. S. N. Ranade: Trends in Social Work. In S. K. Khinduka (Ed.): *Social Work in India*, op. cit. p. 325.
42. A. V. S. Lochhead: op. cit. p. 51.

Chapter 7
1. United Nations: *Training for Social Welfare: Fifth International Survey*, New York: 1971, p. 48.
2. H. Stein: Cross-National Themes in Social Work Education. In International Association of Schools of Social Work: *Proceedings of the XVI Congress of Schools of Social Work*, New York: 1973, p. 161.

3. United Nations: *Proceedings of the International Conference of Ministers Responsible for Social Welfare*, New York: 1969, p. 6.

4. Philippines, Department of Social Welfare: *Report of the First Asian Conference of Ministers Responsible for Social Welfare*, Manila: 1971, p. 18.

5. United Nations, Economic and Social Commission for Asia and the Pacific: *Report of the Expert Group Meeting on the Determinants of Social Development Content in Social Work Education Curricula*, Bangkok: 1974, p. 3.

6. D. B. Lasan: Indigenization with a Purpose. *International Social Work* Vol. 18, no. 1 (1975) p. 24.

7. W. Clifford: *A Primer of Social Casework in Africa*, Nairobi: Oxford University Press, 1966, p. 6.

8. S. Farman-Farmaian: Social Work Education and Training. In India, Planning Commission: *Social Welfare in a Developing Economy*, Faridabad: 1964, p. 51.

9. J. F. Bulsara: Social Welfare in Indian Conditions. In S. K. Khinduka (Ed.): *Social Work in India*, Allahabad: Kitab Mahal, 1965, p. 316.

10. Ibid.

11. E. M. Clarkson: The Contribution of Casework to Development. *International Social Work* Vol. 17, no. 3 (1974) p. 47.

12. Ibid. p. 45.

13. See, for example, K. Little: *West African Urbanization: A Study of Voluntary Organizations in Social Change*, Cambridge: Cambridge University Press, 1965 and P. C. W. Gutkind: African Urbanism, Mobility and the Social Network. In G. Breeze (Ed.): *The City in Newly Developing Countries*, Englewood Cliffs: Prentice Hall, 1969, pp. 389–400.

14. See, for example, A. Gunder-Frank's scathing critique of these theories in his *Sociology of Development and Underdevelopment of Sociology*, London: Pluto, 1971.

15. S. K. Khinduka: Social Work in the Third World, *Social Service Review* Vol. 45 (1971) p. 71.

16. S. Florendo: Family Planning and Population Dynamics: The Role of Social Work, *International Social Work* Vol. 16, no. 2 (1973) pp. 27–34.

17. United Nations, Economic and Social Commission for Asia and the Pacific: op. cit. p. 45.

18. K. Kendall (Ed.): *Population Dynamics and Family Planning: A New Responsibility for Social Work Education*, New York: Council on Social Work Education, 1971, p. 59.

19. Ibid.

20. Ibid.

21. Ibid. p. 61.

22. Ibid.

23. Ibid. See also L. Rapoport: Education and Training of Social Workers for Roles and Functions in Family Planning. *Journal of Education in Social Work* Vol. 6 (1970) pp. 27–38 and S. E. Francis: Case Study of the Role of Short Term Teaching in Family Planning. *International Social Work* Vol. 16, no. 4 (1973) pp. 33–7.

24. S. Florendo: op. cit. p. 31.

25. D. Brokensha and P. Hodge: *Community Development: An Interpretation*, San Francisco: Chandler, 1969, pp. 43–5.

26. United Kingdon, Central Office of Information: *Community Development: The British Contribution*, London: 1962, p. 23.
27. Ibid.
28. K. Cama: Casework in a Community Development Setting. In J. A. Ponsioen (Ed.): *Social Welfare Policy*, The Hague: Mouton, 1963, p. 24.
29. S. Dasgupta: *Social Work and Social Change*, Boston: Porter Sargent, 1968.
30. Ibid. p. 40.
31. Ibid. p. 41.
32. J. Midgley and D. Hamilton: Local Initiative and the Role of Government in Community Development: Policy Implications of a Study in Sierra Leone. *International Social Work* Vol. 21, no. 2 (1978) pp. 2–11.
33. See, for example, R. Bailey and M. Brake (Eds): *Radical Social Work*, London: Edward Arnold, 1975. R. Nickmeyer: A Marxist Approach to Social Work. *Social Work* Vol. 17 (1972) pp. 58–65. P. Corrigan and P. Leonard: *Social Work Practice under Capitalism: A Marxist Approach*, London: Macmillan, 1978.
34. Also, there has been much controversy about this question in developing countries. See, for example, J. Narayan: Revolutionary Social Work and V. M. Kulkarni: Social Workers are not Revolutionaries. In S. Dasgupta (Ed.): *Toward a Philosophy of Social Work in India*, New Delhi: Popular Book Service, 1967.
35. United Nations: *1974 Report on the World Social Situation*, New York: 1975, p. 255.
36. R. P. Resnick: Conscientization: An Indigenous Approach to International Social Work. *International Social Work* Vol. 19, no. 2 (1976) pp. 21–9. K. Kendall: Dream or Nightmare: The Future of Social Work Education. *International Social Work* Vol. 16, no. 2 (1973) pp. 5–15. P. Leonard: Towards a Paradigm for Radical Practice. In R. Bailey and M. Brake (Eds): op. cit. pp. 46–61. L. A. Alfero: Conscientization. In International Association of Schools of Social Work: op. cit. pp. 72–81.
37. P. Freire: *Pedagogy of the Oppressed*, Harmondsworth: Penguin, 1972 and *Cultural Action for Freedom*, Harmondsworth: Penguin, 1972.
38. R. P. Resnick: op. cit. p. 24.
39. L. A. Alfero: op. cit. p. 80.
40. J. F. C. Turner: *Housing by People*, London: Marion Boyars, 1976 and J. F. C. Turner and R. Fichter (Eds): *Freedom to Build*, New York: MacMillan, 1972.
41. For a description of some aspects of this project by a local resident see P. Unsongtham: Une initiative locale dans le tuadis de Bangkok: des services communautaries pour l'enfance. *Assignment Children* no. 40 (1977) pp. 49–67.
42. M. Yu Hung: Social Work and Social Action. *International Social Work* Vol. 19, no. 2 (1976) p. 13.
43. Y. W. Gerima: Social Planning: Challenge to Social Work Education. In International Association of Schools of Social Work: op. cit. pp. 135–6.
44. M. C. Hokenstadt: Preparation for Social Development: Issues in Training for Policy and Planning Positions. *International Social Work* Vol. 18, no. 1 (1975) p. 3.
45. S. K. Khinduka: op. cit. p. 71.

46. Z. Butrym: *The Nature of Social Work*, London: Macmillan, 1976, p. 126.
47. E. L. Younghusband: The Future of Social Work. *International Social Work* Vol. 16, no. 4 (1973) p. 4.
48. S. K. Khinduka: op. cit. p. 69.
49. Y. Nakamura: Role of Social Welfare in Social Planning. In *Proceedings of the International Council of Social Welfare Regional Conference for Asia and the Pacific*, Hong Kong: 1976, p. 59.
50. V. Jagganadham: Social Policy and Social Work. In S. K. Khinduka (Ed.): op. cit. p. 157.
51. S. K. Khinduka: Bureaucracy in Social Welfare. In ibid. p. 216.
52. Ibid. p. 212. V. Jagganadham: op. cit. p. 157.

Chapter 8

1. J. Midgley: Developmental Roles for Social Work in the Third World: The Prospect of Social Planning, *Journal of Social Policy* Vol. 7 (1978) pp. 173–88.
2. *Evening Post*, 17 September 1976.
3. V. Hebbert *et al.*: *Social Work Practice: A Philippine Casebook*, Quezon City: New Day, 1972.
4. Philippines, Department of Social Services and Development: *Basic Social Services to Meet Basic Human Needs*, Manila: 1978.
5. Ibid.
6. Philippines, Department of Social Welfare: *Report of the First Asian Conference of Ministers Responsible for Social Welfare*, Manila: 1971, p. 31.
7. Ibid. p. 15.
8. Philippines: Presidential Decree no. 994 of 8 September 1976.
9. Philippines, Department of Social Services and Development: *Annual Report '77*, Manila: 1978, p. 42.
10. Philippines, Department of Social Services and Development, Region III: *Annual Report: Calendar Year 1977*, San Fernando: 1978, p. 3.
11. Philippines, Department of Social Services and Development: *Annual Report '77*, op. cit. p. 18.
12. Philippines, Department of Social Services and Development, Region VI: *1978 Accomplishment Report*, Iloilo City: 1978, p. 6.
13. Philippines, Department of Social Services and Development, Region III: op. cit. p. 9.
14. Philippines, Department of Social Services and Development, Region VI: op. cit. p. 9.
15. Sierra Leone and International Development Association, National Training Centre Survey Project: *Progress Report no. 2: The Interpretation Report*, Freetown: 1977, p. 111.
16. Ibid. pp. 117–20.
17. For an account of the role of the foreign consultants in this project see M. Hardiman and J. Midgley: Foreign Consultants and Development Projects: The Need for an Alternative Approach. *Journal of Administration Overseas* Vol. 17 (1978) pp. 232–44.
18. J. Midgley and D. Hamilton: Local Initiative and the Role of Government in Community Development: Policy Implications of a Study in Sierra Leone, *International Social Work* Vol. 21, no. 2 (1978) pp. 2–11.

19. Sierra Leone and International Development Association: op. cit. p. 139.
20. J. Midgley and D. Hamilton: op. cit.
21. Sierra Leone and International Development Association: op. cit. p. 137.

Index

Hill, O., 20, 23
Hokenstadt, M., 147
Hopkins, H., 30
Hoselitz, B., 47
Huang, K., 92
Hung, M., 146

Imperialism, *see* colonialism, 40–44, 50
Individuation, 7, 12
Industrialisation, 48–50, 131–3
International Association of Schools of Social Work, 61, 64, 65, 77

Jagannadham, V., 117, 149
Jarrett, M., 28
Jones, R., 74
Juvenile justice, 27–8, 51, 96, 163

Kendall, K., 61
Khinduka, S., 134, 147, 148
Konopka, G., 1, 9, 34, 81, 88

Lasan, D., 130
Lewis, A., 46, 47
Liberalism, 17, 29, 85–92, 97, 140
Liyanage, L., 95
Loch, C., 20, 23, 29, 87
Lochhead, A., 115, 118

Maas, H., 6
Marxism, 91, 143, 145, 148
Meyer, A., 28
Missionaries, 43, 53, 54
Modernisation, 44–50, 55, 85, 131–4

Nagpaul, H., 74, 76, 77, 82
Nakamura, Y., 148

Paraiso, V., 74
Participation, 9, 143
Perlman, H., 6, 81
Philanthropy, 2–4, 18, 24, 25–6, 29, 35–6, 87
Poor laws, 4, 17–20, 26
Poor relief, 2–3, 17–23, 26, 36, 86–7
Population problems, 48, 113–14, 135
Probation, 29, 51, 96, 125, 162, 164

Psychology, 28–9, 32–3, 47, 78, 85, 123
Psychiatry, 28–9, 32, 133–4
Pumphreys, M., 88, 93

Queen, S., 22

Rashid, R., 92, 95, 116
Religion, 2–3, 8, 21, 43–4, 92–6
Residential institutions, 18–19, 51, 82, 89, 96, 120, 163–4
Resnick, R., 144
Richmond, M., 7, 28, 31, 32, 33, 34, 87
Roof, M., 3
Rostow, W., 46, 47
Rural problems, 49–51, 114–15, 131, 141
Rural development, 52–3, 124, 138–142, 145, 165–7, 168

Settlements, 22, 31, 34
Shawkey, A., 73
Slavery, 42–4
Socialism, 88, 143, 145, 148
Social needs, 6, 106–15, 125, 147, 169–70
Social problems, 1–6, 8, 31, 51–3, 82, 105–15, 124–6, 131–4, 154–155, 158, 169
Social planning, 9–10, 146–9
Social policy and administration, 4–5, 29–31, 50–56, 73–5, 79, 88, 146–9
Social security, 30, 51–2, 159
Social welfare services, 29–31, 38, 51–53, 55–6, 116–18, 119–27, 147, 154–5, 157–62, 163–6
Social work
 defined, ix–x, 1, 6, 168
 casework, 6–8, 11–12, 21, 31–5, 37, 79–80, 98–102, 116, 120, 125, 140, 151, 159, 164–6
 community work, 9–11, 12, 22, 26, 34–5, 79–80, 83, 136, 148, 166
 education and training, 11, 21, 23–26, 31, 36–9, 56–60, 61–84, 116, 119, 123, 136–7, 145, 148, 152–153, 162, 169, 171–3